D1337255

# CREDIT RISK MODELING

*Design and Application*

ELIZABETH MAYS, EDITOR

**GLENLAKE PUBLISHING COMPANY, LTD.**
Chicago • London • New Delhi

**FITZROY DEARBORN PUBLISHERS**
Chicago and London

© 1998 Robert A. Klein
ISBN: 1-888998-38-5

Library edition: Fitzroy Dearborn Publishers, Chicago and London
ISBN: 1-57958-005-X

All rights reserved. No part of this book may be reproduced in any form or by
any means, electronic, mechanical, photocopying, recording, or otherwise
without the prior written permission of the publisher.

Printed in the United States of America

GPCo
1261 West Glenlake
Chicago, Illinois 60660
glenlake@ix.netcom.com

# CONTENTS

# PREFACE

Credit scoring has long been used in the consumer lending arena for products such as automobile loans and credit cards. More recently, credit scoring systems have been applied to mortgage lending, small business lending, and agricultural lending. Credit risk models are everywhere and more and more credit decisions are being made using automated systems. Credit grantors recognize the benefit of implementing scoring systems to lower costs associated with traditional underwriting, decrease credit losses, and provide consistent credit decisions across groups of borrowers.

*Credit Risk Modeling: Design and Application* combines the expertise of leaders in the credit scoring field into a comprehensive guide that will enable both new and experienced model users to improve their techniques and practices at every step of the way in the model design, implementation, and monitoring process.

Section I provides an overview of credit risk modeling, describing the various ways scoring models are being used today. It discusses the pros and cons of developing a model internally versus using an external consultant and provides a description of consumer credit data critical to many applications. This section explains the difference between generic and customized scoring models, compares their advantages and disadvantages, and describes how the two may be used together for more effective credit decisions. A detailed list of generic score vendors and a description of their scores is also included.

In Section II, modeling experts describe how to build scoring models. A host of important model development issues are covered including factors to consider when compiling a data set for model development, how to segment your scorecards for more powerful performance, and the important problem of reject inference and how to deal with it. The various statistical techniques used to build credit scoring models are explained and contrasted. One chapter is devoted to building application scoring models while another concentrates on behavior scoring.

Finally, Section III describes how to evaluate your models and decide when it is time to build a new one. This section describes a set of critical monitoring and tracking reports users should produce to ensure their scorecards are performing as expected. Also, a bank regulator describes what lenders should do to validate their scorecards both at the development stage and on an ongoing basis.

I'd like to thank the authors for taking the time to write these insightful, informative chapters. I'd also like to express my gratitude to Robert Klein and The Glenlake Publishing Company who made the publication of this unique and important book possible.

**Elizabeth Mays, Editor**

# ABOUT THE EDITOR

## Elizabeth Mays

Elizabeth Mays is a Washington D.C. economist, currently working in the area of credit risk analysis and automated underwriting. She has extensive experience in risk modeling for financial institutions and, while working for the U.S. Treasury's Office of Thrift Supervision, was instrumental in the development of one of the first "Net Portfolio Value" models for measuring interest rate risk. She has published a number of articles in the risk management area and is co-editor of *Interest Rate Risk Models: Theory and Practice* (Glenlake Publishing Company, Ltd.). Dr. Mays holds a Ph.D. in economics from the University of Cincinnati.

# CONTRIBUTORS

**Gary G. Chandler**
Gary Chandler, a Director and Principal of Risk Management Resources, Inc., provides the firm with expertise in credit scoring, consulting, training, and educational programs. He is also an adjunct research scholar at the Credit Research Center at Georgetown University (formerly at Purdue University) and a member of the American Bankers Association's National/Graduate School of Bank Card Management Advisory Board and faculty. In 1976 he co-founded Management Decision Systems, Inc. (currently Experian, formerly CCN-MDS Division). He holds a B.S. in Physics, and an M.S. in Industrial Administration and Ph.D. in Finance from Purdue University.

**Larry Cordell**
Larry Cordell became a Director of the Loss Forecasting Group in the Servicer Division at Freddie Mac in 1996. He served as a senior economist on the Loan Prospector℠ mortgage origination scorecard team from 1994 to 1996, and was an economist at the Office of Thrift Supervision from 1988 to 1994. He received his Ph.D. in economics from the University of North Carolina at Chapel Hill in 1988.

**Hollis Fishelson-Holstine**
Hollis Fishelson-Holstine, Senior Vice President, joined Fair, Isaac in 1987. She is currently in charge of North American markets. From September 1995 through December 1996, Ms. Fishelson-Holstine was responsible for strategic development in Fair, Isaac's credit unit. Previously she was in charge of opening and managing Fair, Isaac's office in the United Kingdom. She holds an MS in statistics from Oregon State University and a B.S. in biology from Cornell University.

**Dennis C. Glennon**
Dennis Glennon is a Senior Financial Economist in the Risk Analysis Division at the Office of the Comptroller of the Currency. His research interests are in the areas of credit scoring, bank failures, and core deposit analysis. His work has been published in the *Journal of Banking and Finance*, the *Journal of Risk and Insurance*, and the *Journal of Urban Economics*. Glennon earned a Ph.D. in economics from the University of Missouri, Columbia.

## John M. L. Gruenstein

John Gruenstein is Vice President, Risk Management at the Money Store in Sacramento, California. This chapter was written while John was Senior Economic Consultant at PMI Mortgage Insurance Co., where he had previously held the position of Director, Forecasting & Modeling. Before joining PMI, John served in senior level positions in business, government, and academia. He was a founding partner and CEO of BPA Economics, Inc., an economic consulting firm. BPA Economics' projects involved conducting econometric analyses, policy analyses, and credit risk modeling for business and government clients. John also has served as Vice President at the Federal Reserve Banks of Philadelphia and San Francisco, Senior Vice President at Rosen Consulting Group, and Director of Economic Analysis for the Mayor of San Francisco. John's academic career includes teaching real estate and land economics courses at the University of California at Berkeley, and economics at the University of Pennsylvania and Haverford College. John has a Ph.D. in Economics from the University of Pennsylvania, dual Bachelor of Science degrees from M.I.T. and has written many papers and reports in real estate finance, regional economics, public policy and other fields.

## David J. Hand

David Hand has been professor of statistics and head of the Statistics Department at the Open University in the United Kingdom since 1988. His wide-ranging research interests include the foundations of statistics, the relationship between statistics and computing, and multivariate statistics, especially classification methods. He has extensive consultancy experience with bodies ranging from banks through pharmaceutical companies to governments. He has served as editor of the *Journal of the Royal Statistical Society, Series C, Applied Statistics,* and is founding and continuing editor-in-chief of *Statistics and Computing.* He has published over 100 research papers and 15 books, including *Discrimination and Classification, The Statistical Consultant in Action, Construction and Assessment of Classification Rules,* and *Statistics in Finance.*

## Allen Jost

Allen Jost is Vice President of business development for HNC Software, Inc., in San Diego. Before joining HNC he worked in risk management for Commercial Credit Finance Corporation and Citibank, and in market research at Metromail Corporation. His decision systems experience includes traditional statistical score modeling and neural network score development in credit risk management and direct mail marketing. He holds a Ph.D. in applied statistics.

## Matthew Klena

Matthew Klena has been a Senior Economist at Freddie Mac since 1996. He was an economist at the Federal Deposit Insurance Corporation from 1995-1996 and at the Resolution Trust Corporation from 1990-1995. He did graduate studies in economics at the University of North Carolina at Chapel Hill and has an undergraduate degree in economics from Georgetown University.

## William M. Makuch

Bill Makuch is the Managing Director of Structured Transactions and Analytical Research (STAR) for First Union Capital Markets. In this capacity, Bill leads First Union's transaction structuring, prepayment and loss model development, structured products quantitative research, valuation and surveillance, and portfolio analytics efforts, and also provides the analytical infrastructure for the trading and sales of asset backed, mortgage backed, and commercial mortgage backed securities. STAR provides a unique organizational bridge which enables First Union to analytically link its origination, trading, and distribution capabilities for its retail, wholesale, and third party channels thereby maximizing both volume and execution.

Prior to First Union, Bill spent 16 years at GE's Corporate Research and Development Center and GE Capital where he most recently held the position of Senior Vice President of Risk Management for GE Capital's Mortgage Insurance Corporation. As the Chief Credit Officer he was responsible for transaction approval, credit policy development and administration, portfolio analysis, customer management, underwriting technology development and integration, and new product assessment and approval. Prior to this, he held various analytical management positions throughout GE including Vice President of Decision Technology where he and his team developed and applied OmniScore[SM] Analytics. While at the Research and Development Center he developed and implemented risk management and scoring technology for many of GE Capital's domestic and international consumer credit businesses including GE Capital's private label credit card, bank card, auto leasing, mutual fund, and mortgage businesses.

Over the years Bill's consumer credit work has earned him several recognitions including the Franz Edelman International Management Science Competition and IndustryWeek's "50 R&D Stars to Watch." Bill holds the B.A. and M.S. degrees in Mathematics from The State University of New York at Albany, a Ph.D. in operations research and statistics from Rensselaer Polytechnic Institute, and a M.B.A. from Union College.

**Timothy J. Malamphy**

Tim Malamphy is Senior Financial Analyst on the Early*Indicator*$^{SM}$ development team at Freddie Mac after spending three years in the loss forecasting group. He received his M.B.A. from Virginia Polytechnic Institute and State University and holds a B.S. in systems engineering from the University of Virginia.

**Leonard J. McCahill**

Len McCahill recently joined Fair, Isaac's Consulting subsidiary, Credit & Risk Management Associates (CRMA) as Managing Director of its Asia Pacific and South America Divisions. Len served in a similar position with Citibank International, where he developed an MIS system for Latin America that became the prototype for the International Consumer Bank. He also led the Citibank team responsible for evaluating the credit quality of potential Latin American acquisition portfolios.

Len was the founder and principal of Credit Partners, a credit score development and risk management consulting company that provided financial institutions throughout Latin America and Asia Pacific with credit cycle and credit consulting services. He also created and taught two courses now being offered by MasterCard University, "Managing Consumer Credit," and "Strategic Management of Scoring Models." He has also served as Vice President of CCN and Manager of Statistical Analysis for General Electric Credit Corporation. McCahill holds a B.S. in accounting from Fordham University, and has completed the two-year Financial Management Program sponsored by General Electric.

**Maria T. Pincetich**

Ms. Pincetich began her career in 1985 with Security Pacific National Bank in Southern California in the Consumer Lending Division, where she worked on bankcard and direct installment portfolios. Her responsibilities included collections, underwriting, and regulatory compliance. At Sears, Roebuck and Co., she gained experience in the Credit Policy Department in Acquisitions and Underwriting and also in Credit Marketing, where she was responsible for Hispanic marketing. Ms. Pincetich currently heads up Acquisition Management Services at Trans Union, where she and her team are responsible for the support and development of the target marketing products. She holds a B.A. in economics and a B.A. in Spanish from California State University at Northridge and a Masters in international management from the American Graduate School of International Management (Thunderbird).

## Balvinder S. Sangha

Balvinder Sangha is a Senior Economist with Ernst & Young's Policy Economics and Quantitative Analysis (PEQA) Group, specializing in econometric modeling. He is PEQA's principal analyst in the validation and fair lending review of credit scoring models used in consumer and mortgage underwriting. He is also involved in provision of other consulting services to financial institutions such as determining the intercompany allocation of income from complex financial products, and developing models for testing the viability of new lending products. He has conducted training seminars for bank personnel in the use of sophisticated statistical models. Dr. Sangha holds a Ph.D. and an M.A. in economics from Brown University, and a B.B.A. from Loyola University of Chicago.

## Richard Schiffman

Richard Schiffman has been with Fair, Isaac since 1992. In his current position as Senior Product Manager, he leads product development and implementation efforts, having worked most recently on the redevelopment effort that resulted in Fair, Isaac's new FastTrack™ data analysis and reporting software. He also managed the development of a suite of desktop tools designed to improve data analysts' productivity. Mr. Schiffman holds a B.S. in industrial engineering from Lehigh University and an M.S. in operations research from the University of California at Berkeley.

## Wan-Qi Ting

Wan-Qi Ting is a Senior Risk Analyst who has been with Freddie Mac since June 1996. Before joining Freddie Mac, she worked for years in medical outcome research and six years in actuarial risk forecasting. Ms. Ting holds an M.S. in actuarial science and a B.S. in computer science from the University of Nebraska.

## Kristin M. Tobin

Ms. Tobin has worked with Trans Union's Acquisition and Risk Management Services for five years. Her responsibilities as Senior Product Research Manager have ranged from the management and support of risk scores throughout the United States to the development of target marketing and account monitoring programs in Canada, Mexico, and South Africa. As Manager of International Scoring Services, she is currently looking for new opportunities to enhance the credit information that Trans Union offers around the world with analytical products and services. She holds a B.S. in marketing from the University of Illinois and is completing her M.B.A. at DePaul University in Chicago.

**Mark M. Zandi**

Mark M. Zandi is Chief Economist and co-founder of Regional Financial Associates, Inc., where he directs research and consulting activities. His research interests include macroeconomic, financial, and regional economics. Recent studies have treated household credit conditions, the location of high-technology centers, and the impact of globalization and technological change on real estate markets. Zandi earned a Ph.D. in economics from the University of Pennsylvania, and a B.S. in economics from the Wharton School at the University of Pennsylvania.

# 1

# SCORING APPLICATIONS

**William M. Makuch**
*Managing Director of Structured
Transactions and Analytical Research
First Union Capital Markets*

## INTRODUCTION

At the beginning of 1998, U.S. domestic consumer credit debt outstanding totaled approximately $5 trillion.[1] Given this phenomenal loss exposure, the evaluation of a consumer applicant for credit, the sale of the asset into the secondary market, and the subsequent account management all receive intense risk management focus. Despite the differences between the various consumer credit products, this focus has resulted in a clear evolution to a score based approach. Although the timing of this evolution has been vastly different for the credit card, mortgage, auto, and commercial lending industries, the results have been similar: a faster, more consistent, unbiased, and more accurate approach to lending based on scoring technology.

Today, good data, development expertise, and score development technology are necessary but not sufficient conditions for a competitive advantage in the market place. In fact, score based origination of new accounts is now the status quo in essentially all consumer lending industries. Over time, as the score development data becomes more accurate, it becomes more available and representative of the total market, and the development techniques approach a terminal level for extracting information from the data, the scores produced by the vari-

---

1 Regional Financial Associates (RFA) estimates that total consumer credit debt outstanding (including mortgage debt) at year end 1997 was $4.972 trillion. Total residential mortgage debt alone was $3.758 trillion.

ous independent development efforts can be expected to converge. At that point, the competitive race will be won based purely on the number, scope, and creativity of score based applications, as well as the level of understanding and the degree to which the score is leveraged in each application.

This introductory chapter discusses applications of scoring systems in the consumer credit industries. The intention is to share the breadth of applications, not the detail, since each application would require its own book if the detail were to be covered. Many applications are therefore simply mentioned. A measure of the benefit of the scoring application is also provided wherever possible. Of course, no sooner is a chapter like this written than it is obsolete—new applications of scores are introduced annually.

Before attempting the following discussion, it is important to unify our terminology. Specifically, the difference between "credit" or "generic" scores and "application specific" or "custom" scores requires clarification. Credit scores are built to predict a borrower's future repayment performance using only credit bureau information, such as the borrower's past repayment performance, credit exposure or utilization, and appetite for additional exposure. The most popular examples are the FICO credit scores. These scores have no access to income, capacity to repay, or product information in making their prediction of the borrower's future performance. FICO credit scores have been demonstrated to be statistically significant predictors of a borrower's repayment performance for many consumer credit products. Application specific or custom scores, e.g., mortgage scores, are developed to predict a specific outcome, such as foreclosure on the mortgage, and typically have access to all the application data, e.g., credit bureau, borrower's income, product, collateral, and regional economic data.

Advantages of generic credit scores include low cost, universal acceptance, and availability. Advantages of custom scores include accuracy—potentially two to three times that of a generic score—and the fact that they are fully understood by the user and not a "black box." Although both credit and custom scores have their place in consumer credit risk management, they are not interchangeable. Certain conclusions reached for custom scores do not apply to credit scores and thus we should respect the differences and exercise the nomenclature properly.

It is also worth a three-sentence mention that the applications mentioned can be used equally across all credit products or "asset classes." Specifically, the bank card, private label credit card, phone card, mortgage, auto loan, and commercial lending industries have all benefited from the applications of scoring technology. Other products, such as home equity and sub prime lending, are just beginning to apply this technology.

Our discussion of the applications will follow the chronology of the credit life cycle: origination, securitization, and servicing. Since most of the risk is booked at the time of credit underwriting, it is appropriate that we start with the application of score based underwriting.

## ORIGINATIONS

It is estimated that as much as 80 percent of the "measurable and controllable" risk is decided upon at the time of underwriting.[2] Stated another way, once the account or loan is approved, servicing and loss mitigation techniques can control future losses only to a limited extent relative to the control or loss avoidance offered by making the correct decision in the first place.[3]

Because of this, an obvious area of scoring application is that of evaluating new credit applicants. It is difficult to know which company was the first to pioneer this application but discussions with several industry veterans acknowledge Montgomery Ward's early 1960's scoring application for credit card applicants as one of the earliest.[4] In contrast, one of the latest consumer credit industries to take the plunge is the mortgage industry. Because this industry is representative of the process, events, and challenges faced by all industries in utilizing scoring for the approval of credit, it makes a great summary case study.

Until the mid-1990s, who was granted a mortgage and for what cost was largely determined by decision rules. These "underwriting guidelines" were optimized over several decades in an attempt to assure profitable yet generous lending practices. Guidelines were created for different quality grades (A, B, C) of mortgagees by those that assumed, insured, or rated, the default risk; i.e., investors, mortgage insurers, rating agencies, and portfolio lenders.

---

2 Imagine for a moment that one could segment the entity called credit "risk" into three mutually exclusive types: measurable/controllable risk, measurable/uncontrollable risk, and non measurable/uncontrollable risk. The objective of scoring systems, portfolio analyses, etc., is to maximize *measurable* risk. Credit policy then devises ways to use this increase in predictive capability to increase the amount of risk controlled. Based on the performance of many different asset classes, I would estimate that as much as 80% of the products total measurable and controllable risk can be identified at the time of underwriting for use in the decision making process.

3 Different asset classes will have different levels of controllable risk. For example, until the recent wave of bankruptcies, the credit card product was considered to have a greater level of controllable risk than, say, the mortgage product. The mortgage product is basically a consumer held 30-year "call" option (30-year, fixed rate mortgages are today's most popular product). A 30-year window of performance is at best difficult to predict. It is the appreciation of the collateral that offsets this relatively high level of uncontrollable risk.

4 For an excellent historical review, see Edward M. Lewis (1992), *An Introduction to Credit Scoring* (The Athena Press, 53 Circle Road, San Rafael, California).

For the most part these guidelines were generally shared among the players in the mortgage industry with only minor tweaks for niche market focus, competitive spirit, or some form of perceived informational arbitrage. Significant modifications were shared by all and resulted from each oil patch, southern California, or failed product debacle. The mortgage industry continued independently along this path while other consumer lending industries profitably employed the data-driven technique of scoring. Not until about 1995 did the industry begin to demonstrate comprehensive acceptance of this technology.

Scoring's uphill battle against manual guideline underwriting in the mortgage industry was similar to the resistance it had faced in other industries. In many cases, the value of scoring was discounted before it was evaluated. After all, how could a mathematical model evaluate the risk associated with the complex mortgage/borrower/collateral relationship? This attitude, coupled with the fact that relatively smaller data sets were available in the mortgage industry than in the card industry, resulted in scoring's late arrival.

In the interim, the mortgage industry, being no less competitive than the card industry, developed its own technology solution, which for the most part came and went between 1990 and 1995. During this period "mentored AI" systems were developed that attempted to reproduce the decision process of a human underwriter. Though these systems gave speed and consistency to the underwriting process, by 1995 their accuracy was seriously questioned. These systems were built to reproduce manual underwriting without much consideration of whether the manual underwriting thought process was optimal. The obvious question is: what is the most accurate approach for avoiding delinquencies and losses while satisfying the mortgage lending demands of Americans? Scoring technology is developed using actual loan performance data—the assessment of risk is substantiated based on a significant and representative sample absent of opinions and bias.

Because the industry is driven by profit, a randomized side-by-side comparison of the various underwriting technologies may never be conducted.[5] However, practically speaking, a few defensible production comparisons do exist. Figure 1-1 illustrates the results of such a comparison.[6]

---

5 Statistical experimental design requires observing the performance of those applicants identified as "declines." In the mortgage industry, where each failed mortgage can amount to tens of thousands of dollars in losses, it is unlikely that we will ever be allowed to randomly sample this group for comparison purposes. However, due to the low declination rate and high override rate of industry guidelines in the early 1990s a production sampling of this group does exist that is adequate to support our conclusions.

6 GE Capital devotes a constant research effort to assure its underwriting practices are not only consistent and unbiased but also as accurate as possible. GE capital Mortgage Insurance data are presented here.

# FIGURE 1-1

### Scoring vs. Guideline Underwriting Performance by Path—1992 Applicants

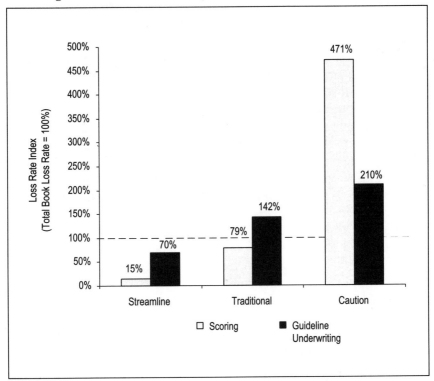

It presents an indexed foreclosure rate comparison of 1992 applicants whose mortgages were approved as a result of underwriting guidelines and of a mortgage scoring approach.[7]

The use of the mortgage score could have substantially reduced the foreclosure rate.[8] In this comparison, the approval rate for the score based approach was set equal to that of manual underwriting.[9] Although mortgage scoring is now generally recognized as beneficial by the industry, the magnitude of this benefit is seldom understood.

---

7 An early version of OmniScore[SM], built by GE Capital's Mortgage Corporation, was used in this comparison.

8 Since the future performance of a loan also depends on other factors that are neither predictable nor controllable, scoring should not be viewed as a substitute for portfolio geographic dispersion.

9 The percentage of applicants approved was first established by the guideline technique at, say, X percent for "streamline" approvals and Y percent for "traditional" approvals. The score was then used to rank the same applicant population and the best X percent of this ranking was used as the score's streamline approval population and the following Y percent as the score's traditional approval population.

Although this example comes from the mortgage industry, the loss avoidance benefit due to scoring is believed to be similar across all asset classes where there is meaningful data on which to develop scores. The benefit of loss avoidance is only one of many. Equally important is the benefit of fast, consistent, unbiased, and defensible decision making. This is especially true in today's environment of pre-approvals, on-line banking, Internet Web sites, and Fair Lending considerations.

Application scoring ranges in degree of scope from providing supplemental information to the underwriter (who makes the final decision) to totally automated decision making independent of an underwriter's intervention. In the card industry it is estimated that more than 95 percent of all applicants are processed without any assistance from a human underwriter. In the mortgage industry, the application of scoring for underwriting purposes is less mature. There, scoring is used to determine the "processing path" or degree of underwriting and level of documentation required. Score-suggested declinations typically are reviewed by a human underwriter before a declination is issued. This too is changing as the scores' declination messaging or "adverse action reasons" improve and Fair Lending recommendations are updated. In fact, the OCC has now identified an area of concern entitled "disparate treatment" designed to address what happens when an underwriter overrides a score suggested declination and approves a loan.[10] The OCC's intention here is to eliminate any bias introduced after the use of, and independent from, the scoring model.

Score based underwriting is typically the first application explored when scoring technology is introduced to a new product type. A natural extension of this is risk based or score based pricing.

## RISK BASED PRICING

Risk based pricing is not a new idea. The mortgage industry, for example, has offered different note rates for different levels of risk for decades, and for those who put less than 20 percent of the house's value into the down payment, the industry requires that mortgage insurance premiums be paid. These higher loan to value (LTV) ratio loans have been demonstrated to be of significantly higher risk. The mortgage insurance industry itself uses risk based pricing, as evidenced by a premium structure based on the LTV, product type, and level of coverage.

---

10 The appendix of OCC document number OCC 97-24 dated May 20, 1997, provides an excellent discussion of potential discriminatory score application issues.

In the card industry, the practice of different credit card annual percentage rates (APR) for those of varying risk is commonplace. Recently, however, the metrics used in risk based pricing structures are being replaced by scoring technology. Once again, the card industry leads in this area—the score based pricing mechanism has been used for some time at a somewhat coarse level in the card industry, whereas it is only beginning to transform the mortgage industry. What the entire lending industry is now beginning to see is the evolution from risk based pricing to score based pricing.

The basic premise is the same for score based and risk based pricing—provide a more competitively priced product to the deserving consumer by reducing the cross subsidization of losses and expenses, while better stabilizing the return. Score based pricing algorithms more accurately support multiple pricing tranches, each of which is independently priced for the target return.

Many factors go into a score based pricing algorithm beyond the expected loss level for the score tranche. These factors include, but are not limited to, the volatility of performance of the score tranche, its unique capital reserve requirement, specific servicing cost, cash flow, and other product-specific characteristics differing by score tranche, such as attrition rate for the card product and prepayment rate for the mortgage product. Basically, we have to comprehensively consider all the factors that will determine the future value of the asset. Essentially, we are valuing each score tranche independently. An optimal score based pricing algorithm should also fully integrate the secondary market or "execution" price of the individual score tranche in a real time fashion—a linkage which is in its infancy.

An obvious strategic question arises when one considers a score based pricing approach: why participate? Isn't inefficiency of information a good thing when competition and pricing are considered? As is the case with many changes, this too will be driven by competition. If a single major issuer/lender offers a lower rate to lower risk borrowers, the competition will be adversely selected. Very simply, borrowers seek the lowest rates for which they qualify. If not matched by the competition, lower rates in exchange for lower risk will result in not only a higher quality portfolio but also a larger share of this market. Similarly, higher rates for higher credit risks, if not matched, will also adversely select the competition since, once again, borrowers seek the lowest rates for which they qualify.

How are any of these strategic issues impacted by scoring, or, more specifically, the quality and accuracy of a score? First, in an efficient score based pricing market, the issuer with the most accurate technology will have the advantage. The reason is obvious—the rate charged will be optimally determined based on the future value of the asset. Borrowers shopping for a better rate will find pricing inefficiencies created by a less accurate scoring technology, which will cause adverse selection and reduce the returns of these issuers. Second, if an issuer bases its risk based pricing algorithm on a non-proprietary score, such as a generic credit score, price discounting can be easily matched by the competition causing product margin erosion. And when the competitor undercuts the price for a given score tranche, margin erosion accelerates. Score based pricing algorithms based on generic credit scores are too easily matched to provide any sustained competitive advantage.

Obviously, a score based pricing strategy requires that both the applicant information and the scoring technology be available at the point of sale before the price can be determined. This requirement is usually the major hurdle in the implementation of score based pricing algorithms based on custom built scores and is one of the reasons for the success of generic credit scores—credit scores are readily available in an online fashion from credit bureaus at relatively low cost. Although not as powerful as well developed custom built scores, generic scores typically do offer a level of risk separation capable of supporting at least minimal levels of pricing differentiation.

## PORTFOLIO ANALYSIS AND CREDIT ADMINISTRATION

Two other areas that closely follow the originations function chronologically and that are rapidly finding numerous applications of scoring technology are portfolio analysis and credit administration or auditing. In portfolio analysis, the score has become a single number surrogate measure for the quality of a loan or account. Unlike reactive measures such as delinquency or write-off rates, the score's value is proactive, allowing future portfolio performance to be quantified today. Score distributions across time, geography, and channel or source of origination (e.g., retail, wholesale, third party, branch office, underwriter, etc.) all produce meaningful insights in detecting portfolio quality drifts and the subsequent management of these drifts. The score has now become a meaningful and accepted segmenting variable for most analyses.

Scores are also becoming rapidly integrated throughout the credit administration function. Just as scores are applied in the underwriting process to identify loans that require full and careful review, they also can be used in the audit process to identify loans that have a higher probability of negative performance to make sure they were underwritten thoroughly based on properly calculated inputs. Once score based pricing becomes more of a reality in the mortgage industry, it will be necessary to also target for audits those loans that scored in the higher quality score range(s) and received a discount, to assure that the discount truly went to the deserving loans.

## FINANCE AND FORECASTING

The value of scoring technology is now beginning to be integrated within the traditional functions of Finance. A common application is in loss forecasting and reserving. Traditional techniques rely on past "roll rates" or transition matrices applied to current volume. These can be made more proactive when a score is used to assess the distribution of the quality of the current volume.[11] Any shifts in distribution are then incorporated into the calculation of the forecast.

When forecasts are based on a loss curve approach, scores can also be used to improve the forecast based on detected shifts in the distribution of current volume relative to past distribution. A newer technique is to develop different loss curves and total loss assumptions for different score ranges. These ideas also apply to improving prepayment and attrition forecasts.

## SECURITIZATION AND EXECUTION

The entire process of securitization is a relatively new outlet into the secondary market, which will undergo numerous innovations in the years to come. Many of these innovations will be based on the increased precision in determining both the magnitude and timing of future losses and prepayments that scoring will provide. Many feel that score based as well as future generations of loan level modeling will revolutionize the structures and investment products available through securitization today as much as or more than the change scoring has created in the origination process.

An obvious but new application area is in determining the credit enhancement level and bond class sizes based on a multivariate consideration of the loan level detail. Here, scoring is expected to both

---

11 It is important always to consider the bad rates of the scoring *distribution* of the portfolio and not simply the bad rate associated with the average or median score for the portfolio. The reason is that most scores are not scaled linearly; therefore, the bad rate associated with the average score is not necessarily the same as average bad rate for the portfolio. A simple example illustrates this. Consider a portfolio composed of only two loans, one of high quality and one of low quality, with credit scores of 800 and 600. The average credit score for this portfolio is 700, which has an associated bad rate of approximately 4 percent. An 800 credit score has a bad rate of 2 percent, while a 600 has a bad rate of 14 percent. [The bad rates quoted here are actual.] The actual expected bad rate of this portfolio of two loans is therefore easily computed to be 8 percent—twice the rate associated with the average score of the portfolio.

increase the accuracy of and reduce the variance associated with the prediction of future performance. Providing more predictable bond returns for the end investor will improve bond liquidity.[12] The reduction in variance around the future expected performance of a group of loans is of benefit to both the investor and the issuer, since credit enhancement levels incorporate a component due to the variance.

This, of course, does not mean that credit enhancement levels will decline once scoring becomes common in the rating process. In fact, pools of loans with a disproportionately higher percentage of poorer quality loans, as indicated by the pool's score distribution, will see their enhancement level increase. Many rating agency models result not only in credit enhancement reductions for score tranches of higher than average quality, but also enhancement increases for tranches of lower quality. As an example, for the highest quality tranches of jumbo mortgage loans, enhancement reductions can approach 200 basis points.[13] Enhancement increases for the lowest quality tranches are multiples of the average level. Duff & Phelps, Fitch IBCA, Moody's, and Standard and Poor's have now modified their rating technology to accept loan level scoring information for use in predicting the frequency of default associated with a group of loans. Many rating agencies have also begun to build their own scoring technology.

Another area of application is to better predict the timing of both losses and prepayments based on loan level information. Empirical evidence suggests that not only do score tranches have different loss and prepayment rates but the shape of their loss and prepayment curves may also be quite different. An improved understanding of the loss and prepay timing will not only aid in the valuation of bonds but also support the creation of new bond structures—and further hasten the securitization of new assets and other cash flows such as insurance risk and residuals currently held by the issuers.

Finally, any true risk or score based pricing approach needs to also incorporate the execution or secondary market price paid for the resulting security. Ideally, this should happen in real time, i.e., the note rate the consumer pays is the instantaneous result of a comprehensive consideration of many factors including prepayment, losses, and the price the market is willing to pay for this level of risk and expected net cash flow.

---

12 For some investment institutions, the fact that scoring increases informational efficiency "up stream" in the origination, pricing, and structuring processes is unwelcome news because it is expected to reduce the opportunity for arbitrage.

13 The benefits quoted here are based on GE Capital Mortgage Insurance's OmniScore[SM]. The actual benefit will depend on many factors and can only be determined by the rating agency.

## SERVICING AND COLLECTIONS

The success of scoring in the originations area has caused many to examine its application in both servicing and collections. Over time, servicing and collection information systems have improved to support the gathering of numerous account or loan characteristics, borrower attributes, and past repayment behavior data. Much of this information becomes available after origination or may have changed significantly after the account was scored during the origination process. Using this new information, especially account performance, to predict future performance is the goal of servicing and collection scoring models. See Chapter 7 for a detailed discussion of these types of models.

Servicing and collection scores differ from origination scores primarily because of the input data, not the technological approach to building the model.[14] Though these scores have access to the past origination data, they usually derive a large portion of their predictive power from recent account performance.[15] Servicing and collection scores also have access to the account's vintage, activity, and updated credit bureau data. It should be no surprise that servicing and collection models can typically be 25 to 50 percent more accurate than origination models.[16] The only problem is that the account is already on the books—there is no longer an option to decline the applicant or suggest another product. In terms of our earlier discussion about measurable and controllable risk, servicing and collection scores do a relatively good job at maximizing the measurable risk, but unfortunately collection and loss mitigation strategies are not as effective at avoiding the loss as not approving the risk in the first place.

Nonetheless, score based collection optimization techniques do produce welcomed benefits. These techniques range from simply prioritizing the dialer queues, based on the "need to call" as indicated by the collection score, to optimally choosing which collection resource to apply in order to maximize the net dollars collected. It is important to consider the cost of the collection resource in this optimization and therefore we choose to maximize the net dollars collected. In the card

---

14 This is beginning to change. Significant predictive power is now gained by incorporating the payment pattern as an indicator variable.

15 For example, credit bureau, collateral, and product information are the primary informational components of mortgage origination models. However, in collection scores, the recent past repayment performance on the mortgage plus related performance measures compose the most important predictive components.

16 As measured by the ability to separate "goods" from "bads" using the KS measure for comparing mortgage origination and collection models.

industry, improvements of 3 percent in actual dollars collected have been demonstrated.[17] Score based collection approaches in the mortgage industry have recently been motivated by the availability of servicing and collection scores from Fannie Mae and Freddie Mac. Benefits in this industry include an approximate 25 to 50 percent decrease in outbound collection calls, with no negative impact on dollars collected as well as a significant reduction in inbound calls.[18]

The servicing of performing accounts has also benefited from the application of scoring technology. Beneficial applications include credit line management for the credit card product and prescreen risk filter applications during retention and cross sell campaigns.

## CONCLUSION

Yes, today scoring is an accepted, stable, and accurate technology. There already exist many successful applications of scoring technology throughout the credit life cycle. These applications have led to a simpler, more consistent, unbiased, faster, and more accurate decision making process. As you go through this collection of chapters, the more important thing to remember is that there is always a better way—the next generation of scoring applications is expected to lead to a new credit process, not merely an optimization of the current one.

---

17 See Makuch, W.M., Dodge, J.L., Ecker, J.G., Granfors, D.C., Hahn, G.J. (1992), "Managing Consumer Credit Delinquency in the U.S. Economy: A Multi-Billion Dollar Management Science Application," *Interfaces Special Issue: Franz Edelman Award Papers,* Volume 22, Number 1, pp. 90-109.
18 Sample results achieved by major servicers using Fannie Mae's Risk Profiler™ and Freddie Mac's Early Indicator℠. Reductions in delinquencies are also beginning to be identified. See for instance, Sakole, Risk Profiler™, Mortgage Bankers Association, National Mortgage Servicing Conference, June 4th, 1998 presentation.

# 2

# ORGANIZATIONAL ISSUES IN BUILDING AND MAINTAINING CREDIT RISK MODELS

**Leonard J. McCahill**
*Credit & Risk Management Associates*
*Copyright 1998 Fair, Isaac and Companies, Inc.*

The ultimate success of an organization that uses credit risk models is not measured by the statistical power of the models but by the delinquency and loss performance of the its credit portfolios. The best statistical models do not guarantee success; experienced risk management and consistent application of sound credit practices do. This is not to say that the power of the credit risk models is not important, but rather that maximizing profitability is a function of how the models are developed, used, applied, monitored and managed.

The most successful organizations do not always have better models, but they always have risk management people who are experts in actuarial management, knowledgeable about the industry and the latest technology, and highly analytical. They manage credit risk models in accordance with the goals and objectives of the organization, and constantly challenge the models by aggressively testing new strategies. Data retention and sophisticated use of the management information system for reporting are the lifeblood of today's most successful financial institutions.

## MODEL DEVELOPMENT

The first step in the development process is to decide who will develop the risk models. This can be an internal statistical group or an external vendor. There are advantages and disadvantages associated with both.

## Internal Development

Using staff resources may be a cost-effective and efficient way to develop credit risk models. Internal staff should be knowledgeable about the product, the market, and organizational issues that may affect the sample and implementation process. Internal development may also make it more cost-effective to develop homogeneous models that take advantage of unique product, customer, or geographic differences, thus greatly improving their performance by focusing them on more similar credit products or users.

The use of internal resources will generally result in more model experimentation, testing several models, with different characteristics or performance definitions for the same products, in order to create the best predictive and most cost-effective model.

As models age, they begin to lose power. Credit risk models built internally can be updated or redeveloped quickly and at lower cost than those built by an external vendor. It is also possible with internal resources to schedule periodic updates to keep the models current and minimize the impact of changes in the economy or product.

In spite of these advantages, internal development does have disadvantages. First, the development of risk models requires special skills and experience. It is truly an art. It is always possible to develop credit risk models with excellent statistical indicators. However, a model that tests as statistically strong in the development sample may not work in the credit marketplace. There are dozens of reasons for a model to look good in the laboratory and not in the real world, including:

- The sample definition of "good and "bad" accounts
- The sample selection process
- How the sample treats rejects
- Previous organization and operational factors
- Changes in product terms and conditions
- Historical and future marketing efforts
- Credit policy exclusions and changes

The desire for people to grow and advance within an organization will typically make it difficult to keep knowledgeable model developers long enough to reap the rewards of their experience. It is therefore very important that a definite career path and potential for senior status be established for statisticians and risk managers who do model development.

Another potential weakness of internal development is isolation from technical and statistical advances in the area of model development. It is therefore a good idea to maintain good working relationships with credit scoring vendors and to periodically use them to develop models with the assistance of internal people. Participation in related technical and industry conferences is also a good way to ensure that the internal group stays current. This will keep them abreast of advances and "tricks" vendors learn from developing different types of models.

## External Development

The decision to use external resources is not always a matter of who has the best technology, but of who will design and deliver a model suited to the business goals and market. Although technology is necessary to the predictive power of the models, the difference in power between the different technologies (discriminant analysis, neural networks, decision trees, etc.) is not significant. Differences in predictive power between credit risk models are more a function of the differences in the skill, experience, and care of the model developers than of the technologies used.

The best gauges of vendor value are the composition of the project team, their experience with similar situations, familiarity with the system on which the model will be implemented, the thoroughness of their plan, flexibility, willingness to experiment, and project schedule.

As the credit market becomes more competitive and saturated, it is important that a vendor be willing to look at different characteristics and unique performance groups that may enhance the model's effectiveness and differentiate your model from the competition's.

A major advantage of going outside is the vast experience external vendors have gained from developing models for a wide variety of clients, products and situations. Their people are generally more expert than in-house staff can be and have more varied knowledge. The disadvantages of employing an external vendor may be cost, time to develop the model, and inflexibility.

## Development Sample

Regardless of who develops the model or what statistical techniques are employed, the single most important aspect of any development effort is the quality of the data sample that will be used to create the model. Factors that must be considered before acquiring the sample include all of the following:

**Products**  There are obvious products that do not typically belong together; secured and unsecured; installment and revolving; mortgage and credit card. However, even apparently similar products may not be compatible; classic and gold credit cards; new and used auto; credit card and revolving lines; large lines and small lines. It is often difficult to determine at the outset which products can be combined within the same scoring model. Delinquency, charge-off, and roll rates can give an indication, but the only reliable way is to take large enough samples to be able to test actual performance of each with a combined model. If performance of individual products is poor, then the same sample could be used to develop more targeted models. Past experience with combined product models may also help determine the most advantageous combination of products in a single model. However, the only truly reliable method is to analyze the effectiveness of the individual products in a single model, removing products that perform poorly from the sample, and develop unique models.

The goal is to optimize the predictive ability of the score model for each product. This optimization decision is one that considers the additional lift to be had from individual models relative to the cost of development, implementation and use.

***Definition of Creditworthiness***   The next decision relates to how the sample defines "good" and "bad" customers. The definition is based on the number of times an account reaches a specific delinquency stage or worse. Many different methods have been used in making this important decision. There is the old standby of gathering a team of experts from credit, collections, and marketing to debate the definition until consensus is reached. A popular and fairly effective method is to look at account roll rates. The accepted standard for "bads" is the delinquency bucket where more than 50 percent of the accounts roll to the next bucket. In choosing this method, it is important to understand the collection process employed during the roll rate period. If more than 50 percent of the accounts roll once they reach 60 days past due, but aggressive collection activity does not occur until the account reaches 90 days, then a 60-day definition might be too conservative. However, if strong collection activity commences at 30-days, a 60-day definition might be a good one.

In defining creditworthiness, it is important to keep in mind why the organization is developing the risk model. If the goal is to increase revenue and market share, a more delinquent definition might be appropriate. If the goal is to reduce collection costs and loss rates, a less delinquent definition might be appropriate. More often than not, the final definition is a combination of roll rate analysis and business decision. This is a good way to do it.

It is also a good idea to keep the definition simple. Determination of "goods" and "bads" is fairly imprecise and arbitrary. Many cases organizations have come up with very complicated definitions (e.g., a "bad" is an account that has been 30 days late six or more times; or 60 days three or more times; or 90 days one or more times in the past twelve months). While this may initially seem like a good idea, it has some serious problems:

- How can you tell if this is a reliable definition?
- Accounts that are chronic 30s and never 60 may be very profitable.
- It is very difficult to track involved definitions.

It is a better idea to include an "indeterminate" in the definition. This is a group of accounts that cannot be classified as either "good" or "bad." The "indeterminate" accounts would be sampled, but would not be used in the actual development of the risk model. They would, however, be used to create the performance forecast of the model. If an "indeterminate" group is established, it is important that it does not represent more than 10 percent of the entire portfolio. If it were greater than 10 percent, there is a possibility that a unique group of accounts might be excluded from the development sample. For example, if it is decided that accounts that have been more than three times 30 days are "indeterminate," and if you have a customer base of farmers or teachers who may become 30 days delinquent during certain seasons, a large "indeterminate" sample might exclude them.

Another consideration in deciding upon the "good" and "bad" definition is the performance time frame. Accounts need to be on the books long enough to be classified as "good." This is typically a minimum of twelve months. "Bad" accounts on the other hand, can be classified as such with as little as three to four months on the books, depending upon the delinquency stage used in the definition.

On the other side of the performance definition, accounts used in the development sample need to be relatively current. Depending upon the product, this can range from as little as 24 months (personal loans) to as much as seven years (mortgages). The objective is to try to keep the application information as current as possible within the expected life cycle of the product.

It is always a good idea to include the criteria used in the performance definition as a coded characteristic available for analysis. This should be done to make it possible to change the "good" and "bad" definition if necessary, rather than having to pull an entirely new sample.

***Exclusions***   The design of the development sample must also consider what needs to be excluded from the sample. The exclusion list should include application types that will not be scored as well as any credit policy exclusions. The actual list will vary by product and organization and may include:

- Employees
- Deceased customers
- Frauds
- VIPs
- Voluntary cancellations
- Pre-approved accounts
- Underage applicants
- Out of market
- Bankruptcies
- No credit bureau file
- Inactive accounts

The goal is to create a development sample that will match the population upon which the model can make a credit decision, has had a chance to perform, and is based on reliable application information. If a credit policy mandates that, without exception, applicants must be at least eighteen years old in order to be approved, then younger applicants must be excluded from the sample. Similary, accounts that have not had any activity in the last year lack the performance criteria to be classified as either "good," "bad" or "indeterminate."

***Unique Groups***    When designing the sample, it is also a good idea to consider the make up of the portfolio and market. If the market is in a military area or a university town, it might be useful to consider whether individual models for military and young adults might be beneficial. It is important that the sample size be large enough to (1) accommodate the need to test the unique groups on the single model and (2) be the basis for developing individual models.

***Prescreen Criteria***    Likewise, it is important to include applicants who have routinely been pre-screened and declined in the past who, due to a policy or market change, may become candidates for approval with the new risk model. This would include applicants who were consistently eliminated due to debt burden criteria, thin credit bureau files, or a 90-day delinquency. These accounts need to be included within the development sample as part of the "decline" sample.

***Sample Selection***    Selection of applications to be included in the sample (good, bad, indeterminate, decline) needs to be random, representative of the product, and include only account types identified in the sample design process. The list of accounts eligible should include information to make the selection and development process more reliable and flexible, such as:

- Account number
- Date booked or declined
- Delinquency history (number of times 30, 60, 90 etc.)
- Original loan/line amount
- Amount of charge-off
- Debt burden

*Sample Data*   The application and credit bureau data used to develop the risk model may be either manually coded or secured from an automated application system. Coding data manually is very time-consuming, and the input must be audited for correctness. Manually coded credit bureau data generally do not contain all the detail necessary to develop a sophisticated risk model.

Automated data is much more convenient and efficient, though it is still important to audit the accuracy of the data input process. It is also very important that there not be any changes to the database during the sample time frame, whether the changes are capturing new data, eliminating certain characteristics, changing the way data are stored, adding new accounts, or changing demographic or credit bureau codes.

Another consideration in the use of coded data is the depth of the data archived. Are variables required for the existing credit policy or scoring model the only ones captured? Is data archived in raw form or consolidated into ranges or codes? If the latter, it may be necessary to manually append additional data to the sample file.

As the credit market place and economy change, so too may the characteristics that define "good" from "bad" customers. Often, variables that are not significant identifiers of high-risk accounts today become very important later. It is therefore wise to include a complete data set within any risk model development sample.

*Selection of Variables*   Selection of the variables to be included in the final risk model is not exclusively a statistical decision. While any variable in a risk model must be statistically sound, not all statistically sound variables should be in a model. Variables that are expensive or time consuming to obtain, such as debt burden, should be excluded unless their omission seriously undermines the model's predictive ability. Variables that are influenced by the organization or individual should also be excluded and either replaced by correlated variables or by a separate model be developed for customers with that particular condition. A good example is "cash advance utilization." If an organization actively promotes cash advances, then it is counterproductive to include the variable in the model. Cash advance utilization is typically a very strong negative indicator. A unique model for customers who have obtained cash advances should be developed rather than including a variable that penalizes cash advance utilization in the model. Other factors to be considered in selecting variables for inclusion in a model are:

- Is the variable legal?
- Is it reasonable and factual?
- It is easily interpreted?
- Is it sensitive to inflation?
- Is it difficult to manipulate?

*Implementation*   The best model will fail if the organization does not think through how the model will be used. The most common reason that credit and behavior scores fail is the fact that the models are not properly implemented. Implementation of risk models requires as much attention and care as their development. To ensure the success of the risk model, all the following steps must be taken:

- Business processes must be re-engineered to take advantage of the model.
- Management must actively support the risk model, making certain that it is being used properly.
- Systems to support the functional needs of the model must be installed.
- The systems must be audited to insure that they correctly calculate the scores.
- Users and management must be trained on the development history and how the model is to be used and managed.
- The model should be tested on a sample of recent accounts that were not included in the development sample to make sure that the model and the its forecast (through-the-door and approval rate, etc.) are reasonably compatible with the current applicant or customer population. If significant differences occur, the test needs to be verified and the cause of the deviation resolved.
- Credit policy and procedures must be updated to account for the use of the risk model. This should include setting the cutoff score, score strategies, limit assignment matrices, signing authorities, information verification, exceptions, and override rules.
- The only overrides that should be allowed are those that can be controlled and tracked. Specific reasons for allowable overrides must be coded so that they can be included in the masterfile and performance tracking MIS. Both highside and lowside overrides should be allowed. By definition, lowside override performance can

be tracked but highside overrides cannot because they are not booked. It is therefore a good idea to book a sample of highside overrides so that their performance can be tracked. The delinquency performance of each override category should then be constantly compared to the performance of accounts in the non-override group. If the performance is worse for a lowside override group, then this override should no longer be allowed. If performance is better, the policy should be changed to permit it. The situation is the opposite for highside overrides. If in the process of monitoring performance of the overrides it is learned that lowside overrides perform fairly well and highside perform poorly, the performance of the entire risk model needs to be questioned.

■ An excellent way to identify the best risk management strategy is to experiment vigorously with appropriate management information systems.

■ Management and users should be kept constantly informed of the performance of the risk model and any exceptions to the model recommendation.

*MIS*    Management information system reporting is absolutely critical to the success of any credit risk model implementation. Without meaningful reports, it is not possible to know how well the risk model is accomplishing its objectives or how well the organization's strategies dependent on the model are performing. Risk models are very powerful and effective tools that can significantly improve profitability and productivity. However, a model that is not properly managed through MIS can cause great harm, in the form of higher delinquency and charge-off or in revenue lost because good customers are declined. Consistent and timely MIS reports are therefore crucial. The system needs to describe the performance not only of the model but also of alternative strategies applied to specific risk categories.

If credit risk models are to be managed effectively, the reports produced must provide information on population stability, delinquency and loss results by risk category, experience by individual characteristic, and results compared to forecast and product norms, in a form that allows comparison of similar vintages at the same point in time. The objective is to make the reports as recent as possible so as to warn of changes and trends as early as possible. All MIS reports should be designed as early warning indicators. Traditional MIS reports depend too much on full term performance. This is not acceptable in today's competitive environment.

***Essential Ingredients for Success***    If the risk models developed are to be effective:

- Members of the project team must be seasoned professionals from each operational unit that may be impacted by the risk model: senior management, product manager, credit, marketing, collections, operations, legal, audit, customer service, and authorizations.
- The project team must be involved in all phases of the process, from selection of the development resource through implementation and ongoing validation.
- The sample design—which is more important than the development technique—must take into account the past and future as well as portfolio profile and business objectives.
- Reporting standards for the MIS area are absolutely critical and must be established before the system can be implemented.
- Senior management must actively support the risk model.
- Policies and procedures must be written and communicated to all involved in the application and management of the risk model.
- Performance results should be communicated to all members of the project team.
- It is important to test and track the performance of different strategies using test and control groups.
- Model validation must be a formal process requiring senior management sign-off.

## CONCLUSION

Only application of sound risk management practices by experienced risk managers will ensure success in today's competitive environment. World class organizations employ state-of-the-art credit technologies only when comprehensive management information systems are in place to monitor credit and revenue performance of the portfolios impacted by the technologies. Risk models are developed in concert with the goals and skills of the organization and tracked with a focus on dollar performance of the models rather than the more traditional emphasis on account performance. The best organizations are willing to test different strategies to enhance market penetration and portfolio profitability. It is important that we keep sight of risk management basics, not allowing old or new technologies to run credit operations without the assistance of appropriate MIS, professional analysis, and experienced management.

# 3

# USING CONSUMER CREDIT INFORMATION

**Maria T. Pincetich**
**Kristin M. Tobin**
*Senior Product Research Managers*
*Trans Union*

In today's highly competitive world the business landscape is changing rapidly. Every day newspaper business sections announce mergers, buy-outs, and acquisitions that turn small businesses into divisions of large corporations. Staying ahead of the competition and protecting market share means finding new, more efficient, ways of doing business. This is reflected in the increasing demand for objective information to help make profitable business decisions at the consumer level.

Not so long ago, creditors had a personal basis for offering credit. Often they were small town neighbors or social acquaintances. As organizations grew or were acquired by larger companies, however, the community structure disintegrated. As decisionmaking became more centralized, the traditional method of judgmental review by a loan officer was no longer feasible. Nor was it cost efficient.

To make the decision process more streamlined and quantifiable, access to more predictive information became imperative. Credit bureau information became extremely valuable because it is objective, diverse, and current. In the 1960s, the first computer-driven scoring model was developed using credit bureau information. Using information included on the credit application, cross-referenced to consumer payment history as described in a credit report, key factors were identified as characteristics that could be used to predict future behavior.

# CREDIT REPORTING

Everyone who has applied for or uses credit or has a public record in the United States has a credit report. The report verifies financial and account-related information, such as current employment, use and types of credit, collections, and reported legal encumbrances. This information is updated to credit bureaus monthly by credit grantors, court houses, and collection agencies. Among the methods for gathering data are account receivable tapes, manual credit updates from computer terminals, inquiries via remote terminals, and consumer relations systems.

Even though any creditor can report information to a credit bureau as long as quality standards are met, a creditor must show proof of permissible purpose to obtain a credit report for evaluation. The Fair Credit Reporting Act (FCRA) defines *permissible purpose* as a legitimate business need in connection with a business transaction that is initiated by the consumer; or the review of an account to determine whether the consumer continues to meet the terms of the account.

A legitimate business need can be an extension of credit, review of a current account, an employment decision, a question of insurance eligibility, or a court order. Sound lending decisions rely on credit bureau information because the shared credit information allows creditors to assess a consumer's *total* credit experiences. Access to a complete credit history is the most powerful tool a lender can have. Credit bureau information makes lending decisions more cost-effective, more consistent, and more objective. This will be illustrated throughout this chapter.

## Components of the Credit Report

There are four essential sections in a credit report:

1. *indicative information,* the consumer's demographics;
2. *public record and collection information,* court actions and third-party recovery efforts;
3. *payment history,* past and current credit relationships and behavior; and
4. *inquiry information,* potential creditors and other parties who have requested a copy of a consumer's file.

Each of these is discussed below. An example of a credit report is shown in Figure 3-1.

*Indicative Information*   The first section of the credit report displays the date of the request and the name of the creditor requesting the report, followed by the consumer's demographic details:

## FIGURE 3–1

### Sample Credit Report

**CREDIT REPORT**

```
   GOi duncan,elizabeth*2 9932,,woodbine,,chicago,il,60693*5 001-01-0418**

                                      TRANS UNION CREDIT REPORT
❶ <FOR>        <SUB NAME>             <MKT SUB>      <INFILE>      <DATE>       <TIME>
  (1) D248     ABC DEPT STORE         06 CH          4/74          2/15/97    09:36CT

  <SUBJECT>                                                  <SSN>            <BIRTH DATE>
❷ DUNCAN, ELIZABETH                                          002-02-2222        2/53
  <ALSO KNOWN AS>                                                             <TELEPHONE>
  COOK, ELIZABETH                                                             555-5555

  <CURRENT ADDRESS>                                                           <DATE RPTD>
  9932 WOODBINE, #9B CHICAGO IL. 60693                                          1/96
  <FORMER ADDRESS>
  10 N. CAMINO, OAKLAND CA. 94583                                               4/94
                                                    <POSITION>
  <CURRENT EMPLOYER AND ADDRESS>                    <INCOME>   <VERF>   <RPTD>   <HIRE>
  MARRIOTT HOTELS                                   CONCIERGE
  8638 GRAND, ANYTOWN IL.                            32500Y    3/96     3/96     3/93
  ------------------------------------------------------------------------------------
  S P E C I A L   M E S S A G E S
❸ ***TRANS-ALERT: INPUT SSN DOES NOT MATCH FILE SSN***
❹ ***HAWK-ALERT: INPUT SSN ISSUED: 1936 - 1950; ST: NH
                 FILE SSN NOT ISSUED BY SOCIAL SECURITY ADMINISTRATION***
  ------------------------------------------------------------------------------------
  M O D E L   P R O F I L E         ❻* * * A L E R T* * *
❼ ***NEW DELPHI ALERT: SCORE❺+775: 26, 03, 06, 25 ***
  ------------------------------------------------------------------------------------
  C R E D I T   S U M M A R Y     * * *     T O T A L   F I L E   H I S T O R Y
❽ PR=1 ❾COL=1 ❿NEG=1 ⓫HSTNEG=1-6 ⓬TRD=2 ⓭RVL=1 ⓮INST=1 ⓯MTG=0 ⓰OPN=0 ⓱INQ=2
              ⓲HIGH CRED ⓳CRED LIM ⓴BALANCE ㉑PAST DUE ㉒MNTHLY PAY AVAILABLE
  REVOLVING:   $500       $1000      $100       $          $20          ㉓90%
  INSTALLMENT: $16.0K     $          $12.4K     $1974      $282
㉔ TOTALS:      $16.5K     $1000      $12.5K     $1974      $302
  ------------------------------------------------------------------------------------
㉕ P U B L I C   R E C O R D S
  SOURCE       DATE       LIAB       ECOA        ASSETS       DOCKET#
  TYPE                               COURT LOC                PLAINTIFF/ATTORNEY
  Z 4932059    10/95R     $13.0K     C           $0           93B38521
  CHAPTER 11 BANKRUPTCY              CHICAGO, IL              R. SMITH/D. WINSLOW
  ------------------------------------------------------------------------------------
㉖ C O L L E C T I O N S
  SUBNAME        SUBCODE      ECOA   OPENED     CLOSED    $PLACED    CREDITOR         MOP
  ACCOUNT#                           VERIFIED             BALANCE    REMARKS
  ADVANCED COL  Y 999C004      I     5/93       5/93F     $2500      ABC BANK         09P
  12345                              4/96A                $1000      MAKING PAYMENTS
  ------------------------------------------------------------------------------------
  T R A D E S
㉗ SUBNAME     ㉚SUBCODE  ㉜OPENED  ㉟HIGHCRED  ㊳TERMS  ㊶MAXDELQ  ㊸PAYPAT    1-12 ㊻MOP
㉘ ACCOUNT#               ㉝VERFIED ㊱CREDLIM   ㊴PASTDUE㊷AMT-MOP  ㊹PAYPAT   13-24
㉙ ECOA㉛COLLATRL/LOANTYP㉞CLSD/PD ㊲BALANCE   ㊵REMARKS            ㊺MO     30/60/90

  AMERICAN BK B 6661001 10/94    $16.0K      60M282    1/96     545543211111      I05
  9876543210            4/96V                $1974   $1974   05 11111111
  I    AUTOMOBILE                $12.4K      *CONTACT SUBSCRIBER    19V   1/ 1/ 5

  FILENES      D 3847002 8/91    $500        MIN20              111111111111      R01
  2212345678            3/96V    $1000                          111111111111
  C    /CREDITCARD               $100                                 24V   0/ 0/ 0
  ------------------------------------------------------------------------------------
㊼ I N Q U I R I E S
  DATE        SUBCODE          SUBNAME            DATE         SUBCODE          SUBNAME
  4/17/96     DCH248           ABC DEPT STORE     3/7/96       BPH9999          TEST BANK
  ------------------------------------------------------------------------------------
㊽ E N D   O F   C R E D I T   R E P O R T   -   S E R V I C E D   B Y :
  TRANS UNION CORPORATION                                                  NNN-NNN-NNNN
  PO BOX 390, SPRINGFIELD, PA. 19064
```

- consumer's name (and any aliases)
- current address and date reported
- up to two previous addresses and date reported
- social security number (if available)
- date of birth (if available)
- telephone number (if available)
- most current employer
- one previous employer (including addresses, position, income, and date employment verified, reported and/or hired, if available).

The next section, Special Messages, alerts the creditor to conditions in the data, such as suspected fraud, inconsistencies between the consumer's name and social security number, or the presence of a consumer statement. Consumers may write a statement that articulates their issues to be incorporated into their credit report. A consumer statement would be included, for instance, if the consumer was a victim of fraudulent account activity or had experienced a personal hardship that had caused delinquency. For example, a consumer might explain that late payments were due to a job lay-off.

If a creditor has requested one or more scoring models, the numeric scores are listed after Special Messages. (Scores will be explained in the next section and a discussed in more detail in Chapter 4.)

Finally, a snapshot view is provided under the Credit Summary, listing data by type of credit (installment, revolving, etc.), high credit, credit limit, balance, past due amount, and monthly payment available. *High credit* is the highest outstanding balance a cardholder account has ever had. *Past due* are payments that have become due but have not been made according to the terms and conditions of the account. *Monthly payment available* is the average monthly payment amount the consumer owes as defined by the creditor.

***Public Records and Collections***   Next comes the public record and collection information, which must comply with the Fair Credit Reporting Act (FCRA). Public record information, obtained from county, state and federal courts, notifies inquirers about civil judgments and tax liens in the past seven years and bankruptcies filed in the past ten years. Collections are accounts that have been transferred to a professional debt-collection firm. Accounts that go to collections are typically classified as charge-offs, where the creditor assumes the loss if the consumer fails to repay the debt.

***Payment History***   The payment history section, also known as trades or tradelines, contains the data that is most valuable for assessing credit risk.

Tradelines are the consumer's credit accounts. Each tradeline provides an ongoing record of the consumer's usage and payments. In this category are mortgages, bank cards, retail credit cards, installment loans for automobiles, and personal lines of credit (secured or unsecured).

*Inquiries*    The final section of the report lists the businesses that have requested a credit report for a particular consumer. Depending on the intention of the creditor, each may be either a *hard inquiry* and a *promotional inquiry*. A creditor seeking a credit report because a consumer has applied for credit posts a hard inquiry. A hard inquiry is. initiated by the consumer's action.

A creditor that wants to market a product to a consumer with whom there is no current account relationship may use credit bureau information, including objective criteria and scoring models, to determine whether to extend a firm offer of credit. This is a promotional inquiry, representing the creditor's efforts to market a credit product. Because promotional inquiries are not seen by creditors, they do not adversely effect the consumer's ability to obtain credit.

## Credit Bureau Scores

Credit bureau data has proven to be very powerful in predicting a variety of consumer behaviors, from delinquency to revenue potential. Credit bureau information is predictive because it is objective, current, and based on actual payment performance. It is also extremely diverse because it encompasses all credit-active individuals in the United States regardless of geography, race, religion, or type of credit used. This allows for the study of almost every type of credit experience possible.

Creditors must evaluate the profitability of applicants and current account holders; credit bureau scores aid in this evaluation. Credit bureau scores use the most current record of a consumer's payment behavior across all reported credit accounts, as well as public records and inquiries, to predict a variety of behaviors, such as the likelihood of account repayment, revenue potential, or account closure. Specific examples of these uses are provided in sections to follow.

*Credit Bureau Score Design*    Credit bureau scores are composed of characteristics, attributes, and points resulting in a score. The score, usually three or four digits, is associated with specific performance outcome. For example, a score may predict the odds that an individual will go delinquent, or it may predict the amount an individual is likely to repay on a past due balance. A *characteristic* is a predictive element of a credit report, such as "number of tradelines." An *attribute* is the value of a specific characteristic. For example, if an individual has four tradelines on file, the attribute for the characteristic "number of tradelines" would be 4. Points are assigned based on the relative importance of the attribute in predicting a given outcome.

Characteristics are derived from the public record, collection, tradeline, and inquiry sections of the credit report. Indicative information is not used in generic credit bureau scores because it is not as predictive as account information and could be perceived as discriminatory. Some common characteristics used in scoring models are:

(1) Previous credit performance, meaning reliability in paying past debts, across all obligations.
(2) Current indebtedness: how much is owed today?
(3) Need for new credit: is the consumer shopping for more credit?
(4) Types of credit accounts available, including installment loans, credit cards, etc., and
(5) Length of time credit has been in use.

The relationships among characteristics have proven to be highly predictive of future credit performance. Because characteristics are reported by creditors, they are objective records of actual payment behavior.

Though the model development process can be summarized simply; the actual process can be lengthy and rigorously detail-oriented. In general, building a predictive credit bureau model is reliant on a diverse, unbiased development sample of hundreds of thousands of credit reports. This sample is used to determine which characteristics best predict a specific performance outcome. Once the characteristics are identified, the attributes that assign value are defined in points that reflect the relative importance of the attributes to the overall model. For the example "number of tradelines," the number of points to be awarded for a file with 4 tradelines, which may differ from the number awarded for 5 tradelines, based on statistical techniques that show that 4 tradelines is more or less predictive than 5 tradelines. The credit bureau scorecard illustrates how the system works:

| Characteristic | Attributes | Points |
|---|---|---|
| Number of Trades | 0 | 10 |
| | 1-3 | 20 |
| | 4 or more | 30 |
| Age of Trades | 0-6 months | 5 |
| | 7-12 months | 15 |
| | 13 months or more | 30 |
| Average Revolving Balance | $0-$200 | 40 |
| | $201 - $500 | 25 |
| | $501- $1500 | 10 |

Points assigned to each characteristic add up to the score associated with a specific performance measure. For a risk score, the model must show clear separation and rank-ordering of "goods" and "bads." To predict a continuous performance outcome like annual revenue potential, the model must rank accounts from the lowest revenue generators to the highest.

*Validation*   Before releasing a model for general use, the credit bureau and model developer will validate it on a portion of the development sample. A percentage of credit files selected randomly from those that were provided to determine the characteristics and weights, or points, in a model is withheld for the validation. The "hold-out" sample is scored with the new model. Actual performance is then evaluated to determine the number of goods and bads for each score interval. A model that demonstrates separation and rank ordering on the hold-out sample is statistically valid. Before releasing a model, developers often perform additional validations on independent samples to reassure themselves about the model's predictive capability.

To use a credit bureau score effectively, accounts should be analyzed to determine how the score relates to a specific situation, such as delinquency or bankruptcy. A cut-off score acceptable to one company may not be acceptable to another. Although the scoring algorithm remains the same, the odds of performance associated with each score interval will vary by user. For example, a score of 100 may translate to a delinquency rate of 2 percent in the development sample, 3 percent for Company A, and 5 percent for Company B, because of variation in the composition of the samples, such as the type of accounts, age of the accounts, marketing strategies, or account management strategies. It is recommended that each company "validate" a credit bureau score on a sample from its own portfolio by scoring the portfolio at a previous point in time and then comparing the score intervals to current performance measures, such as delinquency rates. The company can then determine what level of risk is acceptable for certain actions. This concept will be discussed further below.

*Applications of Credit Bureau Scores*   Initially, credit bureau scores were developed to evaluate risk—"good" versus "bad" performance—across all accounts reported on a credit report. Today, enhancements in data availability and customer sophistication and acceptance mean that scores can be used to predict different performance measures for different industries and different stages in a customer relationship.

Industry-specific credit bureau models provide a predictive lift over generic risk scores for specific types of accounts. The first models employed a general definition of delinquency, such as bankruptcy or ninety days delinquency on any credit account type. Industry-specific models define delinquency according to a typical bad rating on that particular industry's tradeline, giving them additional predictive power.

The need for industry-specific models is illustrated in the diversity of "bad" definitions. For example, in mortgage models a bad account is typically a mortgage tradeline that showed a foreclosure, write-off, or bankruptcy. Bank card risk models define a bad as a bank card tradeline that showed a 90 day delinquency or worse. Industry-specific risk scores are available for auto loans, bank cards, installment loans, personal finance loans, mortgages, insurance policies, retail cards, and cellular accounts.

As credit bureau scores have become more widely accepted, models have been developed to predict a variety of performance measures that can be linked to decisions made throughout the account lifecycle. Lifecycle refers to the different phases that a company and a consumer pass through as they establish and sustain a relationship. The three major phases are typically (1) targeting/acquisition, (2) application review/ booking, and (3) account management/portfolio review.

Within these stages, creditors must face a variety of decisions that can be managed more efficiently and accurately with a scoring model. Within the acquisition stage, "adverse selection" must be addressed, since the worst credit risks will be most responsive to a product offer. Marketing programs therefore use scoring models to identify the best risks that will respond. In the application review and booking stage, approval or decline decisions and pricing terms are based on risk and fraud potential, among other performance measures. Finally, in the account management or portfolio review stage, a myriad of decisions about cross-selling, usage, attrition, revenue generation, and collection procedures can be addressed with different credit bureau scores. The following sections describe the use of credit bureau scores in each of these account lifecycle stages.

*Targeting/Acquisition*   The key to target marketing is identifying the appropriate targets for a product up-front, so that resources can be optimally allocated and activation rates and profitability can be maximized. Targeting with credit information can expand the base of acceptable consumers, increase response rates, and assist in setting product terms.

A common source of targeting information is reported at the neighborhood or household level. In contrast, credit bureau data is provided at the individual level, providing the credit history of a specific consumer who may have behaviors and preferences that differ from those of another family member or neighbor. Because individual data is more effective at placing the right product in the hands of a likely user, it improves the cost effectiveness of marketing campaigns.

It is crucial to incorporate three measures of performance into any acquisition program: response, risk, and revenue potential. There are credit bureau models for each of these behaviors. A *response* model predicts the likelihood that a consumer will respond to a product offering by classifying individuals with similar credit behaviors into clusters. A *risk* model predicts future delinquent or creditworthy behavior. A *revenue* model predicts how much revenue is likely to be generated from a new account. Ideally, these three models together pinpoint the consumers who have the highest response rates, lowest risk for delinquency, and highest revenue potential.

A revenue model often adds tremendous value to a marketing strategy. Eliminating individuals who have a low likelihood for delinquency but a low revenue potential from a target marketing program allows resources to be allocated to those people who have an average to low risk for delinquency and high revenue potential. Overall, these types of models, whether used independently or simultaneously, will help improve profitability by attracting consumers who will respond, generate revenue, and remain creditworthy over time.

***Application Review/Booking***  When an application for a product is reviewed, credit bureau scores can be used to make three basic decisions: (1) whether to approve or decline; (2) the terms of the account, and (3) the appropriate price.

A credit bureau risk score can be used alone, with judgmental criteria, or with a custom application score to determine if the likelihood for delinquency is low enough to book an account. Typically, it is necessary to identify the risk score cut-off that denotes an acceptable level of risk or bad rate. Through validation procedures like those mentioned earlier, bad rates can be associated with each risk score interval. Then, all applicants who score above the cut-off are approved and those that score below are declined. This approach usually results in a lower overall bad rate and a higher approval rate.

There are compelling reasons why creditors use credit bureau risk scores with judgmental criteria to make approval/decline decisions. Since credit bureau risk scores are empirically derived and consistent across credit files, they allow creditors to make better, more consistent decisions than they could by using judgmental criteria or an application score alone. Also, when a company is attempting to enter a new market, offer a new product, or grant instant credit, there is no performance information available for benchmarking or validation. When there is no history of performance within an industry, credit bureau risk models, which are based on large, diverse samples of credit files, can be used to successfully assess risk.

Another use of credit bureau scores in the application/booking phase is to reduce the risk of application and identity fraud. *Application fraud* occurs when a consumer fills in information on a credit application that is fake or inconsistent with reality. For example, a fraudster might provide a "real" name, but a date of birth that is inconsistent with the social security number. With *identity fraud,* the subject actually attempts to take over another person's identity by providing someone else's name, address, social security number or other sensitive information.

Credit bureau information is useful in predicting both types of fraud. Data on the application can be compared to the credit bureau database. The models can highlight inconsistencies or changing patterns and relationships. By identifying applications with a high likelihood of fraud, creditors are alerted to investigate further and verify before approving an account. Not only does this practice help spare losses to the creditor, it also helps protect consumers against personal losses.

Credit scores can also be used in the new account stage to determine the terms of an account, such as credit limits and minimum payments for revolving credit accounts or choice of a collateral amount and repayment period for installment loans. A low likelihood for delinquency as indicated by a credit bureau risk score could get the consumer preferential terms.

Finally, credit bureau score are used to assign pricing or risk-based interest rates. The better the credit risk, the lower the price or lower the interest rate may be. Risk-based pricing helps identify more accounts to approve, thus increasing the size of the portfolio, while controlling risk and profitability by charging higher rates for higher risks.

*Account Management/Portfolio Review*    Account management involves evaluating and reviewing existing accounts, so that actions can be targeted to minimize exposure to losses and promote portfolio profitability. Such actions might include credit line management, authorizations, cross-selling, retention, and collections. Each of these can be based on a variety of credit bureau scores that predict risk, revenue, attrition, and repayment.

For revolving credit accounts, credit bureau risk scores can be incorporated into an annual account review to determine whether credit limits should be increased or decreased or additional products offered through a cross-selling. Since risk scores are calculated from a credit report, the score can highlight other credit problems that may not yet have affected the inquiring creditor yet. Protection plans can be used to manage credit limits so that the potential for poor performance is controlled.

Another account management decision for revolving accounts is when to authorize an over-limit purchase. These point-of-sale decisions require quick response from the creditor. Credit bureau risk scores are useful in this scenario, because a score can be returned instantly and matrixed with account behavior information; if the risk score is good and the account shows no previous derogatory behavior, the transaction should probably be approved. Again, the credit bureau risk score adds value because it gives a view of all credit obligations, not just how the immediate account is performing.

Account retention is an important consideration for all types of credit accounts, but has been particularly so in the bankcard, retail, and cellular industries. The issue is now becoming crucial to the auto finance and mortgage markets as well, simply because of the increase in competition.

Retention programs should be driven by three factors: attrition, risk, and revenue. Attrition occurs when an account is closed voluntarily by a customer or when the balance is paid down to zero and remains inactive. The first case is easily identified, since the customer is taking the effort to close the account. The second, more common case, "silent" attrition, is more difficult to quantify because the customer does not initiate contact, but simply stops using the account. Both types can be predicted using credit bureau models.

The objective is to identify and take aggressive action to retain accounts that have a high likelihood for attrition, a low likelihood for delinquency, and a high potential to generate revenue. Actions that have proven effective in saving good customers include lowered interest rates, higher credit limits, and convenience checks. The action needs to be tailored to fit the needs of the customer. Personal contact is recommended to determine the best product incentives.

The following chart outlines an account retention strategy based on credit bureau risk, revenue, and attrition scores. The first step is to review risk scores. For an account at high risk for delinquency, no retention action is taken.

## FIGURE 3–2

### Account Retention Strategy

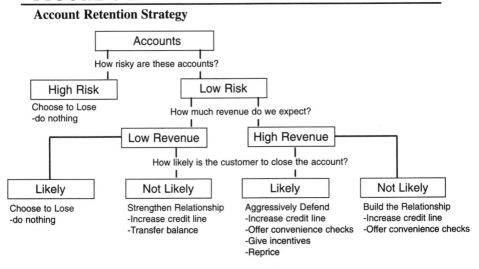

Accounts with a low likelihood for delinquency are then scored with revenue and attrition models. Strategies are developed according to the customer's revenue potential and likelihood of attrition. No action will be taken on accounts with low revenue potential and high attrition likelihood. A low cost strategy may be employed to strengthen the relationship on accounts with low revenue and low attrition potential. Although not highly profitable, these accounts still contribute to the bottom line.

On those extremely profitable accounts that have high revenue and high attrition potential, creditors should move aggressively to keep these valuable customers active and customize strategies according to the type of account and portfolio goals for each creditor.

The final account management strategy using credit bureau scores is in collections. All stages of delinquent accounts can be prioritized according to a credit bureau risk score or a repayment score. A risk score is very effective for managing first payment defaults or early stages of delinquency. Accounts with the lowest likelihood for write-off or bankruptcy are usually prioritized first in the collection queue. For later stages of delinquency, a repayment score is effective at identifying the accounts most likely to repay, so that aggressive action can be taken to collect more outstanding dollars earlier to reduce write-offs.

## Scoring: The Debate

Since its inception, credit scoring has been controversial. Skeptics are concerned that automated review of sensitive data removes the human element from the decision process. In fact, credit scoring is designed to make better, more objective and informed decisions. A score is invaluable in removing personal bias, reducing processing time, and minimizing costs. Additionally, a score provides better targeting by improving response rates, which reduces acquisition costs.

Credit bureau scoring is particularly beneficial because it is based on unbiased, up-to-date, comprehensive, and predictive data. The value of credit bureau information is that it offers a panoramic view of a consumer's credit history, particularly in conjunction with personal information obtained from an application, or account relationship information. This fact will improve overall portfolio performance, as well as assist in meeting fair lending regulations.

# 4

# GENERIC AND CUSTOMIZED SCORING MODELS: A COMPARISON

**Gary G. Chandler**
*Director and Principal*
*Risk Management Resources, Inc.*

## INTRODUCTION AND OVERVIEW

Since generic[1] credit bureau scoring models were introduced in the mid-1980s, the growth in their usage and acceptance has been astonishing. Today more credit decisions are impacted by generic than by customized scoring models, though some creditors use both. Customized credit scoring[2] models are developed for the use of a single creditor while generic credit scoring models are sold in the marketplace for the use of multiple creditors.[3] Typically, a customized model is based on data from a creditor's past lending experience. A generic model is based on data from a number of creditors' past lending experiences. The most popular generic scoring models[4], developed using credit bureau information, are marketed by the three major credit bureaus.

Creditors must decide whether to use customized scoring, generic scoring, or a combination of both.[5] The creditor will also have to choose

---

1 Use of the term "generic" in the credit industry to categorize scoring models does not conform to general usage. Generic scoring models are named, trade or service marked, and advertised by name.

2 Although use of the term "credit scoring" is often limited to the measurement of risk, this chapter will use a broader meaning that also covers marketing, collection, revenue, attrition, etc..

3 Although there are exceptions to the definitions, concepts, discussions of issues and conclusions presented in this chapter, the overall thrust of the chapter remains intact.

4 The most popular generic bureau models are BEACON, New Delphi, Enhanced Delinquency Alert System (EDAS), Experian/Fair, Isaac Model, TRW/MDS Bankruptcy Model, and EMPIRICA. See the next section and Exhibit 1 for an expanded listing.

5 This chapter does not deal with those creditors (mainly smaller ones) that do not use any form of credit scoring, relying entirely on judgmental evaluation.

among competing generic scoring models. Proper evaluation should consider, among other factors, the credit product and type of decisions, the creditor's capabilities, the environment, the target market, and the characteristics and costs of the models available. The primary purpose of this chapter is to provide a framework for these evaluations.

This chapter compares generic with customized credit scoring models in terms of feasibility, development, implementation, economic, and management issues. It presents the advantages and disadvantages of each approach and integrating generic scoring within an overall evaluation system. The generic scoring models available are described in detail.

The first generic credit bureau scoring model was "Prescore," developed by Fair, Isaac and Company, Inc. from credit bureau information in 1984-85 to evaluate new applicant credit risk in direct mail solicitations. In 1987, MDS[6] introduced the first mass-marketed generic credit bureau scoring models (Delphi for Trans Union, Delinquency Alert System for Equifax, and The Gold Report for TRW Information Services) to predict bankruptcy risk. These models resulted in the rapid acceptance of generic bureau scoring. Fair, Isaac soon introduced competing generic credit bureau risk models: Beacon (1989) for Equifax, Empirica (1990) for Trans Union, and the TRW Fair Isaac Model (1991). These models have been periodically redeveloped and many new models have since been added.

Over the years credit scoring venders have also marketed generic scoring models not developed in conjunction with the credit bureau for sale to individual creditors.[7]

## DEFINITIONS AND REGULATIONS

There are two basic processes for credit evaluation, judgmental and credit scoring.[8] In the judgmental process, the traditional method, credit analysts evaluate the information and make decisions based on their experience and judgment. This process of human judgment may also include rules and policy guidelines.

---

6 MDS (Management Decision Systems, Inc.) was founded in 1976 and sold in 1985 to CCN (a United Kingdom company), where it was renamed CCN - MDS Division. In 1996 Great Universal Stores (CCN's parent company) bought Experian (formerly TRW Information Services) and merged CCN - MDS Division into it. Depending on the date, different names will appear in the literature and brochures describing generic scoring models.
7 Examples include The CreditTable by Fair Isaac and Fast Start by Experian.
8 See Gary G. Chandler and John Y. Coffman, "A Comparative Analysis of Empirical Vs. Judgmental Credit Evaluation," *The Journal of Retail Banking,* Vol. 1. No. 2 (September 1979) pp. 15-16.

## Credit Scoring Evaluation and Regulation B

Credit scoring was originally described as the use of a numerical formula assigning points or values to key attributes of applicants to determine whether they were creditworthy. Regulation B,[9] which implements the Equal Credit Opportunity Act, divides credit evaluation processes into two distinct types: *empirically derived, demonstrably and statistically sound, credit scoring systems* (EDDSS) and *judgmental systems.* Any system that does not meet the requirements of EDDSS is defined as a judgmental system. Systems that meet EDDSS requirements may consider (score) applicant age directly; judgmental systems may not.[10] A system that does not score the age of the applicant can be considered a judgmental system under Regulation B regardless of how it was developed and implemented.

Over the years, the consumer credit industry has greatly expanded the use and meaning of credit scoring. Today, scoring models are used to predict not only creditworthiness, but also potential bankruptcy, revenue, response, activation, usage, profitability, collect ability, attrition, and fraud. A working definition for the industry, and this chapter, would be that credit scoring is the use of a numerical formula to assign points to specific items of information to predict an outcome.[11]

## Customized Scoring Systems

Customized scoring systems developed for an individual creditor are based on a sample of the creditor's past decisions. Often the creditor influences the actual scoring model by participating in sampling, characteristic selection, and implementation decisions. Such scoring models are proprietary, available only to the individual creditor. Many of these systems meet the requirements of EDDSS.

## Generic Scoring Systems

Generic scoring systems are typically based on a sample from the past experiences of several lenders. Generic systems are sold to any creditors who believe they will find them useful. The systems are available on a transaction as well as a purchase basis.

EDDSS generic credit scoring systems are described in Regulation B as "borrowed systems" and "pooled data scoring systems."[12] However,

---

9 See Regulation B, 12 C.F.R. Section 202.2 (p).
10 See Regulation B, 12 C.F.R. Section 202.6 (b) (2) (ii-iv).
11 An even broader definition that could include systems that do not assign points would be: Credit scoring is the use of an empirical evaluation of specific information to predict an outcome.
12 See Regulation B, 12 C.F.R. Section 202.2(p)(2)&(3).

they must comply with Regulation B only if they actually score the age of the applicant. If they intend to comply with Regulation B, individual creditors have their own validation and revalidation requirements.[13] Most generic scoring systems do not score applicant age.

### Generic Credit Bureau Models

The most dominant generic models are those available through the three major credit bureaus; they influence most credit decisions made by major creditors. While the actual scoring models are not available to creditors, the bureaus provide generic scores as part of their credit reports (on line) or as a stand-alone product (batch). Each bureau has its own models; the competition is intense.

Generic models were developed both by scoring vendors working with credit bureaus and by internal credit bureau development staffs. Though only information from a single credit bureau is used in model development, sample sizes typically range from the hundreds of thousands to over a million files. In general, the predictive powers of the generic bureau models are outstanding, comparable to those of customized models.

### Non Credit Bureau Generic Scoring Models

Years before the credit bureaus developed models, vendors were marketing their own generic models, which had been created in response to creditors who wanted a systematic way to predict risk without a customized system.

Often data from several creditors were pooled in the development of generic scoring models. Some generic models were specified by the model developer based only on their own past experience. Both approaches yielded a scoring system that closely resembled customized models. The predictive power is significant, though typically lower than customized scoring systems. Applicant age is not scored in most generic systems, since they may not always meet EDDSS requirements.

## GENERIC SCORING MODELS IN THE MARKET

Over 30 generic credit scoring systems containing over 100 different scoring models are listed alphabetically in Figure 4-1, which also lists delivery firms, development firms, types of systems, brief descriptions

---

13 Regardless of legal requirements, the performance of a scoring system should be closely monitored for economic reasons.

# FIGURE 4–1*

## Generic Scoring Models

| Scoring System Name | Delivery Firm | Model Developer | Type | Description/Predicts | Number of Models/Prediction Period |
|---|---|---|---|---|---|
| Bankcard Usage Score | Equifax | Equifax | Balance | Predicts propensity to generate a balance on a bank card over a 12 month period | 1 Model |
| Bankruptcy Risk Prediction Service | Integrated Solutions Concepts, Inc. (ISC) subsidiary of Visa U.S.A. | Fair Isaac/ ISC | Bankruptcy | Predicts bankruptcy using combination of transaction, issuer-supplied account performance, and third party information | Multiple/varies - performance definition varies as defined by opportunities for action |
| Bankruptcy Navigator | Equifax | Equifax | Bankruptcy | Rank order and predicts probability of bankruptcy within 24-month period | Layered approval incorporating delinquency, risk, bankruptcy and economic segmentation 24 mos. |
| BEACON | Equifax | Fair, Isaac | Risk | Predicts bankruptcies, charge-offs, repossessions, defaults and serious delinquencies | 10 - Based on credit behavior and 4 product specific overlays (each with 2 models based on derogatory history |
| CARcredit | Equifax | Equifax | Risk - auto | Predicts risk and rank order risk of serious delinquency for auto trade customers | 4 - Thin, non auto, high inquiry, low inquiry/24 mos. |
| Cardholder Risk Identification Service (CRIS) | Visa | Visa | Fraud | Predicts fraud based on authorization pattern along with cardholder spending profile (neural network model) | Multiple models/multiple time periods |
| CreditTable | | Fair, Isaac | Risk | Empirically derived generic risk models based on pooled data; some tailorization and judgmental models available | Industry and product specific models |
| Desktop Underwriter | Fannie Mae | Fannie Mae | Mortgage risk assessment | Used by mortgage lenders to determine whether loans meet Fannie Mae underwriting guidelines | Statistical underwriting models and collateral assessment models |
| EMPIRICA | TransUnion | Fair, Isaac | Risk | Predicts bankruptcies, charge-offs, repossessions, defaults, and serious delinquencies | 10 - Based on credit behavior and 4 product specific overlays (each with 2 models based on derogatory history) |
| Enhanced Delinquency Alert System (EDAS) | Equifax | CCN/MDS** | Bankruptcy/ risk | Likelihood of bankruptcy within 12 months or serious delinquency | 4 - Regional/12 mos. |
| Equis | Equifax | Equifax | Segmentation | Assigns to one of 64 clusters based on likelihood of similar performance on a preapproved offer | N/A |
| Experian Revenue Opportunity Indicator (ROI) | Experian | Fair, Isaac | Revenue | Rank orders relative amount of revenue likely to be generated on a revolving account over next 12 months | 4 - Recent revolving credit usage/12 mos. |

# FIGURE 4-1 (continued)
## Generic Scoring Models

| Scoring System Name | Delivery Firm | Model Developer | Type | Description/Predicts | Number of Models/Prediction Period |
|---|---|---|---|---|---|
| Experian National Risk Model | Experian | Experian | Risk | Predicts likelihood of bankruptcy, charge-off, and public record derogatory in next 24 months. | 8 - Based on past credit profiles/24 mos. |
| Experian Bankcard Response Model | Experian | Experian | Response | Predicts likelihood of response to a bankcard direct mail solicitation | 4/performance windows vary up a maximum of 5 months |
| Experian CollectScore Model | Experian | Fair, Isaac | Collection | Predicts which delinquent accounts are most likely to result in the highest repayment amount | 2 - General and tailored to lender /6 mos. |
| Experian/Fair, Isaac Model | Experian | Fair, Isaac | Risk | Predicts bankruptcies, charge-offs, repossessions, defaults & serious delinquencies | 10 -Based on credit behavior & 4 product specific overlays (each with 2 models based on derogatory history/24 mos. |
| Experian Recovery Model | Experian | Experian | Recovery | Predicts high to low levels of collectability in 6 months. | 2 - Bankcard & Retail Card/6 mos. |
| FACETS | Trans Union | Scoring Solutions, Inc | Risk segmentation | Risk based clustering system for segmenting accounts into one of 13 clusters | N/A |
| FAST START | | CCN/MDS** | Risk | Empirically-derived generic risk models based on pooled data | Industry and product specific models |
| General Risk Model | Equifax | Equifax | Risk | Predicts risk and rank order probability of serious delinquency, bankruptcy, and charge-off | Based on revolving utilization by thin/thick file/24 mos. |
| HORIZON | Trans Union | Fair, Isaac | Bankruptcy | Predicts bankruptcy loss ratio (dollar losses from bankruptcy divided by net revenue from "good" accounts) | 11 - Based on consumer profile |
| Loan Prospector | Freddie Mac | Freddie Mac | Mortgage risk | Predicts mortgage default risk | Multiple models; segmented on key risk characteristics and by conventional conforming, government, subprime, and jumbo |
| New Delphi | Trans Union | CCN/MDS** | Bankruptcy/ risk | Likelihood of bankruptcy within 12 months; or serious delinquency | 6 - Population segments on risk characteristics/ 12 months |
| Omni Score | GE Capital Mortgage Insurance (GEMICO) | GEMICO | Mortgage risk | Validated to be an effective delinquency and foreclosure predictor over the entire life of the loan | Life of the loan |
| PATROL | Trans Union | CCN/MDS** & Trans Insureco Insurance | Insurance | Likelihood of consumer carrying required collateral insurance | 1 |
| PORTRAIT | Trans Union | Trans Union | Segmentation | Aggregated credit bureau and demographic data used to assign to one of 32 clusters | N/A |
| Retail Usage Score | Equifax | Equifax | Balance | Predicts propensity to generate a balance on a retail account or card over a 12-month period | 1 Model |
| REVEAL | Trans Union | Trans Union | Home market value | Estimates the value of home. Assigns to a range of values | 1 |

## FIGURE 4–1 (continued)
### Generic Scoring Models

| Scoring System Name | Delivery Firm | Model Developer | Type | Description/Predicts | Number of Models/Prediction Period |
|---|---|---|---|---|---|
| Revenue Evaluator (REV) | Equifax | Fair, Isaac | Revenue | Rank orders relative amount of revenue likely to be generated on a revolving account over next 12 months | 4 - Recent revolving credit usage/12 mos. |
| REWARD | Trans Union | Fair, Isaac | Collection | Rank orders delinquent accounts according to likely repayment amount. | 2 - General and tailored to lender/6 mos. |
| RPM (Revenue Projection Model) | Trans Union | Fair, Isaac | Revenue | Rank orders relative revenue likely to be generated on a revolving account over next 12 months | 4 - Recent revolving credit usage/12 mos. |
| SENTRY | Trans Union | Fair, Isaac | Attrition | Likelihood of an account attrition over next 3 to 5 months | 10/3 - 5 mos. |
| SILHOUETTE | Trans Union | CCN/MDS** | Segmentation (marketing) | Assigns to 25 clusters according to similar credit lifestyles (spending and payment behavior) | N/A |
| SOLO | Trans Union | CCN/MDS** | Segmentation | Spending practices & payment patterns used to assign to one of 41 similar lifestyle clusters | N/A |
| SPECTRUM | Trans Union | Scoring Solutions, Inc | Risk | Predicts new account risk for wireless industry | 3 |
| TIE | Trans Union | Trans Union | Income | Analyzes behavioral characteristics for predicting income - debt to income included | 2 |
| TRADE | Trans Union | Credit Strategy Management | Retail revenue | Projects actual dollar balances over 12 month period, taking seasonality of card usage into consideration | |
| TRW/MDS Bankruptcy Model | Experian | CCN/MDS** | Bankruptcy/risk | Likelihood of bankruptcy within 12 months; or serious delinquency | 6 - Level of bureau information and type of primary credit/12 mos. |
| UniQuote | Trans Union | Fair, Isaac | Mortgage risk | Likelihood of delinqueny on mortgage | 5 - Population segments |

*Although the vast majority of the information in Exhibit 1 was obtained from sales brochures and discussions with employees of the firms represented in the accuracy of the material presented is not warranted.
**Currently part of Experian

and predicted outcomes, number of models, and prediction time periods. Exhibit 1 is not exhaustive, however, because new systems enter the market each year and revisions of current models are marketed under the same names as previous versions.

*Scoring System Name*   is simply the trade mark or service mark of the scoring product.

*Delivery Firm*   either provides a service that delivers generic scores to the creditor or sells generic scoring models. Generic credit bureau model scores are generally available on-line and in batch mode from the credit bureaus, both priced per transaction (score).

*Model Developer*   The vast majority of generic models have been developed by either Fair, Isaacs or Experian (or its predecessor, MDS/CCN).

*Type*   Systems are classified according to their intended usage, usually a broad outcome prediction. Systems of the same type developed by the same vendor will tend to produce similar forecasts, given similar credit bureau file content.

*Description/Predicts*   Although different terms may be used in brochures marketing risk systems—"rank orders risk," "predicts risk," "predicts" or "measures" likelihood—they all describe the same effect. Most risk systems analyze outcomes as either "desirable" and "undesirable." While differences in the exact definitions can be important, they tend to overlap, so the models tend to be somewhat similar. For instance, bankruptcy models will also predict charge-offs and serious delinquencies. Risk models will predict bankruptcy as well as charge-offs and serious delinquencies.

The best evaluation of what and how well a model predicts is to examine specific forecasts and validations based on the outcomes the creditor is concerned about.

*Number of Models/Prediction Period*   To increase accuracy, generic scoring systems often contain multiple scoring models. The selection of which model to use will depend on the content of a given credit file. For example, an applicant with numerous delinquencies may be scored with a different model from one with no delinquencies. In almost all cases, each applicant is scored on only one model, which is selected automatically by the bureau. Many creditors believe that more models are always better, but again it is important to look at the forecasts and validations.

The prediction period is the time appearing in marketing brochures, usually the same as the outcome period used in model development. It is not necessary that the two periods be the same; in fact scoring models are often validated on time periods both longer and shorter than the development times. Again, it is wise to examine forecasts and validations over different time periods.

## GENERIC OR CUSTOMIZED?[14]

Conceptually, a customized credit scoring system should be more accurate than a generic one. The customized system is tailor-made from the creditor's own past experience to fit the creditor's lending environment and objectives. However, there are situations in which the development and implementation of a customized scoring system are either not feasible or not the most appropriate alternative.

Important issues in the decision are feasibility, development, and implementation. The discussion will focus primarily on new applicant scoring models, but similar points could be made for other types of models.

### Feasibility

Few credit situations are absolutely perfect for modeling. Therefore, tradeoffs between what would be ideal and what can be done must be considered in decided between customized and generic.

*Historical lending experience*   Since development of a scoring system requires the analysis of past decisions, the creditor must have offered credit in the past. Therefore: no historical data = no customized scoring system. Usually, the question is, what data are available and how close are they to what is really needed? Ideally, the scoring model should be used for the same product, market area, and economic environment that generated the historical experience. Experience in bank card loans, for instance, may not be relevant to a scoring system for auto loans.[15]

Generic credit bureau models are based on historical credit bureau files that contain a vast wealth of credit experience—in fact, they contain nearly all creditors' experiences. Although there are generic models for different types of credit, types of decisions, and in a few cases different geographic regions, these models are not based on a single creditor's experience.

---

14 The focus will be on generic credit bureau scoring models with only limited treatment given to non credit bureau models, because the issues are similar, they play a minor role, and the variation in their development and characteristics cannot be covered in a brief discussion.
15 In some instances, the appropriateness of different strategies can be tested.

***Data retention***   Information used to support past decisions must have been retained in a usable form in order to build a custom model. For example: the credit application and credit bureau report existing when a new applicant was evaluated would be relevant as a data base for model development, but not a more recent credit report or updated application. Although Regulation B requires creditors to retain information for 25 months after notification of the action taken, it is often necessary for model development to retain information for longer periods.[16]

Since the early 1990s credit bureaus have archived their entire file of reports on a monthly or quarterly basis.[17] These archived records are retained for long periods and are used to develop and validate generic scoring models.

***Known Outcomes of Past Decisions***   The outcomes of past decisions must be available in a quantifiable form. Account payment histories can be used to classify outcomes as good or bad loans. The level of detail of historical payment records must be examined, and data archiving and purging procedures can be important. For instance, when creditors purge charged-off accounts from the records, efforts must be made to recover the information on these accounts.

On one hand, credit bureaus have less detailed payment history than most creditors have internally; on the other hand, they have payment histories for more credit relationships. Classifying the outcomes can become more complex for the generic credit bureau models since payment behavior of many individual debtors varies from creditor to creditor.

***Age of Decisions***   The decisions must have aged enough to allow appropriate measurement and classification of the outcomes. For example, bank card accounts approved three months previously are not old enough to be accurately classified as good or bad risk outcomes, whereas accounts approved two years ago probably are.[18] At the other extreme, bank card accounts approved 10 years ago are too old, since the relationships between their historical credit applications and credit bureau reports and their outcomes would not likely reflect current relationships. Model developers will specify a sample time frame in which decisions must have occurred if they are to be included in the development.

***Sample Size***   The number of credit decisions made must have been large enough to allow an appropriate sample size. Credit scoring developers

16 See Regulation B, 12 C.F.R. Section 202.12 (b).
17 In the mid-1980s credit bureaus began annual archiving in order to develop the first generic credit bureau models and to create data bases for the development of a few customized scoring models.
18 The appropriate time will vary with the product and type of decision. Behavioral scoring models are often developed using short aging periods, because the time between the decision (collection effort) and the outcome (payment or no payment) is relatively brief (1 to 3 months).

often ask for a sample of at least 4,500 applicants—1,500 goods, 1,500 bads, and 1,500 rejected applicants—to develop a customized new applicant scoring model. Smaller creditors or smaller product offerings will try to develop customized models with smaller samples, but developers do not like to work with samples that contain less than 400-500 bad accounts.

The least frequent outcome that must be predicted will often determine if a large enough sample can be obtained. Since bad should be the least frequent outcome, the number of available bad accounts would be the limiting factor.[19] In fact, sample availability may influence the sample time frame: a creditor with fewer accounts might sample decisions made from two to four years ago, while a larger creditor might only sample from two to three years ago.

The samples available for generic bureau scoring models are typically huge. Developers often use samples of tens to hundreds of thousands of files and in some cases may use over a million files. Some of the first generic credit bureau models focused on bankruptcy, since very few creditors had enough bankrupts (in those years) to develop customized bankruptcy prediction models.

***Economic Factors***   The costs and benefits of a customized model must be compared to those of a generic scoring model. Costs include costs of developing, implementing, and managing the system. The cost of developing and implementing a customized system has been estimated to be from $30,000 to well over $100,000.

There is no direct cost to the creditor for the development of the generic scoring system. Generic credit bureau scores are purchased on a transaction basis. (Some non credit bureau generic scoring systems can be purchased on a transaction basis.) While the transaction-based pricing of the generic systems can be less expensive at lower volumes, it can be more expensive at higher volumes.

## Model Development Issues

During the development of any credit scoring model, decisions are made that will impact its performance and implementation. Many of the differences between generic and customized models are the result of the individual creditor's interaction with the model developers.[20] These interactions do not occur in the development of generic models.

---

19 If the number of bad accounts is sufficient, the number of good and declined accounts should be more than sufficient.

20 Often the model developers will provide guidance to the creditor and share their experiences, but decisions will vary from creditor to creditor according to the situation.

***Objective of the Model***   In developing a customized scoring model, a creditor selects the objective of the model and the target population. Objectives may be general—reduction in credit losses from new accounts—or specific—reduction in bankruptcy filings by new accounts within a six-month window after approval.[21] The objective will influence decisions ranging from outcome definitions to implementation.

Generic credit bureau scoring models tend to have general objectives that are not modified for individual creditors. However, different generic models have different general objectives. Creditors may agree with the general objective or just feel it is close enough. Generic models try to be a lot of things to a lot of creditors. In general, their approach works.

***Target Population***   Target population refers to the applicants who will be evaluated by the model. For a customized model, applicants who do not fit the target population can be eliminated from the development sample. For instance, if the scoring model will not be used on student loans (decisions will be made judgmentally), data on student loans can be eliminated from the development sample.

It is sometimes difficult for the credit bureau to identify the target population unless it is based on the credit bureau's files. For instance, if the creditor wanted to target low-income applicants, the credit bureau would have to use proxies such as zip codes to estimate income, or use an income-estimating model. A creditor might have an income question on the application that would accurately identify past applicants for a customized development sample. Thus, the individual creditor's objectives can influence the sample and the resulting scoring model.

In addition, generic models will only be developed for larger populations. If the creditor is targeting a relatively small group, a customized model or a general targeted generic model may be the only choices.

***Data/Sample Development***   Creditors may retain historical credit experience in either manual form, such as paper or microfiche, or automated form (computer files), or both. The development of any scoring system requires that the data be in computer readable form. Coding data requires human interpretation and data entry, which is expensive and time consuming. Automated data requires no entry, but may not contain the level of detail contained in the manual records. In addition, historical payment records are often on a computer system separate from application information, thus requiring a match/merge process.

---

21 The variation in objectives in behavioral scoring can be very wide, covering any measure of account performance.

Credit bureau data is entirely computerized. The data base is HUGE, with millions of records all containing detailed information about applicant credit inquiries, credit accounts, and payment records. But they do not contain detailed demographic information.

***Dependent Variable Definitions***   The dependent variable is the outcome. The most traditional dependent variable for a new applicant model is whether payment performance is good or bad. In the development of customized models, creditors can specify the definitions to meet their objectives. For instance, one creditor might require that an account be 60 days or more past due before it is considered a bad account; another might specify 90 days or more. Customized scoring can accommodate either. In addition, the payment history is based on the information on the creditor's master file, which can accommodate complex definitions.

Definitions for generic credit bureau model dependent variables are based on the credit bureau files of individual debtors. For instance, a bad account might be anyone who has any 90 days past due or worse history on the bureau file, with certain exceptions.

Since debtors often pay certain types of debt before other types, different creditors will be looking at the credit bureau dependent variable definitions from different points of view.

***Independent Variable Definitions***   Independent variables are the characteristics that determine the value of the credit score. In a customized model for new applicant scoring, the independent variables are typically taken from the application and the credit bureau report. When working with an outside model developer, the creditor often participates in decisions regarding: which variables will be tested, the construction and structure of the variables, and which variables will be in the final model. This input can be important since the creditor understands the quality of the data elements and their target market, and must live with the ensuing adverse action reasons.[22]

Independent variables used in generic models are selected by the credit bureaus and their developers. Traditionally, only credit bureau data is available for analysis. Little or no input is provided by creditors. In fact, creditors do not see the exact variable definitions or the associated point values. However, creditors must use the adverse action reasons provided by the bureaus.

***Model Development Procedures***   A creditor can select different scoring development techniques by choosing a development firm that uses those

---

22 See *Adverse Action Reasons* below, p. 50, and Regulation B, 12 C.F.R. Section 202.2 (c) and
   Section 202.9 (a) (1)-(2).

techniques or allows creditors to select from alternative techniques in creating a customized model.

A creditor has no input in selecting development techniques for generic credit bureau models. However, most generic and customized scoring models for the same type of application are developed using the same or similar techniques.

*Rejected Applicants*   There is payment history only for applicants who have been extended credit and have used it. Lack of information about the performance of the rejected population creates a statistical and practical problem; model developers attempt to compensate for this with reject inferencing procedures. Chapter 11 provides a thorough treatment of this topic. The higher the rejection rate, the more important the problem and the less effective the compensation. Hence, creditors with higher approval rates have a less significant rejected applicant problem.

Since the credit bureau data base contains payment performances for nearly all potential credit applicants (except for new entries into the credit market), the rejected applicant problem is nearly nonexistent in developing generic credit bureau scoring models.

*Development Time*   It can take from three to twelve months to develop a customized scoring model. Implementation adds more time, ranging from a month to years. Generic scoring systems already in the market are available for use on relatively short notice. Sometimes a creditor's need is so immediate that generic models are the only feasible alternatives.[23]

## Implementation Issues

A creditor must be able to successfully implement the scoring system; implementation can be as important as the predictive accuracy of the system. If you cannot implement it, don't develop it or buy it. Implementation issues include information interpretation and entry, computer automation, forecasts of performance, validations and monitoring, adverse action reasons, shared experience and advice, security, and management.

*Information interpretation and entry*   In order to implement most scoring systems, applicant information must be entered into a computer. The cost of data entry is a function of the number of applicants, the amount of information entered, and the amount of interpretation required.

Accurate and consistent interpretation of some information can be quite difficult, as with classification of employment information into

---

23 Some creditors will use a generic scoring model until a customized model can be developed and implemented.

occupational categories. While high standards of accuracy and consistency can be archived for developing a sample, it is more difficult and expensive to achieve the same results in an ongoing production environment. Customized scoring systems and some non credit bureau generic scoring systems often require extensive data entry. Generic credit bureau models require minimum entry information (identification of the applicant), and are often a by-product of obtaining a credit report on the applicant.

*Computer Automation*    Nearly all credit scoring systems use computers for implementation. Although customized implementations will differ, in general information is entered, edit checks are performed, exclusions and policy rules are implemented, scores[24] are calculated, additional information is requested as needed, actions are recommended, and adverse action reasons determined. Software to implement the customized model can be developed internally or bought. Sometimes implementation is performed by a third party.

Generic models are implemented by the credit bureaus, which deliver scores and adverse action reasons to creditors. These models are not available outside the credit bureau. Of course the creditor, as with customized models, must also be able to input the scores, take actions, and retain scores as needed in order to use the information.

*Forecasts of Performance*    It is relatively simple to develop performance forecasts for customized scoring models. Typically, the developer calculates the scores for a sample of known outcome applicants from the creditor's files, which may be the development sample, a holdout or validation sample, or a sample from a time frame, geographic region, or product entirely different from the model being developed.

Forecasts of score performance for the generic credit bureau models are based on large samples of files applying standard outcome definitions. While the credit bureau can provide several different forecasts, creditors using these models do not have the flexibility that comes with using their own data and models.

However, a creditor can supply a credit bureau with a list of accounts, get historical generic credit bureau scores at the time of decision, and produce customized performance reports for the generic bureau scores. In fact, credit bureaus often offer customized forecasts as a service.

*Validations/Monitoring*    Although the Regulation B requirement to validate applies only to systems that score the age of an applicant, any cred-

---

itor must know how its scoring system is performing in order to manage the system. The predictive power of the model will change as the relationships between variables and outcome change. It is important to monitor changes and react. In addition, proper monitoring of a scoring system provides a wealth of information about customers, marketing efforts, and the overall credit evaluation system.

In order to validate or monitor the performance of any scoring model, the actual score at the time of the credit decision must be retained. With a customized scoring model, retention is often a natural by-product of the computerized system. This information may be easily matched with payment performance to determine outcomes. These scores and the input information are available for analysis.

Using a generic credit bureau scoring model requires additional efforts to retain the scores and merge them with payment performance. Since the creditor does not automatically receive applicant-by-applicant characteristics from the bureau, detailed credit bureau data cannot be analyzed and compared with performance.

*Adverse Action Reasons*   Creditors must inform declined applicants of the specific reasons why they received adverse action or of their right to receive specific reasons. Creditors would like the reasons to make sense to the applicants while being as inoffensive as possible. However, the reasons must comply with the regulatory intent that they be accurate, educational, and informative. The only controls after a scoring model is developed are the method of selecting the reasons and the exact language used to describe a variable.

In a customized scoring environment creditors have complete control over both, within legal boundaries. Creditors using a generic credit bureau scoring model receive only factor codes that refer to specific language supplied by the credit bureaus. Without the ability to change the selection method and without knowledge of the exact definitions of the scored characteristics, creditors have very little control.

*Shared Experience and Advice*   Since every customized scoring model is unique, creditors cannot discuss their experiences with others who are using the same scoring model. The many creditors using exactly the same generic bureau scoring models can and  sometimes do share experiences in order to learn from each other. In addition, credit bureaus and model developers maintain staff to advise creditors on the use of the models.

*Security of the Scoring System*   The details of a scoring system must be secure from those who would manipulate the system. A customized scoring system is a security issue for the individual creditor. Software and implementation procedures must guard against manipulation.

The details of credit bureau generic models are not disclosed to anyone who does not need to know. Creditors using these scoring models do not know the details of the models. Even if these details were disclosed, it would be difficult to manipulate the scores since the content of the credit bureau files would have to be manipulated.

*Management*   The management of any credit scoring system is the critical element for successful implementation. Management must address each of the issues presented in this section during implementation and provide on-going active management of both the scoring system and the overall evaluation system. Management of a generic credit bureau scoring system implementation should be somewhat less demanding than management of a customized scoring system, since several of the factors in this section have been addressed by the generic model provider and are not really under the control of the creditor.

## EVALUATING THE ISSUES

The final factor in choosing between a customized and a generic scoring system (or a combination of both) is the type of credit decisions being made and the generic models available, along with their strengths and weaknesses and their inherent advantages and disadvantages.

### Type of Decisions and Models Available

There are many types of credit decisions, among them targeting a preapproved offer, approving "take one" applicants or young college student applicants, increasing or decreasing credit limits, amount of loan, and collection prioritization.

Some types of decisions are naturals for generic credit bureau models, for instance, prescreened, preapproved credit solicitations. All three credit bureaus offer a range of generic models for this purpose (see Exhibit 1) that have outstanding predictive power. In this case, there is no credit application. Thus, the only information is the credit bureau information. Rarely would a creditor develop a customized model based on historical credit bureau reports from their own offers or other accounts.[25] In fact, a major goal of such a mailing would be to reach

---

25 Before credit bureau generic models were developed, a few large creditors did de\ lop customized scoring models based on their own past offers.

populations of creditworthy individuals that were not part of the creditor's previous experience. Generic credit bureau models have a natural advantage over other applications for which there is very limited application data, such as instant credit.

There could be problems, however; if a creditor attempts to use only generic credit bureau models for certain other credit decisions, such as take-ones or offers-to-apply targeted to young people, for whom credit bureau files contain very limited information. The credit bureaus have developed "thin file" generic models for cases where limited credit information is available. However, the most predictive information for young people could be the credit application. In these circumstances, a customized model based on the lender's past experience with young people could be the most appropriate approach. In such cases, many creditors would use a customized model to provide overall risk evaluation in combination with a generic credit bureau model to eliminate applicants with bad credit.

*Portfolio Valuation and Rating Agencies*   Today, generic credit bureau scoring models play a central role in the valuation of credit portfolios. They create a standard measurement for portfolio risk by which different portfolios can be compared that is usually simple, fast, accurate, and relatively inexpensive. Those who buy and sell portfolios, provide securitization, and rate portfolio quality all use these scores. Customized scoring models cannot compete for these types of decisions.

*Mortgage Evaluation*   Barely four years ago, the mortgage lending industry began a very rapid transition from judgmental mortgage evaluation to credit scoring.[26] While judgmental evaluation is still important, the pace of this transition has far exceeded that experienced by any other segment of the credit granting industry. Both Fannie Mae and Freddie Mac have endorsed the use of existing generic credit bureau scoring models and developed their own generic mortgage scoring models. Generic models are also being used by mortgage insurance companies and rating agencies.

*Creditors' Strengths and Weaknesses*   Creditors should consider their own strengths and weaknesses when choosing between generic and customized models. In general, creditors with extensive experience in the

---

26 Before this transition started, only a few large mortgage lenders had customized credit scoring models and judgmental evaluation processes dominated the industry.

use and management of scoring systems will select customized scoring models when feasible, to use either alone or in conjunction with generic models. Such creditors can derive maximum benefit from customized systems due to their input into the development, their knowledge of how to integrate policy rules with the scoring models, their experience in implementing scoring systems, and their expertise in monitoring and management.

Creditors with limited staff will often opt for generic scoring, as will those who are new to scoring, in order to gain experience before attempting to develop customized models.

## Inherent Advantages and Disadvantages

*Advantages of Generic Systems*    Generic scoring systems have several natural advantages over customized systems. They are:

1. Available to all creditors, even smaller creditors and small volume products. Development feasibility is not an issue.
2. Not limited by the creditor's historical experience with population groups, credit products, and geographic areas.
3. Available immediately, without development time or cost.
4. Less reliant on the user's knowledge of and experience in using scoring.
5. Easy to implement—often the scores are generated by others.
6. Less expensive for small numbers of decisions.
7. Detailed treatment of credit bureau information.
8. Very economical use of credit bureau information.
9. Better able to predict certain outcomes, such as bankruptcies.
10. Supported by a network of advice.

*Disadvantages of Generic Systems*    However, generic scoring systems do have certain disadvantages when compared to customized scoring systems. They are:

1. Potentially less accurate because they are not based on the creditor's own experience, product, and customers.
2. Available to competitors.
3. More expensive for high volume users paying on a transaction basis.
4. Proprietary—details of the scoring system are often confidential.
5. Harder to use in forecasting system performance and monitoring performance.
6. Rigid in their definition of adverse action codes and selection procedures.

# INTEGRATION OF GENERIC SCORING WITH OTHER SYSTEMS

## Overall Evaluation System

The overall evaluation system, even for a single type of decision, will seldom consist of a generic scoring system alone. The components of an evaluation system may include one or more generic scoring systems, a customized scoring system and policy and exception rules, and even judgmental analysis. The importance, the role, and the use of each component will vary with the creditor's strategy, the accuracy of the component, and the type of decision being made.

*Coordination of Components*   The design of the overall evaluation system must consider the impact of all of its components and how they work together. Examining independently the forecasts of the performance of a generic model, a customized model, exclusion criteria, and policy criteria could be very misleading. While the use of each component might produce desirable results independently, the impact when combined into an overall evaluation system could be disastrous. For example, while independently each could be justifiable, combining high cutoffs (low risk) on the generic scoring model, high cutoffs (low risk) on the customized scoring model, broad exclusion criteria, and highly limiting policy criteria, could result in far too few approvals.

*Sequential or Matrix Strategies*   In *sequential* implementation of an overall evaluation system, the components are processed in a sequence of steps. An applicant who fails a step does not proceed to the next step. Such an approach is easy to implement and can minimize labor and information costs. However, it does not allow tradeoffs of the evaluations of the different components.

In a sequential approach a new applicant might be evaluated by a scoring model based on the credit application only as the first step and a model based on credit bureau information as the second step. Applicants could be rejected by a score below the cutoff on the first model, thus eliminating the second step and the expense of a credit bureau report.[27] Because the second model is likely to be more accurate, it is important not to set the first cutoff too high, eliminating potentially good customers in order to save on bureau reports and labor.

In a *matrix* approach the components of the overall evaluation system are used together, with tradeoffs between the forecasts of the individual

---

27 Conceptually, applicants with high scores could be approved at this point, but few creditors are willing to approve applicants without any examination of the credit bureau report.

components. For example, an individual might score low on one scoring model and very high on another scoring model for an overall forecast of satisfactory performance. The matrix approach is more accurate but requires more effort, with higher labor and information costs. It is more difficult to design and manage a matrix approach than sequential strategies. Selecting adverse action reasons can also be more difficult.

Many overall credit evaluation systems will be a hybrid in which some components are used in a sequential format and others are used in a matrix format. For example—exclusion and policy criteria applied in sequential format followed by multiple scoring models applied in a matrix format.

*Accuracy of the Components*  Less accurate components may be adequate for a low volume of easy decisions; more accurate components are necessary for high volume and difficult decisions. In the sequential example, the first step should only reject a few really high risk applicants and the second step should make the bulk of the decisions, including the more difficult ones.

*Data Retention and Monitoring Results*  In order to monitor the performance of the overall evaluation system and its components, the creditor must retain sufficient historical information. The exact specifications of the overall evaluation system and the data required typically include all exclusion and policy criteria, details of all scoring models, all scoring cutoffs, forecasted results, override specifications (if permitted), all data used in the evaluation and decision, all component evaluations, the system recommendation, the decision made, the implementation made, the date of decision and implementation, identification of each applicant, and the source of the applicant. It is very important that this information be archived without any modification. The creditor must match information with performance to produce reports that monitor how well the evaluation system is performing.

The monitoring reports produced over time will be used to modify the overall evaluation system by changing exclusions, policies criteria, cutoff scores, etc. Often larger creditors evaluate different strategies (for instance a change of cutoff score) by designing tests and tracking the results.

*Types of Decisions*  The type of decision will often influence the role that generic models and other components play in the overall credit evaluation process.

- <u>Prescreened Mailings</u>. Generic credit bureau scoring systems will almost always be used as the most important component of the system. Sometimes multiple generic scoring models are used in a matrix format. For example, a creditor could implement generic credit bureau models such as RPM (Revenue Projection Model) and Empirica (Risk), using matrix strategies that considered the tradeoffs between revenue and risk.

While the scoring model will evaluate tradeoffs between good and bad information, there are certain requirements that creditors themselves will often dictate. For instance, individuals with prior bankruptcies may be excluded, or minimum income levels may be required.

Creditors will often use several different strategies (different scoring models, cutoffs, marketing strategies, exclusions, or policy criteria) and monitor the results. It is very important that the different strategies be well designed.[28] These results will help determine new strategies and design new tests.

- New Applicant Evaluation. To evaluate new applicants, creditors may use customized or generic scoring models (bureau and non bureau) depending on the type of decision and the information available. If the credit application is limited (instant credit, for instance), it is more likely that generic credit bureau models will be used. If a complete application is supplied, it is more likely that a customized model will be used. Some will use both. In any case, the creditor will usually incorporate exclusions and policy criteria as components.

Often, generic scores from the credit bureau are used as an additional check in initial credit limit assignments for revolving credit and for cross selling other products, even though the applicant had previously been evaluated with a customized scoring model.

- Managing Existing Accounts. In managing existing accounts the creditor (particularly the revolving creditor) is faced with a stream of decisions: credit limits, renewals, authorizations, cross selling, collections, fraud potential, etc. Many large creditors have developed customized behavioral scoring systems based on the payment histories of their own customers. While such models are accurate,

---

28 If a strategy is strictly a designed test, it is important that the number of decisions be sufficient and that the items tested be limited so that the cause of the resulting behavior can be identified. The number of decisions for a given level of statistical significance is not a function of the size of the portfolio, size of the mailing, etc., as is often stated in the credit industry.

they cannot incorporate information on how their customers are performing with other creditors. It is simply too expensive to get credit bureau reports even in an automated environment for the vast majority of ongoing decisions required. In these cases, generic credit bureau scoring models have a natural advantage and are typically used in addition to customized models.

Most creditors acquire generic credit bureau scores on a periodic basis (monthly, quarterly, etc.) on their existing accounts as well as event-triggered times such as a request for a large increase in a credit limit. The more often generic scores are purchased, the greater the cost; hence the same score is used over and over until replaced. These scores are stored in computer data bases so that they can be easily incorporated into the overall evaluation system. Although old scores are replaced with newer (more relevant) scores for decision purposes, the old scores must be archived, because monitoring reports of the scoring system's performance must be based on the scores used for the decision, not the new scores.

## SUMMARY AND CONCLUSIONS

Creditors must decide whether to use customized or generic scoring systems or a combination of both. This chapter provides a framework for the evaluation of alternatives by comparing generic with customized credit scoring models.

The main conclusions of this chapter are that:

1. Generic scoring systems have taken a major role in credit evaluation. They can level the playing field between smaller and larger creditors. Generic credit bureau scoring systems allow the use of credit bureau information for managing existing accounts economically and efficiently. They provide a standard measurement that can be used to evaluate and price portfolios.

2. The overall credit environment will often determine whether to use customized or generic scoring systems or both. Since generic scoring systems have generic definitions of outcomes, creditors should seek performance forecasts based on outcome definitions that match their own objectives. Many creditors will use both customized and generic systems in order to minimize risk.

3. Any component of an evaluation system, including scoring systems, policy and exception rules and even judgmental analysis must be designed and implemented to fit within the overall evalu-

ation system. Coordination of the components is critical. Sequential evaluation is often desirable but a matrix approach can be more accurate.

4. It is critical that the overall evaluation system and its components be closely monitored in order to properly manage the system.

5. The role of generic scoring will continue to increase and new models and types of applications will emerge. Standardized risk measurements from generic models will have a major impact on credit granting industries. Customized scoring will still have a place, however, though it will rarely be used without generic modeling.

# 5

# THE BASICS OF A BETTER APPLICATION SCORE

### William M. Makuch
*Senior Vice President of Risk Management*
*GE Capital Mortgage Insurance Corporation (GEMICO)*

## INTRODUCTION

Today few question the value of scoring in the consumer credit industry. As a result, it is no surprise that there are numerous scoring systems now available. No better example of this exists than in the mortgage industry, where there are as many scoring products as there are mortgage insurance companies and major investors,[1] in addition to lender models and the scores provided by credit bureaus. And more scores are being added annually by rating agencies, HUD, etc. There may never be an empirically defensible answer to the question, "Which one allows me to make the most good loans?" but there are approaches to an answer.[2]

This chapter will discuss the numerous factors that contribute to the robustness and accuracy of a scoring system and quantify their effects. Though application or origination scores from the mortgage industry will be used as illustrations, the chapter applies equally well to the credit card, auto leasing, commercial credit and other industries where scoring technology can be applied. The principles of this chapter also apply to scores

---

1 Because mortgage insurance companies and investors bear the brunt of the loss if a mortgage defaults, they work continuously to develop the most accurate underwriting technology.

2 A truly definitive comparison would require (a) agreed comparison criteria, e.g., delinquency or default after a specified time, type one or type two error, Kolmogorov-Smirnov separation (KS), KS area, etc.; (b) a large comprehensive data set; ( c) unique input data for each individual score, accurately collected, and (d) the ever precious response variable, identical to the definition agreed upon in (a). Theoretically, this is possible; procedurally and economically, it is unrealistic.

other than origination models, including behavioral, collection, loss mitigation, refinance, retention, fraud, and credit scores.

The words "score" and "model" will be used interchangeably. *Model* is a general term that includes the category of empirically founded, statistically derived, point based models commonly referred to as scores. A *score* or *scoring system* may be composed of many scores. These individual scores, termed *scorecards,* will be explained in the section dealing with segmentation. However, many scores consist of only one scorecard, in which case "scoring system," "score," and "scorecard" all refer to the same thing.

It is also important to understand the difference between a scoring system, a credit policy, and an underwriting system. *Scoring systems* quantify the future performance or profitability of an applicant. *Credit policy* is the collection of rules that use scoring systems to decide whether to approve an applicant. An *underwriting system* is more comprehensive, being used to determine whether the applicant meets program or investor requirements, is adequately documented, etc.; it will contain a scoring system and the surrounding credit policy as its decision module—its "brain." In this capacity the score chosen will impact many areas beyond just the "bad" rate, including total portfolio profitability, customer satisfaction, and fair lending and other regulatory issues.

## THE PHILOSOPHY BEHIND SCORING

For a true understanding of the building blocks required for quality scorecards it is necessary to understand both the basic philosophy of how scoring systems work and certain critical assumptions on which they are founded.

The basic premise is that analytical technology allows us to learn from our past. Scores are developed or "trained" on past data in order to predict the future performance of new applicants. It is assumed that there are relationships among the variables available at the time of underwriting that are different and unique for the "goods" and the "bads" of the applicant population.[3] It is also assumed that analytical technology can accurately capture these relationships (or an empirical approximation of them).

Once these relationships are identified, it is then assumed that the future will resemble the past and these relationships can be used to separate the goods from the bads of today's applicant population. This assumption is like the assumption underlying the expectation that human

---

3 "Goods" and "bads" are standard consumer credit terminology used to denote profitable and nonprofitable customers.

guideline underwriting will work—the underwriter's past experience can be used to separate the goods from the bads. The difference, however, is that scores derive their "experience" from a much, much larger data set. Scores never have a subjective "opinion."

Once the logic and assumptions of scores are understood, the elements of a sound score are easily enumerated: the data; the technology and development expertise; regulatory compliance; and the application. The data is the least recognized yet one of the most important elements of score development. The discussion of score development technology can require several texts on its own. The treatment here provides the minimum background required for the reader to be considered "dangerous," or in other words to allow the practitioner to ask the right questions. The regulatory compliance discussion attempts to summarize the regulations pertaining to scoring today. The focus here is on the requirements for score development, not implementation and management. Lastly, keep in mind in choosing a scoring system that it is important to consider what it was designed to predict and compare this with the user's current needs.

## THE DATA

Since the score derives all its knowledge from past data, one of the most critical components of a score is the data on which it is based.[4] Both the strengths and weaknesses of a score can typically be linked to the data or its preparation. Assuming technology and development expertise, the limiting factor of scorecard accuracy is without a doubt the amount and breadth of the development data set. It is difficult to over-emphasize its importance.

Data is like a country's critical natural resource, such as minerals or oil. If you don't have it, you may have to invade a neighboring country (acquire a market player or transaction) to get it. Like a natural resource, data cannot be invented or manufactured, because of the aging required before it is useful—typically at least two years for scorecard development data. And for both data and natural resources the "purity" varies. Two aspects of purity will be discussed here; data integrity and data dispersion. The intention is not to reveal the technical secrets of score development or how to build the perfect data set, but to arm the practitioner or risk manager with what one needs to identify a superior score and understand its limitations.

---

4 We require our scoring system to satisfy the Equal Credit Opportunity Act's "empirically derived and statistically sound" requirements. Subjectively constructed scorecards will not be considered.

## Cross Applicability

We begin with an intensely debated, critically important, but rarely resolved aspect of score development—how the data set affects the applicability of the model. Whether "The score will not work for my application because it was not developed on my population" is a statement based on true concern for underwriting accuracy or simple resistance to change will always be a mystery to me, but it does raise a legitimate point—possibly the most important data-related issue.

Scores can be no better than the data on which they are based. A score will know nothing more about the relationship between the origination data and the future performance than the information contained in the data set on which it was built. If the development data set is focused in the scope of its observations and these observations have unique predictive "good/bad" relationships not shared by other populations, then the scorecard developed from this data will truly be limited. However, a data set constructed in a comprehensive, heterogeneous fashion can produce a score that will apply to populations beyond those on which it was developed. Consider these illustrations.

The Fair Isaac (FICO) credit score model[5] was developed to predict the future performance of a consumer trade line. Before 1990 it was applied primarily in the consumer credit card industry. The FICO credit score uses only data elements from the credit repositories in its prediction. No special emphasis was given to the mortgage trade line when constructing the FICO development data set and score. In fact, approximately 66 percent of the data observations did not have a reported mortgage trade.[6]

The data set used in the development of this model represented a broad cross section of consumers. The debate raged for years—how can a mathematical model built on generic population predict the performance of the complex mortgage? Yet the mortgage industry now accepts the fact that the FICO credit scores can predict a mortgage applicant's future performance.[7]

The reason should not be surprising: The same relationships between the data and the goods and the bads of the FICO development population hold for the mortgage applicant population. As an example, credit scores consider a consumer's past number of late payments, debt exposure, and

---

5 This model is named Beacon at Equifax, Empirica at Trans Union, and FICO/TRW at TRW.
6 Based on a 1997 Fair Isaacs estimate, approximately one third of the observations in the development sample for a FICO credit score contained a mortgage trade line. However, Fair Isaacs also estimates that only 50 percent of mortgage trades are reported to credit bureaus.
7 About as accurate as a human underwriter or half to a third as accurate as a reputably built custom mortgage score.

desire for additional exposure. A higher number of late payments, larger exposure, and an appetite for additional credit have been found to indicate higher risk. No magic here: this is exactly what you would expect. The same relationships also hold for mortgage customers. The applicant whose credit history profile indicates a tendency not to pay, large existing balances, and more inquiries, etc. will also be a higher risk mortgage customer. This is a clear example of "cross applicability"—a score built on one population (development population) is applicable to a seemingly different population (target population).[8]

Now consider a credit card or mortgage applicant who has minimal or no credit usage history, either by choice or due to an inability to get credit. Is a credit score applicable? Typically we will never find out! A reputable scoring system will contain a screening algorithm referred to as the "unscorable criteria," which will not allow applicants to be scored for whom there is insufficient information. Once such a case is identified, it is then the responsibility of the credit policy to assure that the applicant is manually underwritten in a consistent and unbiased fashion.

Unscorable criteria are nothing more than conditions or rules that assure that the score is appropriate for the applicant about to be scored and enough data exists for meaningful results. Unscorable criteria are developed for many reasons, but the most common one stems from limitations of the score development data set. All data sets that are the result of underwriting guidelines are limited in some way. Since virtually all products have underwriting guidelines, all data sets should be viewed as censored to at least some extent. Examples of unscorable criteria for mortgage scores are limits on loan amount, ratios, cash-out amounts, and prior bankruptcies. Even though an objective is to minimize the number of unscorable applicants, unscorable criteria should not be viewed as a weakness of a score. In fact, just the opposite. Because a reputable score will acknowledge its limitations, it can be trusted to provide more dependable results on the population it does score.

The FICO credit score is an example of a score that without modification reasonably captures the relationship between the credit information and the loan performance for a population somewhat different from that on which it was developed. It derives its robustness from a sample of millions of loans from all types of credit using consumers. Now let us consider a series of brief examples that illustrate cross applications that are not as successful. The data sets used in their development contained

---

8 Admittedly the phrase "is applicable to" requires explanation. There is no standard definition. I would propose "equal to or better than manual underwriting" or, in technical terms, "a KS measure of 20 or greater *at the point the score cutoff is drawn*." Cross applicability should be evaluated case by case using a historical cross validation measure whenever possible.

unique relationships that the score captured, but these relationships were not shared by the population to which the score was meant to be applied.

High loan to value ratio (LTV) loan performance is driven by characteristics and relationships somewhat different from those behind low LTV loan performance. Intuitively, a 60 percent LTV loan is far less likely to default because of an erosion in collateral value than a 97 percent LTV loan. Less obvious is the fact that high and low LTV ratio customers also appear different when credit and capacity relationships are compared. Empirical studies tell us that high and low LTV populations deserve different treatments when developing scoring models.

Or look at the application of originating low documentation (low doc) loans regarding income and/or assets using a mortgage score built on traditionally verified income and asset data sets. Depending on the other product parameters, and especially if a higher note rate is paid by the borrower for the product, the results are usually quite intuitive—the actual performance versus the score's predicted performance can be multiples worse.

Now let us consider a less obvious application. Scoring in the mortgage industry entered its stardom in the mid-1990s. Industry players began building their data sets reaching back as far as practical limitations would allow. This usually meant a sample from the early 1990s or late 1980s at best.[9] As we will soon discuss, the value of a data set is driven more by the number of bads than the total number of observations. Because of the industry's low bad rate, it is assumed there will always be enough good observations in the sample. Now recall the premise behind scores—they learn from the development sample. Given the limited time period of the development data set, the importance of the bad population sample, and the negative performance of the California market in the early 1990s, there is an increased potential for the development of a biased score if California is allowed to contribute a disproportionately high amount of bad observations. The population characteristics of the California market differ from those of, say, the North Central United States, with a higher percentage of high LTV loans and higher loan amounts. No one will dispute the additional risk associated with higher LTV and higher loan balance, but scores built on samples of this data containing a disproportionately high percent of bads from California will typically attribute higher risk to these attributes than actually exists. In the extreme, if the sample contained high LTV and high loan amount observations from only California, because of California's recent negative performance, high LTV and high loan amount characteristics would be found to contribute more risk than appropriate.

---

9 Credit bureau archive data are either not available or are of poorer quality, with a significantly lower match rate, prior to 1990.

This is an example of a bias that could result if the development sample is not carefully built or if adequate geographic dispersion did not exist.

A score will quantify the relationships present within the data set on which it was developed. It is therefore critical that the data set represent, or contain as a subset, the target population to which it is meant to be applied. Ideally, it will be formed entirely from past observations of the target population. To assure accuracy when this is not the case, it is important that the target population be adequately represented in the development data set.

In statistical terms, those target or subpopulations for which we do not specifically create individual models we should include by random sampling. In plain English, this means the development data set should be as comprehensive as possible, including geographic, origination year, interest rate, and applicant income considerations. Obviously this implies both large and extensive past books of business to draw from. Though data set diversity measurements do not readily exist, the risk manager, lender, or investor can ask about how their population is represented in the development data set.

## Reject Inferencing

All data are the result of some preexisting guidelines—the data do not represent an uncensored sample of all future applicants, because some applicants were declined in the past. Because of the guidelines used in originating the population, the resulting data are censored and, if only theoretically, represent those applicants believed to be good credit risks. If the guidelines were perfectly correct and if they were never overridden, we would not expect to see any bads approved. Unfortunately (or fortunately for the score development effort), this is usually not the case. At the same time, we cannot dismiss the fact that some good applicants were also systematically rejected by the guidelines while attempting to avoid the bads, i.e., the guidelines were not optimal.

When building the development data set we should make every attempt to include a representative sample of the entire universe of potential applicants if we desire the resulting score to make the optimal decision on all future applicants and approve as many good customers as possible. We certainly would not want a score to systematically decline profitable customers. Since we have no performance data on those that were declined, we must infer their performance, a topic in score development termed, appropriately, reject inferencing. Several techniques exist today, based either on applying the model to the declined population or on assessing actual performance of the declined applicant on other product(s).

The criticality of reject inferencing is determined largely by the declination rate, the bad rate, and the guideline override rate associated with the development data set. If the declination rate was low and both the bad and override rates were high, reject inferencing is obviously less critical or even not necessary because the sampling of the applicant population was not overly conservative and systematic. Such is usually the case in saturated or no growth markets when manual guideline underwriting is used. Here declination rates can shrink to 5 percent or lower, often with 40 percent or higher override rates. When declination rates are high, resulting in exceptionally good portfolio performance, reject inferencing is necessary. This situation is typical of high end department store credit cards or gold bankcards where declination rates can approach 50 percent. Whatever the situation, the impact of reject inferencing on the model's performance should have been assessed. See Chapter 11 for further discussion of this topic.

## Sample Size

In general, the larger the development sample, the larger the number of variables found to be statistically significant which will result in a more accurate and robust score. This is an over-simplification however.

The size of the development sample alone can be misleading. The value of a data set is usually limited by the number of "bad" observations it contains.[10] If all other elements are the same, a data set with 1,000,000 goods and only 500 bads will generally produce a less accurate model than one based on a data set of 100,000 goods and 5,000 bads. A large number of both goods and bads are required to maximize the power of a score. Once you have 100,000 randomly selected goods, little if any incremental knowledge about the good population is gained from one more good observation, as compared to the incremental knowledge gained from one more bad if you only have 500 bads. Although there are no rules for this phenomenon, typically a minimum of 1,000 goods and 1,000 bads are required for each individual score model.[11] In general, the more of both goods and bads available, the more accurate the resulting score. In consumer credit scorecard development, given the low number of bads relative to the number of goods, the number of bad observations is the limiting factor. Ironically, then, those companies with a higher number of past bad accounts will have a data set advantage for scorecard development.

---

10 Today, the most common type of consumer risk scoring model predicts the probability of a good versus bad outcome, not the dollars gained or lost if the applicant is approved. These models are trained on a data set with a binary outcome response variable, which the discussion here assumes.

11 This has not been proved; it produces different results for different data sets and applications. Scorecards developed on even less data can still produce favorable results compared to manual underwriting. Out-of-sample validations, however, will not be well supported by data set containing only 1,000 goods and 1,000 bads.

## Data Dimensionality

The number of bad observations alone is still only part of the story. The next consideration is what data are available for each observation: How much and what kinds of data were used during the original underwriting of the loan and how much is currently still available? In general, the greater the number of independent sources of data on which a score can be built, the more accurate the score will be. Put another way, if I had an additional dollar that could be spent on virtually anything to produce the most accurate score, I would always choose to buy data from yet another data source. Today, basic level development technology is relatively inexpensive; gathering the minimum development expertise, although a challenge, is also usually not the limiting factor. Often, however, the data cannot be obtained at any cost.

Data dimensionality refers to the number of independent categories or types of predictive data considered for inclusion in the score. For example, FICO credit scores rely on one important source of data, the consumer's credit bureau information. There are hundreds of variables within this single source and the FICO scores are built on many of these variables. Most custom-built mortgage models bring in other dimensions of the loan's characteristics, such as product information and the borrower's capacity to repay. Other independent dimensions worth investigating are the collateral information and economic market rankings data. Figure 5-1 illustrates the contributed power, on a percentage basis, of the categories which compose an early version of GE's OmniScore[SM] mortgage scoring system. FICO scores contributed approximately 28 percent of OmniScore[SM]'s total predictive power with the remaining credit bureau information contributing an additional 11 percent, the borrower's capacity information 8 percent, etc.[12]

## FIGURE 5-1

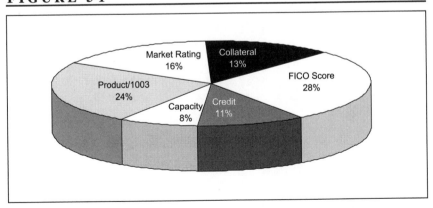

---

12 These percents can be computed in many ways, the two most common being deviation from average value and the individual categories' KS.

These sources are viewed as independent. Each category contains numerous individual data elements or raw variables. Optimal combinations and transformations of these raw variables requires creative work in order to produce the most accurate scores. Seldom is it helpful to combine more than three raw variables into a single variable. Once the category's predictive information is captured, attempting to add additional raw variables from the same category will produce little "lift" or model accuracy improvement. However, finding yet another independent predictive category will always improve accuracy. As an example, consider the fact that the mortgage industry's underwriting guidelines for Southern California and the North Central United States were essentially identical during the late 1980s, yet the Southern California loss rate for these books of business was almost ten times higher than that of the North Central Region. Clearly, there were differentiating factors not used in the underwriting. In this case, regional economic behavior caused the difference. This category of information is essentially exclusive of the data variables used in the underwriting guidelines at the time of origination. If this information were properly considered in the initial underwriting, it is reasonable to expect that underwriting accuracy would have been improved.

Whenever information from more sources is properly combined to make a decision, that decision is better supported and typically more accurate. A similar result holds for scores—those scores that consider information from numerous sources can be expected to produce more accurate and robust results than scores relying on fewer sources of information.

This is a good point to mention the "curse" of good data. Assuming the existence of numerous predictive data variables from many independent sources, and a large enough number of observations, the modeling technique will identify these variables as statistically significant. In general, the larger the number of significant variables, the more accurate the score.[13] However, once the score is created, these same variables will be required to produce a score for a new applicant. Lack of this data is usually a show stopper when attempting to move a score from one environment to another, such as from one origination system to another. Scores with fewer variables may not be as accurate, but can be applied more widely.

## Data Integrity

We close our data discussion with the somewhat obvious requirement of data integrity; i.e., the correlation between reality and what the database

---

13 Diminishing returns do set in, however. Typical custom built scores do not contain more than 20 constructed variables, representing 40 or so individual raw variables.

says. The mere existence of a field of data does not mean that the variable information actually exists or has been captured in an accurate and uniform fashion. This is especially true where the portfolio has grown through acquisitions. Priorities during an acquisition tend to favor the information needed to assume accurate billing, not the data used in underwriting. And when underwriting data have been converted, their uniformity needs to be examined.

Consider the variable "borrower's income" as an example. Underwriting guidelines from different lenders or for different products typically require different inputs. Some may require "total income," others require "protected sources of income" such as alimony and child support, still others require only base income. Such differences are seldom rectified during the conversion. This dilemma also plagues score development efforts that attempt to build a development data set from data sets contributed from various lenders. The degree of uniformity of these data sets will limit the accuracy of the resulting score. Numerous observations of bad loans, with nonuniform or inaccurate information provides little value.

When the data are not available in an electronic format and inputting is manual, data integrity should be audited. The lack of certain information can actually be good news, however. For example, at the point of underwriting it is best to obtain the credit bureau information directly from the credit bureaus instead of relying on what was in the original file, because many variables have been redefined in recent years. If the variables originally defined are used in development but the variables as newly defined are used in production, the score will inevitably be less accurate. Historical archive credit bureau runs are also a good idea because of the numerous variables they provide access to—data not considered during the original underwriting process.

## TECHNOLOGY AND DEVELOPMENT EXPERTISE

Today there are many technologies or algorithms for the development of statistical scoring systems, among them are regression (e.g., classical, logistic, nonlinear, Hazard), neural networks, decision tree approaches (e.g., CHAID, CART), case-based techniques, discriminate analysis, and various hybrids. Expert system technologies are also used when past data are scarce or not available. Each technology has its own independent, dedicated, and competitive following, comparable to the rivalry between Chevrolet, Dodge, and Ford pickup truck owners. Theoretically, each score development technology has its own strengths; practically, these differences seldom lead to consistent and significant benefits beyond those offered by the regression technology that has been used for decades.

To date, there is no conclusive comparison allowing any of these technologies to be declared superior when accuracy alone is considered. Any such comparison must also consider more than accuracy, for instance, such other practical considerations as ease of explanation and implementation in a production environment.

*Regression based technologies* represent the vast majority of scoring systems in actual production use today. The technology is stable and many diagnostics have been developed over the years to assure an interpretation of the performance of the resulting model. Its advantages also include the full understanding of which variables are included in the score and their relative weights and relationships to one another. This is critical for origination or application scores used to grant credit. It is also useful in credit policy and program parameter development. Relatively speaking, regression based models are also among the easiest to implement on today's systems hardware. Regression based techniques, however, require an experienced development team and analysis time to produce the most powerful models.

*Neural networks* are a promising technology with two potential benefits. First, compared with regression based technology, neural networks require less time to construct a comparably accurate score. Second, they can be implemented to automatically update or rebuild scores, making instantaneous use of any new information.

Practically speaking, however, understanding whether a recently approved account will result in a good or bad requires an aging period of at least several months, if not years, which makes instantaneous updating less important. And although much research has been conducted and diagnostics have been developed, neural network technology is still largely regarded as producing a black box system compared to regression approaches. Regression techniques today provide a better understanding of the relationships among the variables included in the scoring model. This understanding is necessary when evaluating a score for fair lending and other legal compliance requirements. Although not common in origination or application scores, neural network applications do include credit card fraud detection and various marketing applications.

*Tree-based technology* is also relatively new and promising. Its primary benefit is that it can be used to produce "rules" as its output as compared to a three digit number or some other numerical output—the common output of most regression and neural network based scores. Because traditional credit underwriting has normally followed rules or guidelines, the traditional underwriter or risk manager is more receptive to the output from tree technology. Tree based approaches can be used to optimize guidelines based on past data. This technology is better adapted to smaller data sets with fewer predictor variables. Its applications include credit card line management, collection rule generation, and market segmentation and response modeling. Relatively few tree based origination applications exist.

Regardless of the technology employed, it is commonly assumed that the approach to score development is a standard process. This assumption is far from the truth. Truly elegant and accurate scoring systems are actually the result of reproducible mathematical "art" rather than a cookbook process. To date there are no step-by-step textbooks to guide the layman through the score development process to a high-quality end product. Each score development application is unique. Therefore, score development expertise is critical. Without it today's development technology is nothing more than a space shuttle waiting for a team of experienced astronauts. An experienced score development team can cut the development time by 50 percent while increasing score accuracy by as much as 40 percent.[14] Development experience is essential for applications involving the granting of credit, since the resulting score is expected to optimize the competing objectives of maximizing the approval rate and minimizing the bad rate, while simultaneously avoiding discriminatory bias. Development experience is also critical in implementing segmentation schemes to increase scorecard accuracy.

## Segmentation

Identifying subpopulations deserving of their own scorecard is referred to as segmentation. Formally, segmentation is the process of identifying homogeneous populations with respect to their predictive relationships. The groupings are based on relationships shared in behavior, not in outcome.[15] The objective of segmentation is not to separate the goods from the bads but to group like populations, allowing a different scorecard to be built for each population. It is the objective of the different scorecards to then separate the goods from the bads better than a single scorecard could, thus improving overall accuracy. The theory is that different seg-

---

14 Author's estimates based on numerous score developments and implementations.
15 Often, however, segments are created based on process or business requirements rather than to increase predictive accuracy. For example, many collection scorecards are segmented with respect to the stage of the delinquency. And usually managers for individual product lines will ask for (demand) scorecards built on their own population, despite the similarities of their product to other products underwritten or processed by the same system.

ments of the population have unique relationships that cause an applicant to become a good or a bad. Building different scorecards for individual populations allows the unique relationships or structures to be leveraged optimally in the prediction.[16] Unlike socks, one size does not fit all.

Examples of possible segments are numerous. Intuitively, we would expect high loan amount customers, i.e., the jumbo market, to behave differently than the conforming loan amount market. Large predictive relationship differences also exist between "low doc" or "no doc" loans versus those loans originated with full documentation requirements. Similarly, those with past delinquencies or bankruptcy are different in behavior when compared to those with clean credit. And although it can be shown that a reputably built "prime paper" scorecard will separate risk when applied to subprime populations, the volatility associated with subprime performance deserves individual consideration. The basic relationships within the data used to separate the goods from the bads for the prime population will for the most part hold true for the subprime populations. However, the volatility or variance around the expected performance suggests other factors, currently not considered by scores built on prime loan data, that need to be incorporated when scoring subprime loans.[17]

There are many other equally powerful but less obvious examples, such as adjustable rate versus fixed-rate mortgage customers or purchase versus refinance customers. Segmentation groupings can also be layered. For example, within the high LTV segment we can segment for adjustable and fixed-rate product. These are proven segmentation groupings. Building individual scorecards for each group will allow us to separate the goods from the bads more accurately than if one model were built to handle all groups.

Not all intuitively appealing segments make analytical sense, however, and the optimal segmentation scheme to group the limited data (data are always "limited") is rarely determined by intuition. In fact, one of the most promising areas for score accuracy improvement is segmentation or interaction research. Segmentation should be performed when it will improve the score's ability to separate the goods from the bads, not because it intuitively seems reasonable. Once again, there is no such thing

---

16 Although this section promotes the merits of segmentation, there is a more advanced single scorecard approach that models variable interactions and results in similar or improved accuracy over a traditional single scorecard. Modeling variable interactions in a single scorecard also provides more efficient use of the sample size and eliminates the potential for disagreement between multiple scorecards.

17 Subprime customers have cash-out amounts that greatly exceed the prime market and reserve amounts that are significantly less than those of the prime market. The servicer will also play a big part in the performance of subprime paper.

as a free lunch: Every time one more segment is identified, the development data set must be divided one more time. The data set on which the scorecard for the new segment is to be built are data which apply to only that segment. In a segmentation approach these data are no longer available for use in developing scores for the other segments. However, the accuracy of a score is also proportionate to the size of the development data set, typically the number of bads, since that is the limiting quantity. Although the segment may deserve its own scorecard, there may not be enough data to accurately support the development and testing of this scorecard. To build another scorecard would reduce the data set to be used for scorecards for the remaining populations. Although there are general rules on the number of sample observations and the number of segments that can be supported, it is best to decide whether or not to segment based on empirical results for each individual application.

Here again, score development and risk management expertise can identify likely candidates for segmenting variables. If the sample size is adequate and the segmentation is meaningful, then segmenting will usually increase accuracy by 5 to 10 percent compared to a single scorecard system. The following table illustrates the accuracy benefit due to segmentation using an indexed KS performance of scores built on high LTV loans, on low LTV loans, and on both, using single and multiple scorecard approaches. The table also documents the relative performance of a single scorecard system which incorporates variable interactions.[18] An index value of 100 percent indicates that the KS achieved by this model on the specified data set was equal to the maximum KS observed for this data set.

Note the increase in accuracy of the multiple scorecard system on this data set compared to the single scorecard system. The multiple scorecard

## TABLE 5–1

| | Data Sets | | |
|---|---|---|---|
| Type of Scorecard | High LTV | Low LTV | Combined LTV |
| Single Scorecard | 95% | 93% | 94% |
| Multiple Scorecards | 100% | 100% | 100% |
| High LTV Scorecard | 100% | 68% | 81% |
| Low LTV Scorecard | 79% | 100% | 80% |
| Single Scorecard (with interactions) | 105% | 104% | 104% |

18 This illustration is based on results from various versions of GE's OmniScoreSM developed by the immensely capable team of Chris Jolly, Matt Palmgren, and Wei Wang—the finest score development organization I have ever worked with. All results are approximate.

system is composed of the same high and low LTV scorecards documented in the following two lines of the table; hence the high LTV scorecard applied to the high LTV data set obtains 100 percent of the KS the multiple scorecard system achieved. The result for the low LTV scorecard on the low LTV data set is similar. Also note that for this data set a scorecard developed on low LTV loans is only 79 percent as accurate on high LTV data as a high LTV scorecard. A high LTV model is only 68 percent as accurate on low LTV loans as a low LTV scorecard.

Note also the increase in accuracy from a single scorecard that incorporates variable interactions—a benefit that results from the opportunity to use a larger development data set due to not having to split the data set into mutually exclusive segments. Discussions of variable interactions are beyond the scope of this chapter but they can be simply summarized as the unique and different relationships produced by one variable due to the values taken on by another variable—the effect of a variable on the good/bad outcome will depend on the value of another variable.

Segmentation results in a multiple scorecard system. Multiple scorecard systems are transparent to the user. For example, if LTV is the segmenting variable and the Smith's 60 percent LTV loan scores a 712 from the low LTV scorecard while the Jones' 95 percent LTV loan scores a 712 from the high LTV scorecard, then the future performance of both loans is expected to be identical even though the loans were scored by different scorecards.[19] The scorecards in multiple scorecard systems are scaled to have the same meaning even though the algorithm for the prediction is different.

## FAIR LENDING CONSIDERATIONS

Developers, implementers, managers, and users of scoring systems must realize that along with the advantages of a score-based approach comes the responsibility to ensure that they do not discriminate in performance. Since one of the benefits of score-based origination is consistent application, any bias either contained within the score or introduced by the scoring process will unfortunately also be consistently applied. According to the Comptroller of Currency (OCC) Eugene A. Ludwig, "Like all tools, credit scoring models can be used well or badly. Because they are so powerful their potential for good, or ill, is magnified. That means they must be developed, implemented, tested, and maintained with extreme

---

19 Assuming the score was built to predict incidence or frequency of the "bad" outcome both Smith and Jones will perform identically. However, if the Jones's 95 percent LTV loan defaults, the severity of loss will typically be greater than if the Smith's 60 percent LTV loan defaults.

care." The OCC also acknowledges that when developed, implemented, and maintained correctly, scoring systems can both ensure that the lending approval criteria are sound and consistently applied, which will further improve the compliance with fair lending laws.

Today two primary laws impact the use of scoring models. The first is the Equal Credit Opportunity Act (ECOA), which prohibits the use of race, color, national origin, religion, marital status, age, sex, or level of involvement with public assistance or other right granted under the Consumer Credit Protection Act in the decision to grant credit. The details pertaining to scoring systems can be found in ECOA Regulation B.[20] The Fair Housing Act is similar to the ECOA but specifically governs real estate lending. It ensures that the credit decision will be made without consideration of race, color, national origin, religion, sex, handicap, or family status.

The ECOA also categorizes scoring systems into those that are empirically derived and demonstrably and statistically sound, and those that are not, which it defines as judgmental systems.

These laws place two types of requirements on scoring systems: those that address (1) potential protected class discrimination bias introduced during score development and (2) biases introduced during score application. We review here only the development aspects.[21]

When considering a score for potential use in granting credit, regardless of whether the score was developed internally or provided by a vendor, the practitioner needs to evaluate the likelihood of two types of discrimination against protected classes.[22] The first and most obvious is overt discrimination. Use of a scoring system that contains factors such as race, color, sex, or any other prohibited factor will constitute overt discrimination.[23] A score is said to be "face valid" or "face neutral" if it does not include any of the ECOA's or Fair Housing Act's prohibited factors among the predictors.

Use of segmentation to include potentially predictive correlations associated with prohibited factors will also constitute overt discrimination. For example, separate male and female scorecards could be developed which never use a male/female identifier variable in their calculations. Any difference in the overall performance between men and women could be hidden within the constants of the two models or the

---

20 See the appendix of the OCC's Safety and Soundness and Compliance Issues on Credit Scoring Models; see document OCC 97-24, dated May 20, 1997.

21 The appendix of document OCC 97-24, dated May 20, 1997, has an excellent discussion of potential discriminatory score application issues.

22 Protected class discrimination is defined to be an adverse impact against one of the government protected classes, which as of 1997 classes included females, Blacks, Hispanics, and Asians.

23 The one exception is the use of an applicant's age. This factor is permitted provided that an applicant 62 years or greater must be treated at least as favorably with respect to the points assigned to their age class as any other age class.

weights or structure of their variables. This example, or segmenting by any ECOA or Fair Housing Act prohibited factor, is illegal.[24] Segmentation algorithms that result in the development of surrogates for the ECOA and Fair Housing Act prohibited factors may also be judged illegal. The score development organization should fully disclose the variables considered by the score to facilitate an overt discrimination review. Alternatively, a recognized third party can mediate the review if externally developed proprietary scores are to be used. Overt discrimination is reasonably easy to identify. Even so, the opinion of legal counsel is recommended.

The second type of protected class discrimination has become known as disparate impact, or, more recently, disproportionate impact. Disproportionate impact results when a seemingly innocent variable (face valid) adversely affects applicants from a protected government class more than applicants from a non-protected class and the use of this variable was "avoidable." The use of a variable is considered avoidable if the variable can not be supported due to its statistical relationship with loan performance (no business necessity), or another variable with comparable predictive power can be identified that has a less discriminatory effect. In order to eliminate disproportionate impact, score development should take into account the effect on protected classes of each variable included within the score. For any offending variables the development effort should consider surrogate variables that are comparable in predictive strength to the original variable yet minimize adverse impact on the protected classes. The OCC recognizes, however, that a variable is justifiable due to business necessity if the variable is statistically significant and has an intuitively understandable relationship to the future performance of the borrower.

A third area of concern is that of disparate treatment, which results from biased actions introduced after the use of, and independent from, the scoring model. The most common example would be score override rates significantly different for protected populations compared to non-protected populations.[25]

---

24 Again, age is the only exception. Age is an allowable segmenting variable provided no more than two segments are created, one of which is a narrow age segment (e.g., less than 20 years of age at first credit application) containing variables uniquely predictive for that segment while the other segment is broader and contains variables predictive for that segment. The result should not negatively impact those 62 years of age or older unless they are members of the broader segment and are impacted equally negatively as others in that segment.

25 Score overrides result when the credit policy recommendation for a given score is not followed because additional information, not initially considered by the score, has been introduced. "High side" overrides are committed when an applicant is declined which the score said to approve. "Low side" overrides are committed when an applicant is approved which the score recommended to decline.

# THE APPLICATION

Since all scores are built to predict a specific outcome, the best built system does not necessarily imply superior accuracy in all applications. This is an under-emphasized consideration when comparing scoring systems, largely because the outcomes which the various models are trained to predict are usually an overly protected secret. Not knowing the objective of a score prevents the user from comparing it to the objective of the application. Hence, even if the score's objective is achieved in development, if this objective is not similar to the intended use, operational accuracy may not be achieved.

In the development of today's scores the definition of good and bad outcomes must be rigorous. Once goods and bads are defined, the score is developed to numerically separate goods from bads. The defining of goods and bads is referred to as defining the response variable. Examples of response variable definitions for mortgage origination scores could include:[26]

### Definition A
*Bads*   All loans that went into foreclosure within three years after origination
*Goods*   All other loans

### Definition B
*Bads*   All loans that went into foreclosure within three years after origination
*Goods*   All loans that were never delinquent within three years after origination
*Excluded*   Loans that became delinquent within three years after origination but were not foreclosed

### Definition C
*Bads*   All loans 60 days or more delinquent within two years after origination
*Goods*   All other loans

In definition A we are most interested in identifying those loans that will reach foreclosure. Scores built from this definition would satisfy the prediction objectives of mortgage insurers, investors, and rating agencies.[27] Definition B, a modification of definition A, places greater emphasis on assuring the purity of those loans identified as goods. Such a score

---

26 The definitions given here are simplified for illustrative purposes; missing are consideration of those initially declined for a loan and those that prepaid on the mortgage during the observation time window.

27 In actuality, scores to predict longer term foreclosures can be built using a late stage delinquency surrogate definition. Because of the increase in the number of bads produced by these alternative definitions and the elimination of the noise introduced by loss mitigation efforts during the late stages of delinquency, models built using the alternative definitions are usually more powerful at predicting foreclosures than those based on the foreclosures themselves.

also satisfies the prediction objectives of mortgage insurers, investors, and rating agencies but better supports risk based pricing-specifically, discounts for loans identified as the high end of the goods. Definition C, however, would produce a score appropriate for those whose profitability was driven by delinquency, such as lenders or servicers.

Although a score built using definition A is also predictive when validated using definitions B or C, the results are not necessarily optimal. In comparisons using the same development data set, scores that were optimized to predict default over longer time periods were approximately 20 percent less effective at identifying delinquent loans over a shorter time period when compared with scores built for this objective.[28] Similarly, delinquency scores were approximately 45 percent less effective at identifying foreclosures.

This is a very interesting result on its own. The likely reason is that the profile of foreclosure loans resembles that of the delinquent loans more than the profile of delinquent loans resembles that of foreclosure loans. Put another way, foreclosures are a subset of delinquent loans. Those that default typically become delinquent first. There is a class of foreclosures, however, that from a credit and capacity perspective, bears no resemblance to that of a delinquent-the foreclosure is driven almost exclusively by excessive deterioration of the collateral value. From a technical perspective the reason is also quite simple. Scores that predict long-term foreclosure will have different weights or variables from scores that predict shorter-term delinquency. Examples are easily identified: FICO scores, when used as a component of mortgage scores, will have a greater contributed value in predicting delinquency over shorter time periods than in predicting foreclosure over longer time periods. Numerous examples exist but, in general, foreclosure predicting models over longer observation periods will tend to contain more variables and place more emphasis on regional economic and collateral related variables than delinquency scores do.

Using a scoring system developed to predict foreclosure for applications that are most interested in predicting delinquencies can usually be justified because the accuracy is typically greater than the alternative of manual guideline underwriting, not to mention the other advantages such as speed, consistency, and omission of discriminatory bias.

## CROSS VALIDATION AND CONCLUSION

Admittedly, it is somewhat inconclusive to assess the accuracy of a score from a review of the scorecards, the development data set, the tech-

---

28 Based on numerous GE Capital comparisons conducted during the period 1994 through 1997.

nology and segmentation, and the development definitions. When such a review is not possible, or when a more quantified result is required, this question can only be answered with a cross validation. A cross validation is a simple procedure for assessing the expected performance of a score on a specified population. A cross validation consists of taking an aged sample of a population for which we know the good/bad outcome and scoring it with the score under consideration. The score distribution is assessed and the traditional performance measures, such as KS separation, are computed. The assumption is that performance on the future applicant population will be similar to that of the performance on the aged sample. It may sound simple but few organizations have the time, patience, and budget to go back and collect the data required for retroactively scoring the aged sample at the point of origination. Many short cuts can be applied to hasten validation, but they come with compromised results.

The real comparison to keep in mind is not that between cross validation results and stated score performance, but that between cross validation results and the performance of the underwriting technique currently in use. A well-developed scoring system built on a comprehensive data set is likely to be not only more consistent, with less potential for discriminatory bias, but also significantly more accurate than manual guideline underwriting.

# 6

# OPTIMAL USE OF STATISTICAL TECHNIQUES IN MODEL BUILDING

**John M. L. Gruenstein**
*Vice President, Risk Management*
*The Money Store*

Model builders face many decisions. What kind of modeling approach should be used: regression analysis, neural networks, case-based reasoning, rules-based, or other? Once the approach is chosen, a host of technical issues must be decided. What functional forms should be tried for a particular approach—linear, polynomial, exponential, or logistic for regression analysis, for example, or the number of hidden layers and the input node-output node connections, for a neural network? For all techniques, decisions must be made about which variables should be used. And do we include all the data or use a sample? How do we measure how well the model will work in a production environment? And numerous others.

Model users also face decisions. Which approach is best for a particular application? What is the best way to use it? Can it be used in all situations? How much confidence should we put in its results? These decisions are based partly on the techniques used to construct the model. Users may want to know that the "best" techniques were employed, assuming that the model will then work best for their application. Model users rarely know as much about techniques as model builders. The model builder can tell the user about the techniques used (those that are not considered proprietary) but the user may find it hard to relate the technical aspects of the model to its application.

Technical choices in credit risk modeling depend on the available data, tools, and computational resources, and on the application, as well as on the skill and experience of the modeler. For some technical choices there is no agreement on an optimal method, and there are large obstacles to determining which technique is better. Some differences among approaches appear to be greater than they really are: for instance, neural network and traditional statistical analysis are both learning-based systems, an aspect they share with many other methods.

This chapter discusses the potential range of choices for making technical modeling decisions and explains why different techniques are used in different situations. The first section lays out a general framework—pattern classification systems estimated using automated learning procedures—for understanding different credit risk modeling approaches, including traditional statistical models and neural networks. The second section discusses the key issue for optimizing any credit risk pattern recognition system—answering the question that the user needs to make a decision. The next section uses the automated learning procedure framework to compare three approaches: rules-based systems, regression analysis and neural networks. The following sections discuss choices in technique regarding training sets, evaluation procedures, and feedback loops, which have similar optimization considerations across different approaches.

## PATTERN RECOGNITION SYSTEMS AND AUTOMATED LEARNING

Schurmann (1996) describes pattern classification systems embedded within automated learning procedures. This framework encompasses all kinds of modeling approaches, including regression modeling, neural networks, and case-based reasoning. Schurmann nicely demonstrates that, despite their individual complexities, each approach is constructed to do the same job, each has the same underlying general structure, and each is optimized in the same general way.

Schurmann also shows that each major credit risk modeling approach is inherently statistical. The same issues regarding the optimal use of statistical techniques arise in all the common approaches. We will use the pattern recognition system/automated learning procedure framework to show how similar considerations apply when trying to optimize any credit risk modeling approach.

## Pattern Classification Systems

A *pattern classification system* is a method for deciding to which of several discrete classes an observation should be assigned, based on measurements of the observation's characteristics. For credit risk pattern classification systems, the measurements are made on variables that determine credit risk—characteristics like number of previous delinquencies for the borrower or the loan-to-value ratio of the loan. For simplicity we will discuss credit risk pattern classification systems having only two classes, *acceptable* risk and *not acceptable* risk. The two class system will allow us to discuss all the types of choices that need to be made in statistical modeling. More generally, credit risk modeling can involve multiple classifications. A hypothetical set of five classes might be high accept, accept, low accept, refer to an underwriter, and refer to a senior underwriter, where different actions would be undertaken based on the class.

Credit risk modeling can also involve modeling continuous variables, such as the frequency or severity of a loss, which in a sense involve infinite classes. Generally, though, decisions will be made based on the value of the continuous variable being modeled. These decisions fall into a small number of categories, so the full decision system is actually a pattern classification system with a finite number of classes, even though the classes themselves are determined by the value of a continuous variable.[1]

Pattern recognition systems have *adjustable parameters.* Different values of the adjustable parameters make the system give different results. We create a pattern recognition system by using an automated learning procedure to estimate the system—that is, to set the adjustable parameters. We optimize the system by choosing a set of parameters that does the best job possible, in some sense. While it is possible with the simplest systems to optimize manually, usually we use an automated learning procedure to optimize them.

## Automated Learning Procedures

An automated learning procedure has four components:

1. A pattern classification system with adjustable parameters.
2. A training set.
3. An evaluation procedure.
4. A training feedback loop.

---

1 Credit-risk modeling used to set risk-based prices would require continuous variables. The main points of this article carry over to the case of modeling a continuous variable.

## FIGURE 6–1

**Automated Learning Procedure**

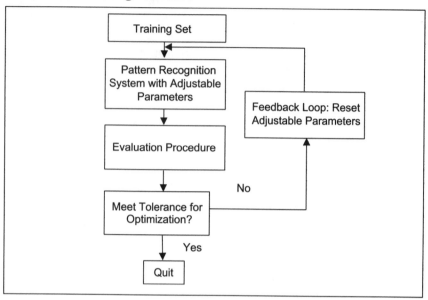

The components of the automated learning system interact to produce a pattern classification system with parameters set to minimize the classification error rate (Figure 6–1).

The *training set* consists of observations on both the measurement variables and the known outcomes the system is designed to predict. For example, a training set could consist of measurement variables for closed mortgage applications and a performance measure, such as whether the mortgage paid off fully or whether there was a loss. The *evaluation procedure* compares the prediction with the known outcome in the training set. The *training feedback loop* adjusts the parameters of the system to make predicted outcomes align more closely with the known outcomes, minimizing prediction errors.

Any pattern recognition system that is estimated using an automated learning procedure is inherently statistical, as long as the training set is a statistical sample. Since the errors of prediction are calculated from the training set, these also have a statistical distribution. What is inherently statistical is the use of errors of prediction. Because all the common credit risk approaches use automated learning procedures they are all statistical.[2]

---

2 Users of regression techniques may find the reference to automated learning procedures unusual, since linear regressions are estimated using closed-form solutions. This point will be clarified later in the chapter, for instance, the section on batch versus incremental learning modes.

## FIGURE 6-2
### Meta-Loop Surrounding Automated Learning Procedure

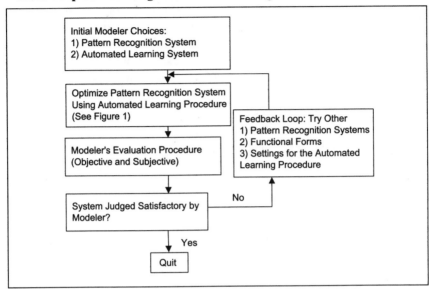

An automated learning procedure clarifies both the differences and similarities among different modeling approaches and the decisions about modeling techniques each approach requires. Because each approach has the same
components, many of the technical issues are the same. An automated learning procedure makes it possible to organize and classify modeling decisions
according to which part of the automated learning procedure they affect.

The choices the modeler makes are part of a meta-loop surrounding the
automated learning procedure (Figure 6–2). The first choices must be
about the components of the pattern recognition system and the automated learning procedure itself. As the modeler gains information from estimation of the model, he will respecify certain aspects of the system whol-
ly or partly outside the automated learning procedure—functional form,
choice of variables, structure, etc.—in ways that go beyond the automated learning function, and will then rerun the automated learning procedure to optimize again.[3]

## WHAT'S THE QUESTION?

The most important criterion in optimizing a pattern recognition system
is answering the right question. By optimization, we mean that the system

---

3 This "meta-loop" procedure is a generalized interpretation of specification search as described by
Leamer (1978).

is designed and created (estimated) to give the "best" answer to the question the user needs answered to make a decision—not to some similar but distinct question. This vital point seems obvious, but for several reasons is often not adequately addressed. One reason is that users' questions are often stated in general terms, but systems are designed to answer a specific question. Another reason is that the simplifying assumptions often used to make estimation easier, such as normality of probability distributions, make questions that in practice have different answers appear to be equivalent.

The general credit risk question—"How good a credit risk is this loan?"—can be answered by a pattern recognition system in many different ways. We must decide what we mean by risk: risk of a loss, a foreclosure (which may not entail a loss, just as a loss might come from a non-foreclosure situation like a short sale of the collateral underlying a mortgage), a delinquency—and if so, how long: 30, 60, 90 days?—or some other measure? Should severity of the loss be included in the measure of risk, or only frequency? Even when we settle on the type of risk, we must choose whether the system should tell us the most likely or the worst outcome. We also have to consider the period over which we are assessing the risk: 2 years, 4 years, and life of loan are time frames often incorporated into credit risk systems.

## The X-Y-Z Question

Two very different questions—both of which can be loosely translated as "what is the credit risk of this loan?"—are the expected frequency and what we will call the X-Y-Z question:

A.  Expected frequency question: What is the expected value of the frequency of a loss on this type of loan?

B.  X-Y-Z question: What is the probability $(X)$ that loans of this type will show a loss frequency greater than Y over the next Z years?

These are not the same question. A is a single question. B is a family of questions indexed by Y and Z. Most regression systems are optimally designed to give an answer to A, but many credit decision-makers may implicitly act as if they were getting an answer to B, with some specification for Y and Z—say a loss frequency greater than 10 percent over the next 2 years. Both questions relate to the probability distribution of losses, but question A asks about the central tendency (mean), whereas question B asks about the upper tail of risk beyond Y.

Any pattern recognition system can be estimated to directly answer either question, but the optimal value of the parameters will differ depending on the question. For example, for a regression, statistical optimization of the regression works best if we decide ahead of time which

**FIGURE 6–3**

**Normal Distribution vs. "Fat-Tailed" Distribution**

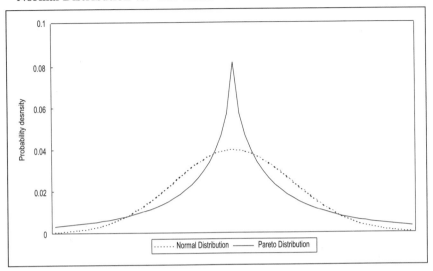

regression we want to run. It is common to make assumptions, particularly normality, so that we can get the answer to B from A (using the variance estimated from the regression), but theoretical and empirical work in finance suggests that the tails of the distribution may be thicker than a normal distribution (Peters, 1991). While the deviation from normality may be small throughout most of the curve, the deviation in the tails could be enough to make the risk for X-Y-Z twice as great, say, as one would calculate from the mean loss frequency and an assumption of normality. This makes a very big difference in worst case planning. Figure 6–3 shows how even with the same mean, a normal and a Pareto distribution will generally have very different probabilities of extreme events.

For optimization, the modeler must first learn how the system will be used to make decisions and embody that decision-making process in the question the system answers. In mathematical terms, the answer the system gives us is the value of the left hand side or dependent variable—for instance, the credit score for a loan combined with a cutoff score for decision-making. The modeler must then choose a credit risk modeling approach, which can be viewed as selecting a general structure that relates the left-hand side to the right-hand side variables.

## FLEXIBILITY VERSUS COMPUTATION

The essential difference among the various credit risk modeling approaches—regression, rules-based systems, neural networks, and case-based logic—is the form of the function that relates the measurements to

## FIGURE 6–4

**Rules-Based System with One Adjustable Parameter**

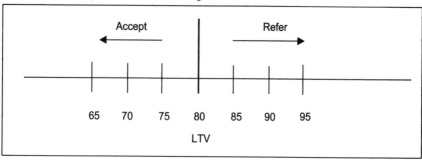

the classes, the inputs to the outputs, the independent variables to the dependent variable. Some functional forms allow for more flexibility than others. Greater flexibility allows for more predictive power but usually requires more computation. We will look at four types of approaches to illustrate that trade-off:

1. Rules-based systems
2. Linear regression
3. Non-linear regression
4. Neural networks

### Rules-based Systems

The simplest credit risk pattern recognition system is a rules-based system with a single rule, such as a system for mortgage credit risk based only on the loan-to-value ratio (LTV):

**Rule 1:** If the LTV is <= b percent, accept the loan; otherwise refer.

(We use "refer," meaning "refer to an underwriter for further consideration, as the alternative to "accept," because referral, rather than rejection, is the accepted practice in the residential mortgage industry with regard to automated underwriting systems.)

This very simple system qualifies as a pattern classification system because it takes the value of a variable for a particular observation (a loan application) and uses it to assign the observation to a particular class (accept or refer). The adjustable parameter, b, sets the assignments.

For every pattern classification system there is an associated diagram showing how the system assigns the observations to the various classes, which we call the system's *class diagram*. The class diagram of a rules-based system with one adjustable parameter is a line (Figure 6–4), divid-

## FIGURE 6–5

**Rules-Based System with Two Adjustable Parameters**

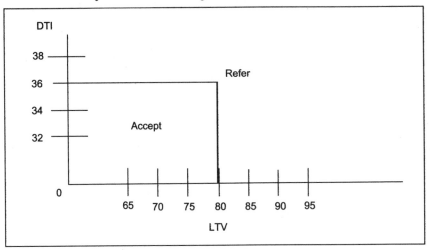

ed into two regions, one for acceptance (all points to the left of and including the value b) and one for referral (all points to the right of b).

Because it has only one adjustable parameter, the single variable rules-based system has very little flexibility, which means it has a low computational burden. On the other hand, the system is so simple that it is not likely to be a very realistic representation of the relationship between measurements and classes, and therefore not a very useful tool for making decisions.

***Adding flexibility with a second variable***   The functional form of a rules-based system with two variables—say LTV and the debt-to-income ratio (DTI)—requires a two dimensional diagram (Figure 5):

**Rule 2:**  If the LTV <= 80 percent and the DTI <= 36 percent, accept; otherwise refer.

Rule 2 divides the space into two regions, accept and refer. The accept region is the rectangle in the lower left hand area, bounded by 80 LTV on the horizontal axis and 36 DTI on the vertical axis. The refer region is everything outside the accept region (note that because the overall decision space includes only positive values of LTV and DTI, we are dealing only with the upper right hand quadrant of the full space.)

Rules-based systems can be made much more flexible with more variables and more complex rules. The variables can be continuous (a credit score) or discrete (loan purpose, with such categories as purchase, refi-

## FIGURE 6–6

**Rules-Based System with Two Adjustable Parameters—Compound Rules**

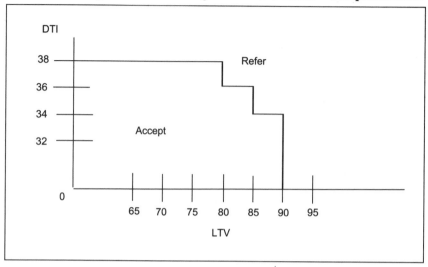

nance with no cash out, or refinance with cash out). Each variable adds a dimension to the class diagram. Adding a credit score would require a three dimensional diagram, adding loan purpose a four dimensional diagram, and so forth. With a two class system, however, no matter how many dimensions, the class diagram will be divided into two regions: accept and refer.

*Modeling risk trade-offs with compound rules*   More complex rules-based systems can embody trade-offs or other relationships among variables. Consider a two variable system with compound rules (Figure 6–6):

**Rule 3:** If the LTV <= 80 percent and the DTI <= 38 percent, accept;

otherwise: if the LTV <= 85 percent and the DTI <= 36 percent, accept;

otherwise: if the LTV <= 90 percent and the DTI <= 34 percent, accept; otherwise refer.

This system embodies a tradeoff between the higher risk of increased LTV and the lower risk of lower DTI. In principle, it is possible to build as elaborate a system of rules as required for any degree of flexibility. In practice, trade-offs are often easier to model and to understand using a system like linear regression.

**FIGURE 6–7**

Linear Regression (Hypothetical)

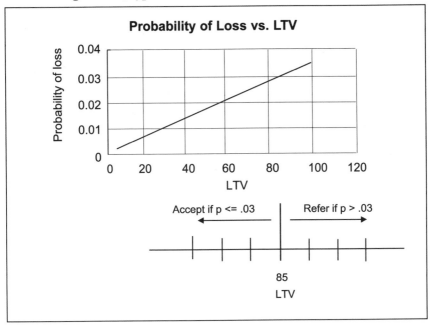

## Linear Regression

Because trade-offs are an essential feature of credit risk, regression is an improvement over pure rules-based systems. The linear regression illustrated in Figure 7 has a single independent variable, LTV, and a single dependent variable, the proportion of losses in each LTV category. Because it does not separate the data into discrete classes, the regression line by itself is not a complete pattern recognition system. Rather it creates a function that relates the probability of a loss to the LTV. As the bottom half of Figure 6–7 shows, this function can be combined with a rule to create a pattern recognition system that accepts or refers the loan. The full system using this single variable, linear regression model, gives the same general pattern of accepts and refers as the simplest rules-based system, Rule 1—it accepts only those loans with LTVs of b percent or below, with b now equal to 85.

The regression-based system's ability to handle trade-offs among variables becomes apparent when we increase the number of variables. The linear regression will generally create an acceptance region that is trian-

## FIGURE 6–8

**Linear Regression (Hypothetical)**

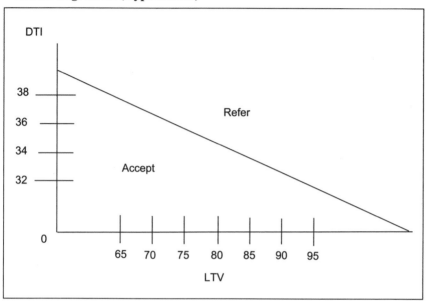

gular in shape, rather than a set of boxes. The regression equation is also simpler in form than the compound rules. Figure 6–8 shows the acceptance region that results from a multiple linear regression that uses both LTV and DTI to predict the probability of a loss. The general form of the regression equation is

1.  $P = a + b * LTV + c * DTI$,
    where P = the probability of a loss.

The fact that the acceptance region is a triangle shows that there is a risk trade-off between LTV and DTI. The boundary line is the set of all DTI/ LTV combinations that have a risk of 3.5 percent:

2.  $DTI = ((.035 - a) - b * LTV) / c = (.035 - a) / c - (b / c) * LTV$

The lower the DTI, the higher the LTV that can be accepted to achieve the same level of risk.

### Non-linear Regression

Because the systems we have examined so far are relatively simple, their class diagrams are correspondingly simple—rectangles or triangles on a

**FIGURE  6–9**

**Power Function vs. Linear Regression (Hypothetical)**

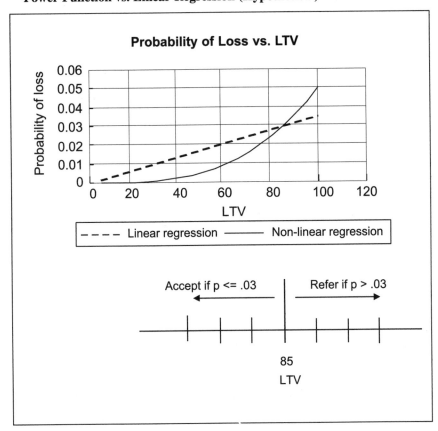

plane. But one of the chief advantages of credit modeling is the ability to account for large numbers of variables that interact in complex ways. In order to model this complexity, the pattern recognition system must be rich enough to produce a wide variety of different accept-refer regions of different shapes. One type of system that can provide this richness is non-linear regression.

A non-linear regression fits a curve rather than a line to a set of observations. The curve may take virtually any form that can be described by a function. Figure 6–9 shows a power curve fitted to the same set of points that was used for the linear regression, probability of a loss versus LTV. (As before, this is hypothetical rather than actual data.) When the power curve is fitted to the previous LTV/DTI data, the accept-refer region again shows a trade-off between LTV and DTI, but this time with

## FIGURE 6–10

**DTI/LTV Tradeoff, Non-Linear Regression (Hypothetical)**

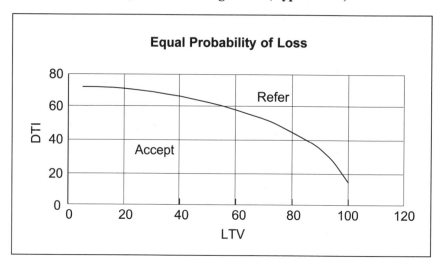

an important difference (Figure 6–10). As with the linear regression, the curve slopes downward, showing that the higher the LTV, the lower must be the DTI in order to maintain a constant probability of loss. But now the boundary line separating the accept from the refer region is curved, bowed out, reflecting a more complex relationship between DTI and LTV.

Start at the top left, where LTV is low and DTI is high. At low levels of LTV, there is not much extra risk from increasing the LTV, say from 50 to 65. But at high levels of DTI, there is a relatively large reduction in risk from lowering the DTI. So the boundary between accept and refer, which is where the risk is constant, is pretty flat at the top left corner. A small drop in DTI compensates for a large increase in LTV.

The situation is reversed at the bottom right. Here LTV is high and DTI is low, so a small increase in LTV produces a great deal of extra risk, and must be balanced by a large decline in DTI from already low levels. So this part of the curve has a steep slope. Thus the slope changes along the boundary, forming a curve instead of a line. Experience in the mortgage industry would indicate that this type of trade-off is more realistic than the straight line boundary. On the other hand, it is not so extreme as the simple rule-based system. In fact, the bowed-out curve, in a sense, is intermediate between the triangle produced by linear regression and the rectangle produced by the rules-based system.

Non-linear regression can take an infinity of forms. One important form used in credit risk modeling is the logistic or sigmoid curve (Figure 6–11). Many applications in credit risk consist of binary data; an event

## FIGURE 6–11
### Logistic (Sigmoid) Function

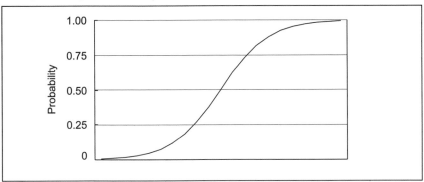

takes place or it does not—foreclosure or no foreclosure, delinquency or no delinquency. Generally, no curve will fit binary data close to perfectly, so the problem is how to fit a curve to the probability of the event. In this case, it is desirable to have the curve be constrained to values between 0 and 1, so that the estimated probability does not take on an impossible value. The logistic satisfies this constraint.

Other common forms used are exponential and polynomial regression, the latter having squares, cubes, and higher powers of the variables, as well as products of the different variables and products of the variables raised to powers—so-called *interaction terms*. These different functional forms may themselves be combined. A logistic or exponential regression may contain polynomials of the variables along with or instead of the variables, or they may contain transformations of a continuous variable into a set of categorical variables. Other transformations, such as gamma functions, are also sometimes used.

This variety of functional forms yields the possibility of virtually any shape for the boundary, including ones that change their curvature from bowed-out to bowed-in. In fact, the accept-refer regions may not even be

## FIGURE 6-12
### Highly Non-Linear System (Hypothetical)

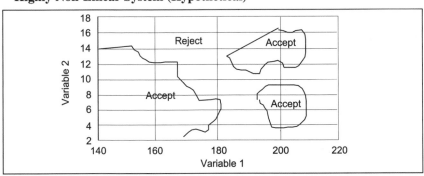

## FIGURE 6-13

**Artificial Neuron—3 Inputs, Logistic Transfer Function**

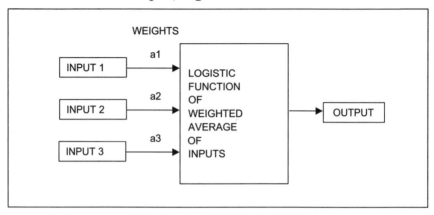

connected, as Figure 6–12 shows. Examples of possible non-connectivity would be where extremely low and extremely high values for the same variable add to the risk—for example, consumers having no bank credit cards and consumers having a large number of bank credit cards may both be higher credit risks than consumers with one or two cards. Further, the number of credit cards might interact positively or negatively, or even in a variable manner, with other credit risk indicators. The key point is that non-linear regressions can provide a model for this complexity.

### Neural Networks

Neural networks are pattern classification systems whose structure is suggested by the interconnection of neurons in the human brain. Figure 6–13 shows a single artificial neuron that takes a weighted sum of the inputs and indexes it with a value from 0 to 1, using a logistic function.[4] In a neural network, there are one or more layers of neurons (Figure 6–14), with outputs from one layer forming the inputs for the subsequent layer. Layers between the input and output layers are considered *hidden* layers, since the values for their operation are hidden from general view. These interconnected neurons form a system that can model highly non-linear processes with complex interactions among the variables.

Despite their apparent differences, neural networks and regression techniques have much in common. The simplest neural network system—a single neuron—is, in fact, essentially a logistic regression with

---

4 Other functions such as step functions or linear functions can be used but are much less common than the logistic.

## FIGURE 6-14

**Neural Network—3 Inputs, 1 Hidden Layer with 2 Neurons**

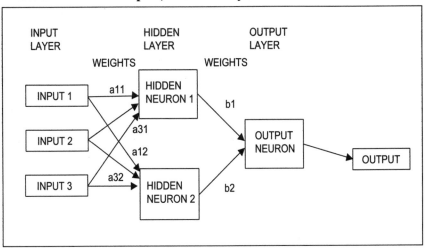

additive inputs. The flexibility of the neural network derives from combining inputs and outputs from many logistic curves. The potential flexibility of regression derives from the use of non-linear functional forms, transformed variables, and interaction terms.

Both neural networks and non-linear regression can be universal approximators to any pattern classification system; no matter how complicated the actual process, either a sufficiently complex neural network (one with sufficient hidden layers and neurons) or a sufficiently complex regression (for instance, a polynomial regression with sufficient high order terms) can model it.[5]

Both neural networks and regressions have adjustable parameters that must be set by the automated learning procedure according to the evaluation system and the feedback rules. The adjustable parameters for the neural network system are the weights applied to each set of input variables by each neuron at each layer. The adjustable parameters of the regression are the coefficients. It is usually easier to interpret the coefficients of a regression than the weights of a multi-layer neural network, but if the regression has many interaction terms, interpretation can get difficult.[6]

---

5 Schurmann (1996) points out that both polynomial regression and neural networks are universal approximators, and so are assymptotoically equivalent (p. 99). He also discusses the case of radial basis functions, local functions that lead to a nearest neighbor approach to pattern classification, which, as a special case of regression, is also a universal approximator. The radial basis function approach is the underpinning for *case-based reasoning,* so the various issues that apply to the other approaches also apply to case-based reasoning as well.

6 For a number of articles which discuss neural network and other techniques, see Freedman, Klein, and Lederman (1995).

## General Considerations for the Functional Form

Each type of pattern recognition system includes certain types of functional forms that are simpler and more natural to model in that system than in others. However, there are a number of issues regarding functional form that are common to all pattern recognition systems.[7]

*Flexibility, Computation, and Overfitting*   There is no limit to the flexibility that can be achieved with a pattern recognition system that is a universal approximator, such as polynomial regression and neural networks. In principle, polynomial regressions can add as many higher order terms as are desired to achieve a better fit. Neural networks can add more hidden layers to achieve the same effect.

But adding more and more terms or hidden layers can cause problems. First, there is an infinite set of choices, and no automatic way to include only those that work best, since an infinite set cannot be searched in a finite time. So the increase in flexibility can only be bought at greater computational cost.

There is also a trade-off between increasing the level of fit on the training set by including higher order terms for a polynomial regression, and overfitting—generating a curve so complex that it picks up essentially random variations that do not carry over to situations outside the training set. Overfitting would also apply to adding hidden layers in a neural network.

*Choice of Independent Variables*   Optimization of any approach requires including all the relevant variables. For credit risk modeling, depending on the type of risk, there are several categories of variables from which variables may be selected: credit history, borrower characteristics, loan characteristics, collateral characteristics, economic conditions, and, for international loans, country risk. If variables excluded from the system affect the risk, then the predictive power of the resultant model will not be as high as it could be.

Variables can be chosen manually or automatically. Manual choices are based on reasonableness, examination of confidence intervals, and signs and sizes of coefficients. The researcher is looking for how much the variable adds to the predictive power of the system, how independent it is of the contributions of other variables, and how well it accords with theory or other prior notions of how the variable should enter, for instance underwriters' experience. Automated methods may be used for the first two criteria, predictive power and independent effect.

Reasonableness of effect becomes more difficult to apply as the system becomes more complex. With linear regression, the size and signs of the coef-

---

7 An excellent, yet fairly non-technical text that goes into much more detail about the issues regarding specification of regressions is Kennedy (1992).

ficients (the weights for each variable) can be examined for reasonableness. With a highly non-linear regression that has many interaction terms, or with a neural network, a sensitivity analysis of the contribution of each variable is required, and the variable must be examined across a range of values.

*Transformations of Independent Variables*   Often, transforming variables before they are included in the model improves predictive power. Ratios of variables are an important and common type of transformation in credit risk. LTV and DTI ratios generally have far more power and also have a different meaning than the raw variables loan size or income.

Variables are also created through summation. For mortgage lending, assets after mortgage close includes many items that are added and subtracted to get a total, which may itself be divided by monthly mortgage payments or by other variables, such as monthly income, to get a transformed variable. What is not always recognized is that how these transformations are carried out should itself be considered part of the model. For example, in assets after close, a decision whether to count assets in a 401K plan at full value or at a reduced amount (e.g., an after tax amount) is really a model decision. These transformations, while affecting the model, are sometimes decisions the modeler inherits from the creators of the data set if the original underlying variables are no longer available.

Other types of transformations include powers, logs, exponentials, or other functions of the independent variables. Continuous variables also may be made into categorical variables, where there may be sharp distinctions at boundaries—e.g., loan size, where there are important institutional differences between conforming mortgage loans (conforming to the Fannie/Freddie loan limits) and jumbo mortgage loans (above the limit). These transformations can improve the power of the model if the underlying variable enters in a non-linear way.

## Choosing a Pattern Recognition System

Choosing among different approaches for a particular application involves a tradeoff between flexibility, which improves predictive power, and computational burden. Greater flexibility also often implies greater complexity, and greater difficulty in making a simple interpretation of the results. As mentioned, too great flexibility can lead to overfitting, which means that the high predictive power of the model on the training set will not carry over to out-of-sample predictions.

In principle, it would seem that a modeler could choose among the different pattern recognition systems to make the optimal choice for a particular application by running each approach—rules-based, regression, neural networks, or other candidate—through an automated learning system to find out which system has the lowest predictive error. But because of the infinite number of choices a modeler has *within* any given approach—functional forms, choice of independent variables, and transformations of the variables—the try-them-all approach is not practical; nor would it guarantee optimization.

Further, the other components of the automated learning procedure also involve a host of technical choices that further complicate the task of optimizing across modeling approaches and the functional choices within those approaches.

## OPTIMIZING THE AUTOMATED
## LEARNING PROCEDURE

To optimize, the modeler must make technical choices with regard to three components of the automated learning procedure in addition to the pattern classification system: the training set, the evaluation procedure, and the feedback loop. Because the issues regarding these choices are often the same for all pattern recognition systems, regardless of the functional form, they can be illustrated with the simple rules-based example.

### Rules-Based Example

A modeler can use an automated learning procedure to estimate the single-rule LTV pattern recognition system by choosing a training set, an evaluation procedure, and a feedback loop and then running the procedure to set b, the cut-off parameter, to an optimal value. Even this simple system illustrates the range of choices that can be made and how they are classified.

The *training set* might be chosen as the set of all first mortgage loans originated over the past five years by this lender. The *classes* might be loans that have or have not gone into foreclosure. The *evaluation system* will test for a particular value of b, say 80 LTV, perhaps by adding up the number of loans that had LTVs of 80 or below that went into foreclosure and the number of loans with above 80 LTVs that did not go into foreclosure. This sum divided by the total number of loans in the training set would equal the error rate of the system for the adjustable parameter set to 80. The *feedback loop* uses the results of the evaluation to adjust the parameters of the system if the result is not yet optimal. If the feedback loop is set to search at intervals of 5 percentage points, the procedure would recalculate the error rate for b = 85 LTV. If the rate were lower than for b = 80, this rate would become the new standard against which the procedure would judge whether b = 90, 95 (and b = 75, 70, etc.) would lower the error rate still further. The feedback loop could be set to stop when it has calculated all possible values of b.

This simple system illustrates many technical choices about the components of the automated learning procedure that will affect the estimated value of the adjustable parameters. The training set used could cover a longer or shorter time, could exclude the most recent loans because they are not seasoned enough to indicate performance, could be a subset of the loans, or could include all loan applications instead of all loans originated. The classes could be set by looking at delinquencies of different lengths or by considering approved versus rejected loans. The evaluation procedure could be based on a loss function that differentiates between different types of errors; classifying a loan that showed a loss as acceptable might be given a higher loss than classifying a loan that showed no loss as not acceptable. The feedback loop could have a smaller step size, such as 1 percentage point. All of these choices will have an effect on the final value of the adjustable parameter.

## The Training Set

The characteristics of the training set are extremely important to predictive power, for it is over the training set that optimization is carried out. Key issues for the training set are quality, size, breadth and sampling bias.

*Quality*   Garbage-in, garbage-out denotes an important truth. When clean data, which accurately measure dependent and independent variables, are used as input to even fairly simple models, much of the time they will beat "dirty" data analyzed using elaborate techniques. Modeling techniques built to deal with so-called "errors in variables"—dirty data—can improve the situation, but in general, they rely on assumptions about the data and the nature and distribution of the errors, which, though plausible, are less reliable than correct information.

Since the model will be used on new observations, it is vital to have clean data going forward as well as in the training set. After cleaning the data in the training set, the modeler needs to incorporate the same cleaning procedures into the production setting. If not, cleaning the data could actually be counterproductive, because the (cleaned) training set data, while more accurate, will not be representative of the (dirty) production data.

*Size*   One of the more common questions asked of a modeler is "How much data do you need?" There is no simple answer. For some models, thousands of observations may be sufficient; for others, it would be best to have millions. Credit risk data sets generally need to be larger than those needed for applications like economic forecasting, for at least two reasons. First, at least for frequency models, the dependent variable is binary—either loss or no loss—so it carries less information than a variable with a magnitude (like a severity variable), and the data set needed to model it must thus be larger.

Second, in credit risk frequency models, on average the frequencies tend to be very low, say a loss rate of 3 percent and almost certainly well below 10 percent. The lower the frequency of the event being modeled, the more observations are needed to get a significant number of negative events. Sampling techniques can be used to reduce the need to actually model on a large data set, for example, by taking a sample where the negative events (losses) are fully represented, but the positive events are randomly sampled at, say, a 50 percent or 10 percent level. In this case, the analysis is carried out using weighting techniques. A key point is that structured sampling of this sort only holds down the computational requirements. The population from which the sample is drawn still needs to be large enough to generate a sufficient number of negatives.

**Breadth**   Whether the training set is representative is as important as its size. A model created from a data set of even millions of mortgage loans all of the same type, with the same type of borrower, from the same part of the country, made under similar economic conditions will be less valuable in many applications than a model created from a smaller data set that has broader representation across all categories.

The breadth of a data set refers to the variety of data types that it includes. A broad mortgage loan database, for instance, would include loans of different sizes (e.g., conforming/jumbo), types (fixed rate/ARM), terms (15/30 year), with a range of LTV ratios, originated in many different parts of the country, over various periods, and with a range of other characteristics as well. To the extent that a particular subset of loans is not well represented—for instance, cash-out refinance loans or loans made under recessionary economic conditions—the training set will not provide strong guidance to the pattern recognition system about how these loans will perform.

To illustrate with a regression example, consider a decision model for mortgage loans to commercial properties. Suppose the training set has very few examples of a type of loan, say, loans to hotels, that we will assume generally performs worse than the office, retail, and apartment loans more common in the training set. In a more complete training set, the modeler could include a dummy variable for hotel loans—0 if no hotel, 1 if hotel—that would show a positive, significant coefficient;[8] but if the num-

---

8 More elaborate types of models could be constructed with slope coefficients or even separate scorecards.

**FIGURE 6–15**

**Sampling Bias (Hypothetical)**

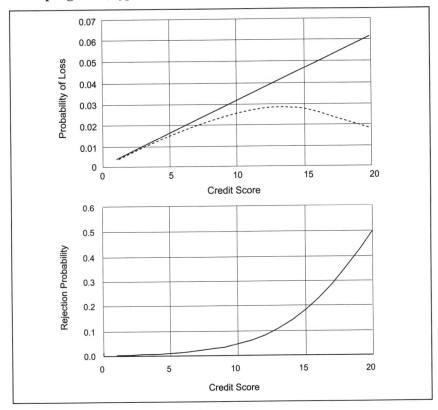

ber of hotels in the training set is not sufficient, the estimated coefficient would be subject to high sampling variance, causing the modeler to conclude that there was no effect or that it was not statistically significant and should be left out of the model. If the model were then used in production, and hotel loans were refinanced more frequently than in the training set, the model would underestimate the risk from this type of loan.

***Sampling Bias***    Sampling bias is another issue that creates problems for the application of credit risk models. A very important example of sampling bias arises in credit risk models trained on only those loans that have been *accepted* in the past when the models are intended to estimate risk on *all applications* in the future.

The problem is illustrated in Figure 6–15. The top graph is a hypothetical example showing the loss frequency of accepted loans only (dotted line) and of all applications (solid line), both plotted against credit score (with low risk to the left and high risk to the right, lower credit score values being associated with lower risk). The bottom graph shows a hypothetical rejection rate at each level of credit risk. For low risk (low score value) applicants, the difference in loss frequencies is very small, the obvious reason being that virtually all low risk applicants are accepted and so there is little difference in the data sets for this type of applicant. But as the credit score increases (the risk increases), an increasing proportion of the applications are rejected.

If the rejections were randomly distributed across applications, the pattern would not create a difference between the loss frequencies on the two samples. But the data set of accepted loans is shaped by the fact that underwriters (either human or automated or a combination of both) are striving to make judgments so that the only loans with riskier credit scores that are accepted have factors that make them low risk for other reasons. In statistical terms, the underwriting is creating a biased data set—not one that discriminates in an illegal or unethical fashion, but one that is biased toward including loans that are less likely to show a loss. The bias in the data set is larger the higher (riskier) the credit score.

When a pattern recognition system is estimated using loss rates only on accepted loans, it will show a much weaker relationship between credit score risk and subsequent performance than would a data set of all applicants. In Figure 6–15 this shows up as a curve with a lower slope for accepted loans than for all applications. In fact, the slope for accepted loans increasingly flattens and eventually turns negative, whereas the slope of the all applications group is constant and positive. But when the system, estimated using accepted loans only, is used to score all applicants, it will tend to underpredict the risk of poor credit scores. Further, the underprediction will get increasingly worse, the higher the risk.

The reader may object that the all-applications curve is a hypothetical construct, since we do not have the data to estimate it. In general this is true, but the effect is real and can be demonstrated indirectly in a variety of ways. For instance, heavily underwritten data sets may show that accepted loans with very poor credit histories actually show *lower* loss frequencies than accepted loans with somewhat better credit histories. The fact that a much smaller proportion of the poor credit history loans are accepted than the fair credit loans, is consistent with sampling bias. The underwriters also clearly recognize that this type of selection is what is going on.

Modelers sometimes suggest, at least half jokingly, that their lending institutions should create a non-biased sample by accepting all applicants for a limited period of time. This could often be a very expensive way to create a dataset in the long run, when high loss rates come about. A less expensive, though less precise, fix for sampling bias is to use statistical techniques to correct for distortions that use information about the criteria for rejection and adjust the credit loss regression to mitigate sampling bias. [9]

# THE EVALUATION PROCEDURE

## Loss Functions

Evaluation of how the model performs on the training set provides feedback to adjust the parameters of the model in the direction of optimization. Evaluation is usually done using a least squares criterion. The deviation between the predictions of the model and the actual values of the dependent variable—e.g., loss frequency—is squared and summed across all observations in the training set. Optimization then means minimization of this sum of squared error terms—hence, least squares.

The least squares criterion is one type of *loss function*, one that evaluates the losses suffered from misprediction. Since squared errors are used, the losses emphasize outliers, so if one misprediction is 0.2 and another is twice as large, 0.4, the loss from the latter will be counted as four times as large. Squared errors also are symmetric with regard to underpredictions and overpredictions. While these characteristics of the loss function can be derived from the characteristics of underlying statistical distributions, which are assumed to apply because they make it easier to do the computations, they may not be realistic descriptions of the losses actually encountered in a credit risk business application.

Other types of loss functions, while much less common, can provide a more accurate assessment of real losses. For loss severity modeling, for example, the absolute value of the loss rather than its square might provide a better description of the losses incurred from misprediction. Regressions using absolute loss functions are sometimes referred to as *robust* regressions, because they are less sensitive to large changes in parameters occurring because of a small number of large outliers. For credit risk frequency, an asymmetric loss function might be more appropriate, because the losses from rejecting a good loan (a so-called Type I error) are generally much lower than those for accepting a loan that will show a loss (a Type II error). Optimization of the system is always relative to a particular loss function: different loss functions will lead to different parameter estimates. [10]

---

9 See Heckman, (1976), Yezer, Philips, and Trost (1994), and Yezer and Phillips (1996) for illustrations of techniques to correct for sampling bias. Gruenstein (1980) uses the Heckman technique in the context of property valuation and land use. A related issue is simultaneous equation bias, where there are several dependent variables, and several distinct relationships among the independent and dependent variables. See Kennedy (1992) for a further discussion.

## Performance on Subsets

How the model performs on subsets of the data should be considered in judging optimal performance. There are many important subsets. Looking at how the model performs for different *time periods* gives information about whether changes in economic conditions, underwriting criteria, loan products, or the applicant pool have had significant effects on the relationships among variables. Performance in different *geographic regions* can point to the effect of differing economic factors as well as demographic or institutional differences. Looking at the model's performance on different *demographic groups* is important from the point of view of legal restrictions and marketing linkages.

More generally, the population can be stratified by any of the variables that are already included or could be included as explanatory variables in the model—e.g., loan sizes and types, credit score, debt-to-income, or LTV ratios. Stratification by variable is a way of finding transformations of the variables or variable interaction terms that would improve the model's predictive power. Suppose a variable such as LTV is included as a linear variable in a mortgage default model, and model performance is then examined for low LTV and high LTV mortgages separately. If the model tends to overpredict defaults for low LTV loans and underpredict defaults for high LTV loans, it would indicate that there is a non-linear transformation of LTV or the dependent variable that would improve the model's performance (see Figure 6–9).

More detailed stratification can uncover more complex relationships. Take a hypothetical interaction between credit score and LTV. Stratifying by LTV and credit score might show that the default probability rises less quickly as LTV increases for groups with poor credit. In this case the model could be improved by including an interaction term between credit score and LTV, which would be expected to have a negative coefficient. In some cases, stratification will show a need for different scorecards—which in essence are different models—where the behavior on different groups is so radically different that it cannot be modeled well using other means. Sometimes separate scorecards are called for because the same data are not available for a particular segment of the population. Along with behavioral differences, lack of complete data would be one reason that new credit users and those with long credit histories might be modeled with separate scorecards.

Another reason to examine model performance on subsets is to demonstrate that the model is robust, in the sense that the performance is the

---

10 Shiller and Weiss (1997) and Manski (1991) discuss the importance and impact of using different loss functions. Manski points out that a step-wise quantile loss function will generate a regression that will answer what we have termed the X-Y-Z question in this chapter.

combined result of many variables, and not just dominated by one or a small number. When a model retains good performance on a highly stratified sample, where the stratification has been created using variables that are known to contribute strongly to the predictive power of the model, it shows that the remaining variables in the model also have power to separate "bads" from "goods".

## Out-of-Sample Tests (Generalization)

Optimization of the model on the training set is fine, but the most important question is how the model will work in production. This is known as generalization, and there are several modeling strategies available to address it. Since the training set is all the modeler has to work with, strategies to address generalization involve splitting the sample into subsamples.

The simplest way to split samples is to use two randomly selected, equal sized subsamples of the full training set. The first subsample is used as the actual training set. The second subsample, called the *holdout* sample, is not used in the initial estimation but later, to test the performance of the estimated model. Similar performance on both the training set and the hold-out sample is an indication that the model will perform at about the same level in production. If the performance of the model deteriorates substantially on the hold-out sample, the model is sensitive to specific aspects of the two sets. Such specifics could include a set of unusual observations, referred to as outliers, that are more prevalent in some data sets. Clusters of observations that show a particular set of relationships that are not always found could also cause performance differences.

Depending on the amount of data available in the full training set and the amount of time and resources available for modeling, more elaborate subsampling strategies can be used to provide more information about actual production performance and to refine the model. One elaboration can be termed iterative hold-out samples: the training set is split into three or more subsamples. The model is estimated on the first. Performance is examined on the second. If there are significant differences in performance, the model is modified to be less sensitive to the random differences among subsamples, for instance, by dropping or modifying variables that showed up as significant on the training sample but not the hold-out sample. The new version is then tested for performance on the combination of subsamples 1 and 2, and this performance is compared to its performance on subsample 3. In principle, this procedure could be carried out with more and more subsamples, until diminishing marginal returns set in.

Other strategies using holdouts can involve attempts to simulate the model's use in practice. For example, instead of a random hold-out sample, the modeler could estimate the model using all data on loans prior to the most recent year available in the training set, and then test the model's performance on the most current year. This method is termed *ex-post prediction*. This procedure will suggest any likely deterioration in performance in the first year a model is used. Using this criterion for optimization, the modeler could try a model with the observations weighted differently by year of observation, weighting more recent years more heavily than years further back. The model used in production would use all years of data, but the optimal weighting scheme could be derived from the ex-post prediction. As with the simpler case of random subsamples, ex-post prediction can also be carried out iteratively.

In an earlier paper (Gruenstein, 1995), I describe a method, rolling ex-post prediction (REP), that tests the predictive power of models by simulating the process that a forecaster would go through generating forecasts for several years, including re-estimation of the models each year. Optimization of the model is carried out by using the simulated goodness-of-prediction (GOP) of these models as a criterion for setting the adjustable parameters, rather than the goodness-of-fit on the full training sample.

## THE FEEDBACK SYSTEM
### Optimization technique

For linear regression, using a least squares loss function, there are well-defined formulas with which the exact value of the optimal parameters of the model can be computed. For complex statistical systems like non-linear regression or neural networks where there are no exact formulas, algorithms that search for the optimal values must be used. These algorithms have several common features that the modeler and the user must take into account.

First, the more complex the system, the more likely it is the search technique will encounter local optima. At a local optimum the parameters give a better performance than any "nearby" sets of values, but the optimum may not be the global optimum—the set of parameter values that give the best performance (on the training set) compared to any other set. Even the global maximum may not be unique or may be "not very" unique. In other words, the search procedure may find, long broad ridges, so to speak, where changes in parameters chosen along certain dimensions make little difference in performance. In principle, all possible combinations of parameters can be searched, so that the true global optimum is found, but with complex systems, including non-linearities, large numbers of variables, and very large data sets, the computational requirements are prohibitive. The final set of parameters chosen as optimal, then, will in general be sensitive to the initial starting point of the search (e.g., if it turns out to be nearer a "high" local optimum than to the "higher" global optimum), the step size used in the search (too large and the search might not converge, too small and the program could use a lot of computation time, especially if the numbers of observations and variables are large), and the specific search technique.

The more complex the system, the less likely that the search procedure will find the exact optimum. Near-optimization rather than global may not make that much difference in the performance of the model on the training set, but it can be a reason for divergences between how the model performs on the training set, on the hold-out sample, and in production. Further, the existence of several near-optima can make model updates more problematic. Model re-estimation based on updates of the data or addition of information could lead to surprisingly large differences in individual parameters if the change shifted the search procedure to another local optimum that is relatively far away.

In most cases the modeler relies on a packaged program, such as SAS or SPSS, that has incorporated one or more search routines. The modeler often can control some search parameters, such as the step size of the search, the tolerance (how much difference in performance is so small that the program stops searching), and even the choice of search technique. In principle, the modeler could try different choices to see whether the result is sensitive to a particular search. In practice, additional choices entail the familiar trade-off between time and results. The modeler may decide to just use the preset defaults of the canned routine.

Hardware can also have an effect. Especially with large datasets, different hardware platforms—PC vs. mainframe, for instance—may give somewhat different results, perhaps because of different degrees of numerical precision. The modeler may have little or no control over this issue, but in implementing the model, it is very important to check where possible for any sensitivity if the model is to be implemented on a platform different from the one on which it was estimated.

## Incremental vs. Batch Learning

It is sometimes claimed that the difference between regression analysis and neural networks is that regression is based on statistical formulas and neural networks on a system that embodies "learning," one that uses a technique where the system evaluates its performance on each new observation and modifies itself based on how well its current parameters predicted this observation. The distinction is really between the way the training set generates feedback to adjust the parameters, and not between the intrinsic characteristics of the two models. In fact, any automated learning system can in principle be run in either of the two modes, which are referred to as *batch learning* and *incremental learning*.

Typically, regression analysis is carried out in batch learning mode, where the entire set of observations from the training set is used in one pass to generate feedback with which to adjust the model. For the simplest form, linear regression, the parameters can actually be calculated using algebraic formulas based on the entire set of observations, so the batch mode is very natural.

In contrast, neural network analysis often adjusts the parameters using the *incremental learning* mode. Incremental learning involves adding observations one-by-one and making marginal adjustments to the parameters based on the information gained from the additional observation.

The decisive factor in the choice between these two modes often is the computational burden. With complex systems and a large training set, it may be more feasible to use incremental learning. As the learning proceeds, the parameter changes can be examined. At a certain point, the effect of the addition of each new observation will fall below a preset tolerance level, and the procedure can be stopped. The result is that the model will have been estimated using a subset of the training set. In a sense, this procedure is like using a subsample for batch learning. However, in incremental learning, the size of the subset will be determined as the procedure goes along, rather than all at once at the beginning. It should be obvious that with incremental learning, the result will depend on the order in which the observations are presented. Different weighting schemes for the observations can be used. This is also true for batch learning, where different weights can be applied to different subsets of the data.

## CONCLUSION

Life would be easier if there were a single set of optimal modeling techniques that could be used in every situation, so that model builders and users could always tell when they had the best model, but that is not the case. The optimal use of statistical techniques for creating pattern recognition systems involves choices that need to be made for all four parts of the automated learning system—the form of the pattern recognition system, the training set, the evaluation procedure, and the feedback loop that adjusts the parameters of the system. An important point, sometimes not fully appreciated, is that the best choices about modeling *techniques* often depend on the modeling *application*. For example, if there are different costs associated with different types of incorrect decisions—accepting a credit risk that should be referred versus referring one that should be accepted—the modeling technique itself ideally ought to reflect this differential.

Although the term "statistical" is sometimes used narrowly to mean only regression-type approaches, in fact, credit risk evaluation systems are all generally statistical. When any pattern recognition system is estimated using an automated learning procedure, it is inherently a statistical system. The parameters are derived from a sample of actual historical experience. The statistical properties of that sample are relevant to the accuracy of the predictions. The parameters and the measures of performance of the system are statistical because they are derived from the training set, which can only be a sample of all the possible observations. The same statistical considerations—such as sampling bias, relationships among the variables, and iterative versus batch learning techniques—are important for all kinds of pattern recognition systems—simple and complex.

## REFERENCES

Freedman, Roy, Robert Klein, and Jess Lederman, eds. *Artificial Intelligence in the Capital Markets.* Chicago: Probus Publishing, 1995.

Gruenstein, John. "Predicting Residential Mortgage Defaults," paper presented at the American Real Estate and Urban Economics Meeting, January 1995.

Heckman, James. "The Common Structure of Statistical Models of Truncation, Sample Selection, and Limited Dependent Variables and a Sample Estimator for Such Models," *Annals of Economic and Social Measurement,* Vol. 5, No. 4 (1976), pp. 475-92.

Kennedy, Peter. *A Guide to Econometrics.* Cambridge, MA: The MIT Press, 1992.

Leamer, E.E. *Specification Searches: Ad Hoc Inference with Nonexperimental Data.* New York: John Wiley & Sons, 1978.

Manski, Charles. "Regression," *Journal of Economic Literature,* Vol. XXIX, No. 1 (1991).

Peters, Edgar. *Chaos and Order in the Capital Markets.* New York: John Wiley & Sons, 1991.

Schurmann, Jurgen. *Pattern Classification: A Unified View of Statistical and Neural Approaches.* New York: John Wiley & Sons, 1996.

Shiller, Robert, and Alan Weiss. "Evaluating Real Estate Valuation Systems," paper presented at the American Real Estate and Urban Economics Meetings, January 1997.

Yezer, Anthony, Robert F. Phillips, and Robert P. Trost. "Bias in Estimates of Discrimination and Default in Mortgage Lending," *Journal of Real Estate Finance and Economics,* Vol. 9, No. 3 (1994), pp. 197-216.

Yezer, Anthony, and Robert Phillips. "Self-Selection and Tests for Bias and Risk in Mortgage Lending: Can You Price the Mortgage if You Don't Know the Process?" *Journal of Real Estate Research,* Vol. 11, No. 1 (1996), pp. 87-102.

CHAPTER

# 7

# Early*Indicator*SM: DESIGN AND VALIDATION OF A COMPREHENSIVE BEHAVIOR SCORING SYSTEM FOR DELINQUENT MORTGAGES


**Larry Cordell,** *Director*
**Matthew Klena,** *Senior Economist*
**Timothy J. Malamphy,** *Economist*
**Wan-Qi Ting,** *Senior Risk Analyst II, Behavior Scoring Modeling Team, Freddie Mac*


## INTRODUCTION

Given that profit margins in the mortgage servicing business have tightened in recent years—and will tighten further—servicers are looking for ways to improve the efficiency of their operations. One area is management of delinquent loans, more specifically the use of aggressive and well-planned collections and loss mitigation campaigns. The recent surge in bankruptcy filings amidst strong economic growth has further heightened the need to deal promptly with delinquent loans.

In 1997, credit scores designed to predict which delinquent accounts are most likely to become more seriously delinquent—called behavior scores—were introduced on a wide scale to mortgage servicing. Freddie Mac and MGIC formed an alliance and released Versions 1 and 2 of their Early*Indicator*SM (EI) behavior scoring software. Fannie Mae threw its support behind a proprietary system, Risk ProfilerSM (RP). Internal systems developed at other mortgage servicers demonstrate a desire in the industry to integrate behavior scoring tools into servicing operations.

Today the mortgage servicing market is characterized by rapid consolidation and large economies of scale, making it an ideal market for automated scoring tools. What is more, payment processing is heavily centralized at large data centers known as service bureaus. The two largest service bureaus (Alltell and Fiserv) process payments for over 60 percent of the $4 trillion mortgage servicing market.

The fact that since the mid-1980s behavior scoring tools have been very successfully implemented in other industries, particularly with credit cards, raises a question about why behavior scoring has not yet become widespread in mortgage servicing.[1] In our view, two major modeling challenges need to be resolved before behavior scoring models are widely adopted in mortgage servicing:

1. A collections model designed to target borrowers at risk during their first month of delinquency needs to incorporate the institutional characteristics of the mortgage business—and demonstrate substantial cost savings.

2. For loans that become more seriously delinquent, models are needed that predict which loans are most likely to result in losses to creditors. To be effective, these "loss mitigation" models need to incorporate estimates of local house price appreciation, combine them with other attributes, and provide accurate risk rankings.

In this chapter we show that highly predictive collections and loss mitigation models for delinquent mortgages are possible through validation of Early*Indicator* (EI) scoring models. By the end of 1997, 24 mortgage servicers, accounting for a third of the nation's $4 trillion in mortgage debt, were in various stages of implementing EI. Whether EI is the scoring system of choice is less important than our demonstration that our two key modeling challenges have been resolved. In our concluding comments, we speculate on how behavior scoring tools will be implemented by mortgage servicers.

## Early*Indicator* AT A GLANCE

As an introduction to the behavior scoring models in Early*Indicator*, it is useful to briefly describe the "splitter logic" in the EI software. The EI scorecards are contained in distributed software designed to run on an IBM-compatible personal computer.

Version 3.0 of EI contains separate models at five different depths of delinquency (Figure 7–1). For the first month of delinquency, a collections score is produced with a range of 000-099. As we will show, the col-

---

1 For a discussion of the development of behavior scoring models in the credit-card industry, see Mary A. Hopper and Edward M. Lewis, "Behavior Scoring and Adaptive Control Systems," a Fair, Isaac Paper (May 1992).

2 For this discussion, a loan 30 days past due (DPD) refers to a loan that owes two payments, a 60DPD loan owes three payments, etc.

## FIGURE 7-1
Early*Indicator* Version 3.0

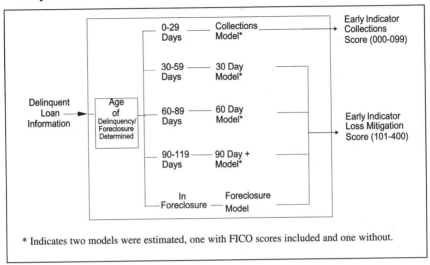

* Indicates two models were estimated, one with FICO scores included and one without.

lections model is related to the likelihood of a mortgage becoming 30 days past due (DPD).[2] Lower scores indicate higher risk of delinquency, higher scores lower risk. Servicers may also use Fair, Isaac (FICO) credit bureau scores as an input to improve the predictiveness of the collections scores, but FICO scores are not required.

Beyond the first month of delinquency, EI loss mitigation scores with a range of 101-400 are produced for mortgages 30+DPD or in foreclosure. These scores predict the likelihood of a loan being at risk of loss to the creditor. Separate models were estimated at 30, 60, and 90+DPD and for mortgages in foreclosure. As with the EI collections score, lower EI loss mitigation scores indicate higher risk of loss, higher scores lower risk. For the 30, 60, 90+DPD scorecards, servicers may use FICO credit bureau scores as an input to improve predictiveness but they are not required. (Because FICO scores were not predictive for loans in foreclosure, a separate model was not needed.)

The EI software has nine statistical models. The current versions of the EI behavior scores are designed for first mortgages, by far the most prevalent form of mortgage debt. Scoring with the EI software is currently not recommended for second mortgages and home equity lines of credit (HELOCs).

## MONTH ONE OF DELINQUENCY:
## THE EI COLLECTIONS SCORE

Version 2.0 of the EI collections score met with great success. Using the EI collections score in combination with the collections strategy outlined in the EI user manual,[3] servicers have reported savings of 30 percent or more, with numerous process improvements. The three largest US mortgage servicers (Norwest, Countrywide, and Chase Manhattan) and many others are regular users of the EI collections model.

The model was designed to capture the institutional characteristics of the mortgage servicing market. By far the most prevalent form of mortgage debt is the first mortgage. Such mortgages are almost always monthly installment payments,[4] typically due on the first of the month, although subprime mortgages may have other due dates. Substantial late fees are typically assessed 16 days after the due date. Collections campaigns designed to bring mortgage borrowers current are thus typically organized to begin around the 16th of the month.

Because as many as 6 to 10 percent of accounts are past due on the 16th day, servicers devote considerable resources to bringing borrowers current. The monthly payment on a mortgage is often the most substantial monthly payment a person will make, often 30 to 40 percent of a borrower's monthly income. Borrowers falling behind even two payments can mean substantial risk of loss to creditors. Collections during the first month of delinquency are often the costliest of a servicers' total delinquency management costs.

The Freddie Mac version of the EI collections model without FICO bureau scores purchased from Jim Carroll of Carroll & Associates represents over 20 years of development work. The results of this variant of the EI collections model are analyzed next, followed by description and validation of a variant of the model that incorporates FICO bureau scores.

## How the EI Collections Score Works

The data servicers need to harness the predictive power of collections scores can actually be found on their own servicing systems, in their transaction file databases, where the dates, amounts, and types of every major transaction are recorded for every mortgage they service. They can pull from the files the last 12 months of payment received and due dates for each mortgage from the transaction file. Analyzed statistically, the 12 payments reveal distinct pay habits that can be classified into unique risk groups for initiating collection campaigns at specified times during the month. These transaction-file data not only provide good predictions of which loans are most at risk of being delinquent at month's end, they also predict when borrowers are expected to pay.

---

3 See Freddie Mac, "Early Indicator $^{SM}$ 2.0: Understanding and Using the Collections Score" (promotional manuscript).

4 The rare bi-weekly or twice a month payments are recorded like monthly payments because servicing systems do not typically advance due dates on mortgages until two payments have been made, enough to equal a single monthly mortgage payment.

## TABLE 7–1

### Description of Early *Indicator*<sup>SM</sup> Collections Scores

| Score | Risk of Nonpayment | Payment Habit |
|---|---|---|
| 001-006 | Highest risk | The borrower has a history of default. The score takes into account how severe and how frequent delinquency has been, and how recently the mortgage was brought current. |
| 007-010 | Very high-risk | The borrower has a consistent history, now breached, of making prompt payments. The degree of consistency and the timing of payment dates are considered in the score. A borrower in this category who does not pay by month-end has demonstrated a changed behavior which may represent a potential loss mitigation candidate. |
| 011-044 | High-risk | The borrower has a consistent history of making payments at month end or shortly thereafter, but recently has always paid by month-end. The degree of consistency and the timing of payment dates are considered in the score. |
| 045-066 | Medium risk | The borrower has a consistent history of payments after the late fee date, but recently has always paid by month-end. The degree of consistency and the timing of payment dates are considered in the score. |
| 067-070 | Low-risk | The borrower has an inconsistent payment record, but no seriously late payment and has always paid by month-end. Recent payment date patterns and the extent of lateness are factored into the score. |
| 097-099 | Very low-risk | The borrower has a consistent record of payment within ranges of payment dates, no seriously late payment, and has always paid by month-end. The degree of consistency and related patterns of payment dates are factored into the score. |

EI scores are reported in three-digit format from 001 to 099.[5] A mortgage is given a score with a *lower number* if there is a high probability that a collection action must be taken on the mortgage to ensure payment is received. A mortgage is given a *higher number* and falls to the end of the queue if there is a high probability that collection action need not be taken. Mortgages that may or may not need intervention fall in the middle. Table 7–1 provides a detailed description of the major risk groups and their EI scores.

---

5 The EI collections model also has scores of '000', consisting primarily of new loans with no payment history. Since they are mainly new loans, they get placed at the very top of the collections campaigns. They are not considered in the analysis that follows.

## TABLE 7-2

**Performance of Early Indicator Collections Model by Major Risk Group
1997 Sample from Several Servicers**

| EI Collections Score Ranges | Risk of Nonpayment | Accounts Delinquent at Day 16 and at Month-end | |
| --- | --- | --- | --- |
| | | % Accounts | % Delinquent Month-end |
| 001-006 | Highest Risk | 23 | 47 |
| 007-010 | Very High-risk | 8 | 12 |
| 011-044 | High-risk | 14 | 37 |
| 045-066 | Medium Risk | 1 | 11 |
| 067-070 | Low-risk | 8 | 13 |
| 097-099 | Very Low-risk | 46 | 11 |
| Total | All Loans | 100 | 23 |

To validate the performance of the EI collections model, we collected a large sample of mortgages from several Servicers using several months of data from late 1997. Our sample includes all mortgages current as of the previous month but past due as of the late fee assessment date on the 16th. A further restriction is that a FICO score had to be available for the loan, something that will be important for completing comparisons with the enhanced collections model in the next section. Table 7-2 reports the results of this analysis.

The predictive power of the collections model is very strong, both statistically and qualitatively. Approximately 23 percent of accounts have the highest risk scores of 001-006. Of these, 47 percent were still delinquent at month-end. Thus, for the highest risk group, roughly half owed two payments at the start of the next month. By scheduling these calls at the very beginning of a collections campaign, servicers will be targeting the very highest risk group of borrowers.

Pay habit cells 007-010 are the next group sequenced for calls. These borrowers represent a unique class of borrowers and demonstrate another unique feature of the EI collections score. They are a fairly small share of the sample (8 percent) and have a relatively low month-end delinquency rate (12 percent). What is unique about them is that they have a habit of paying early in the month, and are now delinquent on the 16th. This is changed behavior that warrants special attention because if these borrowers become delinquent, they are more likely to become seriously so. Thus, the model incorporates some loss-mitigation objectives into the collections scores.

Borrowers with scores of 011-044 (14 percent of the sample) are the next group to sequence for calls. They have a very high month-end delinquency rate of 37 percent. These borrowers, "last minute Charlies," have a habit of paying very near month-end. Their high delinquency rates indicate they are also at risk of being two payments delinquent at the start of the next month.

Borrowers of low- and medium-risk are timed for calls to occur when they breach their expected day of payment. Medium-risk borrowers (scores of 045-066) are those who pay consistently after the late charge assessment date but well before the end of the month. Low-risk borrowers (scores of 067-070) have inconsistent pay habits. Borrowers with scores of 097-099 habitually pay well before month-end.

Note that all three medium and low-risk groups have roughly similar delinquency rates of 11-13 percent. Knowing the day of the month borrowers paid in each of the last twelve months, the EI collections score can predict *when* borrowers are likely to pay.

By adding a timing dimension to the score, servicers can sequence calls to maximize the efficiency of their collections operations. For example, borrowers with scores of 097-099 represent 46 percent of the sample, by far the largest group. Under suggested rules for implementing the EI collections score, these borrowers are scheduled for calling typically on the 25th of the month. Tracking through the borrowers with scores of 097-099 in the sample, roughly 80 percent had paid by the 24th, vastly reducing the number of calls that would need to be made for the lowest risk group of borrowers.

This discussion demonstrates that the 12 months of payment received and due dates found in the transaction file provide the key to an effective collections model. Mortgage tradeline data reported by the three main credit repositories (Equifax, Experian, and Trans Union) will not be as rich in data quality as a servicer's own transaction file. For example, most borrowers with EI collections scores of 007-099 have never been reported as 30 or more days past due on their mortgage. Data captured by the credit repositories will show the same payment histories for these mortgages, and fail to distinguish the very different risks these borrowers represent.

Moreover, because credit repositories receive data directly from servicers, processing time means that, at a minimum, repositories will not incorporate the last month of servicing history in their scores. Still, credit repository data does add important independent information on the overall risk of a borrower, which is considered next.

## Augmenting the EI Collections Score
## with a FICO Credit Bureau Score

The major innovation from Version 2.0 to Version 3.0 of the EI collections model is the option to use FICO credit bureau scores to improve pre-

## FIGURE 7–2

Distributions of Loans 16 Days Past Due Still Delinquent at Month End By FICO Score and Early*Indicator* Collections Score

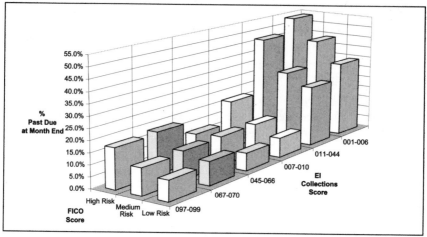

dictive power. Many servicers told us that they wanted to incorporate credit scores into their collections model to better target high-risk borrowers and safely delay calling low-risk borrowers.

The research completed with the sample data indicates that credit scores do improve the ability of the EI collections score to risk-rank borrowers. After extensive testing with FICO scores, we divided the sample into three distinct risk groups: high, medium, and low. As illustrated in Figure 7–2, high-risk FICO scores do indeed report higher 30-day delinquency rates for almost all the major collections score groups. Scores of 001-006 and 011-044 have by far the highest delinquency rates; combining them with FICO scores produces delinquency rates around 50 percent. In contrast, low-risk FICO scores have delinquency rates hovering around 30 percent. Similar patterns between high, medium, and low-risk FICO scores also appear for other major groups organized by collections scores.[6]

Based on these findings, the EI collections scores were rearranged using the FICO scores to give a risk-ranking superior to that provided by the EI collections score alone. We moved certain high-risk FICO groups into higher and riskier EI collections score groups. Likewise, we moved certain low-risk FICO groups into lower EI collections score groups for delayed calling. The results are reported in Table 7–3.

Borrowers with scores of 007-010 are borrowers who typically pay early but have breached that pattern. Using the EI collections model with-

---

6 The single exception are scores of 045-066, where high-risk FICO scores are slightly lower than medium risk. We attribute this to a small number of observations in this particular dataset.

## TABLE 7-3

**Delinquency Rates of Early Indicator Collections Model By Selected Score Ranges With and Without FICO Scores**

| EI Collections Score Ranges | Risk of Non-payment | Early Indicator Collections Model Without FICO Scores | | Early Indicator Collections Model With FICO Scores | |
|---|---|---|---|---|---|
| | | % Accounts | % Delinquent Month-end | % Accounts | % Delinquent Month-end |
| 001-006 | Highest Risk | 23 | 47 | 28 | 49 |
| 007-010 | Very High-risk | 8 | 12 | 2 | 21 |
| 011-044 | High-risk | 14 | 37 | 9 | 23 |
| 045-066 | Medium Risk | 1 | 11 | 2 | 13 |
| 067-070 | Low-risk | 8 | 13 | 13 | 15 |
| 097-099 | Very Low-risk | 46 | 11 | 46 | 10 |

out FICO scores, 8 percent of the sample had scores of 007-010, but these borrowers show low delinquency rates at month's end of 12 percent. Under the EI collections model enhanced with FICO scores, borrowers with high FICO scores were reclassified into scores 097-099. With the readjustment, only 2 percent of loans are in cells 007-010 and those that remain are much riskier, showing a delinquency rate of 21 percent.

The statistical evidence also shows significant improvements when combining an EI collections score with a FICO score. A standard statistic used to evaluate the power of scoring models is the K-S statistic (named after Kolmogorov and Smirnov, two pioneer Russian statisticians). For the FICO score alone, the K-S statistic was 29.6. For the EI collections score alone, the K-S statistic was 39.3. Combining the scores produces a K-S statistic of 43.6.

## MONTH TWO OF DELINQUENCY AND BEYOND: THE EI LOSS MITIGATION SCORES

With the mortgage payment taking up a substantial share of a person's monthly income, creditors typically suffer substantial risk of loss from borrowers who become 30 or more days past due. Figure 7-1 shows the stages of delinquency for which individual loss-mitigation models have been developed: 30, 60, 90+DPD, and loans in foreclosure. For the 30, 60, and 90+DPD models, separate models were also estimated that include FICO scores, for a total of seven EI loss mitigation scorecards.

The most powerful determinant of whether borrowers will default on their mortgage obligation is how much indebtedness still exists relative to the value of the property, summarized as the current estimated loan to value ratio (ELTV). Borrowers who made substantial down payments, who have paid down much of the principal, or whose property has appreciated substantially in value are likely to have enough equity in the property that they offer a reduced risk of loss to the creditor.

The key challenge to developing predictive loss mitigation models is therefore to develop a house-price appreciation index, compute ELTVs, and then combine ELTVs with other borrower and loan attributes into a single score that will successfully risk rank mortgages by their likelihood of loss. The following section describes loss mitigation scorecards with tables and graph illustrations that show the power of the models as well as convey information about expected performance in different EI loss mitigation score ranges.

## Loss Mitigation Scorecards

The data used to estimate and validate the loss mitigation scorecards included over 200,000 mortgages delinquent in the early to mid-1990s. The scorecards are the product of countless hours of research into the variables and their weightings in terms of how well they predict the likelihood of a loan going through foreclosure. The final versions of the models include 18 variables. While the exact variables and their weights are proprietary, the categories they fall in are as follows:

- *Property specific variables,* including ELTV, which includes a measure of house price appreciation from the combined Freddie Mac/Fannie Mae weight of repeat sales index (WRSI).
- *Borrower-specific variables,* including depth of delinquency; number of times 30, 60 or 90+ days delinquent over the last 9 months; and the credit bureau score of the borrower (an optional input to the scorecard).
- *Loan-specific variables,* including loan purpose and type of loan instrument.

The general pattern for variables in the different scorecards is that pay history and credit score, among other factors, tend to matter most in early stages of delinquency (30 and 60DPD); borrower equity and depth of delinquency matter more in the later stages (90+DPD and foreclosure). Having separate scorecards at four different stages of delinquency enables EI to focus on the set of characteristics that will generate the most powerful scorecards. This feature gives EI Version 3.0 a unique advantage over other systems as well as over previous versions of EI.

Another feature unique to EI Version 3.0 is the power of the ELTV. The index, based on over 8 million repeat transactions, is updated quarterly.

Model results are generated on all counties in the U.S., except for about a dozen sparsely populated counties.

## The Meaning of EI Loss Mitigation Scores

The EI loss mitigation scores are scaled between 101 and 400, with higher scores denoting lower risk of loss and lower scores denoting higher risk. We chose this scoring convention so as not to confuse the loss mitigation scores with collections scores, which are scaled from 000-099, or with FICO scores, which are scaled from 400-900.

Each of the loss mitigation models predicts the likelihood of a loan eventually curing, a "positive outcome." Another way of saying this is that the EI score predicts the likelihood of a mortgage *not* at risk of going through foreclosure, a "negative outcome." Since the definitions of positive and negative outcomes are the same in each of the 30, 60, 90+, and foreclosure scorecards, the scores have the same meaning across all depths of delinquency. Thus, a score of 250 has the same risk of default whether it be 30DPD or in foreclosure. This allows servicers to risk-rank loans across all stages of delinquency.

## Model Results

The ultimate test of the loss mitigation scorecards is how well the model predicts which 30+ delinquent loans are most likely to cure on their own and which are most likely to result in loss. An illustration of the power of the EI scores is provided in Figure 7–3.

## FIGURE 7–3

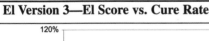

El Version 3—El Score vs. Cure Rate

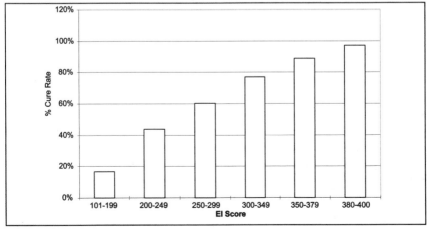

## TABLE 7–4

**Positive/Negative Odds Ratios for All
Scorecards and For Selected Scorecards
Results from 1992-94 Scorecard Development Sample**

| | Positive/Negative Odds Ratios for Overall Scores and For Selected Scorecards | | | | |
|---|---|---|---|---|---|
| Score Range | All Scorecards | 30DPD Scorecard | 60DPD Scorecard | 90+DPD Scorecard | Foreclosure Scorecard |
| 380-400 | 36:1 | 46:1 | 25:1 | 21:1 | 38:1 |
| 350-379 | 8:1 | 8:1 | 8:1 | 8:1 | 7:1 |
| 300-349 | 3:1 | 3:1 | 3:1 | 3:1 | 4:1 |
| 250-299 | 2:1 | 1:1 | 1:1 | 2:1 | 2:1 |
| 200-249 | 1:1 | 1:1 | 1:2 | 1:1 | 1:1 |
| 101-199 | 1:5 | 1:3 | 1:3 | 1:5 | 1:7 |
| K-S Statistic | 61.9% | 55.3% | 51.3% | 51.8% | 57.3% |

Positive = Paid off or current for 12 consecutive months
Negative = REOs, short sales, third party sales, charge offs, and deeds-in-lieu
of foreclosure.

We took the scores in each of the 30, 60, 90+DPD, and foreclosure score-cards in our development sample, combined them, and then plotted their cure rates by selected score ranges. Note the very clear pattern of increasing cure rates with increasing scores. Thus, regardless of the depth of delinquency, servicers can be confident that the EI loss mitigation scores will give them a tool that allows them to effectively risk rank their delinquent mortgages.

To further illustrate the power of the EI loss mitigation scores, Table 7–4 shows the positive/negative odds ratios for overall scores and for each of the individual loss mitigation scorecards.

As shown in the second column in the top row of numbers in Table 7–4, a score of 380-400 shows a positive/negative odds ratio of 36:1. This means that for every 36 loans that become good and cure, one loan will produce a loss. Looking across the columns, we see very high positive/negative odds ratios for each of the individual scorecards as well. Thus, regardless of whether a loan is 30, 60, 90+DPD or in foreclosure, scores of 380 or above mean that almost all the loans will cure.

In the lowest score range of 101-199, most loans have a negative out-come. For all scorecards, there is a positive/negative odds ratio of 1:5. This means that one loan has a positive outcome for every five that have a neg-ative outcome. Looking across the individual scorecards, we see many fewer delinquent loans having a positive outcome than a negative one.

For the middle score ranges, roughly the same number of loans have a positive as a negative outcome. Score ranges of 200-249 have positive/negative odds ratios of 1:1, while scores of 250-299 have posi-tive/negative odds ratios of 2:1.

## TABLE 7–5
### K-S Statistics for All Scores and For Selected Scorecards
### Model Results With and Without FICO Scores

| | K-S Statistics for Overall Scores and For Selected Scorecards | | | | |
| All Models | 30DPD Scorecards | 60DPD Scorecard | 90+DPD Scorecard | Foreclosure Scorecard | Scorecard |
|---|---|---|---|---|---|
| Including FICO Scores | 61.9 | 55.3 | 51.3 | 51.8 | N/A |
| Excluding FICO Scores | 61.5 | 53.6 | 50.6 | 51.4 | 57.3 |

Note that the pattern of declining positive/negative odds ratios with declining scores holds not only for overall scores but also for scores across individual scorecards. These results confirm that EI scores will effectively risk-rank loans across all depths of delinquency. Whether using scores to manage collections on 30DPD accounts or deciding which 90+DPD loans to refer to foreclosure, mortgage servicers can be confident that the EI loss mitigation scores will give them an effective risk-ranking tool.

The K-S statistics for the overall EI scores and for the individual scorecards are reported in the last row of Table 3. For commercially viable models the value of this statistic should be at least 30 percent, with models in the 40 and 50 percent range not uncommon. The K-S statistic for all scorecards is 61.9 percent—significantly higher than for any of the individual scorecards.

The loss mitigation scorecards were also tested on samples of loans other than those used to develop the scorecards. A similar test run on a sample of loans from the first quarter of 1995 yields a K-S statistic of 71 percent, while for 3rd quarter loans in 1996 the K-S statistic is 75 percent. This indicates not only extremely predictive models, but also a great deal of stability in application over time.

It is clear, then, that for each of the individual scorecards as well as the overall group of loans, EI Version 3.0 loss mitigation scores provide superior risk rankings. For the individual servicer, this means improved ability to focus the appropriate resources on a given loan.

### Comparing Results Using Scorecards With and Without FICO Scores

Based on demand, EI Version 3.0 loss mitigation models will give servicers the option of using FICO scores to improve their EI loss mitigation scores. How much will FICO scores improve risk-rankings? We did see above that FICO scores improved the risk-rankings of the collections scores.

With the K-S statistic as the measure, the degree of difference is surprisingly modest. Overall, the K-S statistic is 61.9 for the models using the FICO scores and 61.5 for the models not using the FICO scores (see Table 7–5). This is indeed a very small difference in predictive power.

As expected, the results differ among the scorecards. For the 30DPD scorecard, the measure of separation is greatest (55.3 versus 53.6). For the foreclosure scorecard, the FICO score is not a significant enough variable to be used.

The FICO score declines in importance as the depth of delinquency deepens because it is built to predict which tradelines on a borrower's credit report will go 90DPD or worse. All seriously delinquent borrowers meet that condition on their mortgage tradeline alone.

In the discussion of the collections score, we noted significant improvements in the power of the collections scores when combined with FICO scores. Should servicers opt to use FICO scores for their collections scores, they will also be able to improve the power of the loss mitigation scores as well. Even without using FICO scores or other credit repository data, however, EI loss mitigation scores will give servicers a very powerful risk-ranking tool.

## CONCLUSIONS

Empirical results confirm that behavior scoring tools can successfully risk-rank mortgages at all stages of delinquency. Moreover, recent experience with EarlyIndicator confirms significant cost savings. Whether EI is the scoring system of choice is less important than the demonstration that with it we have overcome the major obstacles to producing highly predictive behavior scores for delinquent mortgage loans.

Given successful models, it is useful to speculate on how behavior scoring can be integrated into management of delinquent mortgage loans. A first observation is that a variant of the EI collections model is likely to be the behavior scoring model of choice for mortgages in the first month of delinquency. Presently, the three largest mortgage servicers are routinely using it, as are many other large- and medium-sized servicers.

It is still too early to tell how behavior scoring tools will be used beyond the first month of delinquency because the EI loss mitigation scores were only introduced in 1997. Given the huge costs associated with referrals to foreclosure, the costs of collecting on seriously delinquent borrowers, the costly process of property valuation, and the costs associated with recent efforts to devise alternatives to foreclosure, cost-savings application for loss mitigation scores should be forthcoming soon. Some servicers may well specialize in servicing high-risk seriously delinquent loans, as has happened in the credit-card industry with seriously delinquent accounts.

For servicers with sufficient data-processing resources, in-house models are likely to be preferred, service bureaus house the EI models and now routinely deliver scores to servicers.

What this says is that credit repositories are not likely to be used as a data-delivery system for scoring delinquent loans. Though credit repository data, such as FICO bureau scores, will be used to score delinquent mortgage loans, we believe such data will be gathered independently and used as inputs into in-house or service-bureau-housed models.

## REFERENCES

Carroll, James R. "A Smarter Approach to Collections." *Mortgage Banking* (February 1995), pp. 59-63.

Cordell, Lawrence R. "Scoring Tools to Battle Delinquencies." *Mortgage Banking* (February 1998), pp. 1-5.

Freddie Mac. "Early Indicator<sup>SM</sup> 2.0: Understanding and Using the Collections Score." Promotional Manuscript.

Hopper, Mary A., and Edward M. Lewis. 1992. "Behavior Scoring and Adaptive Control Systems." A Fair, Isaac Paper (May).

Hoff, John R., and Paul T. Peterson. "Everything in Its Time." *Mortgage Banking* (June 1997), pp. 34-41.

Hoff, John R., and Paul T. Peterson. "Creating Value For All Parties." *Servicing Management* (June 1997), p. 24ff.

# 8

# DATA MINING

**Allen Jost**
*Vice President for Business Development*
*HNC Software, Inc.*

## INTRODUCTION

**A** growing number of companies are making substantial investments in improving their customer information files and building data warehouses. Though these projects need huge amounts of time and money, as well as human and data processing resources, the investments are easily justified in view of the high cost of low quality data.[1] Because data modernization is so daunting, companies tend to spend a great deal of time, effort, and resources on the technical details of building a reliable corporate database. However, most companies do not plan for the operational use of the database. Yet what creates much of the added value and the justification for building the data warehouse is the application of analytical, statistical techniques that use the data to manage the business.

The economics of data and information is changing drastically. New competitors and substitute products are making it more important than ever *not* just to understand your customer but to target action at the customer's willingness to buy. Information represents a large part of the cost structure of most companies in the financial industry. The high cost of distribution makes knowing your customer even more important. Electronic communication with customers makes it crucial to be able to use statistical data analysis techniques. As customers find it easier to switch from one supplier to another, it will be increasingly important to anticipate customer wants and needs and target them with new products.

---

1 Larry P. English, "The High Costs of Low Quality Data," *DM Review,* Vol. 7, No. 6 (January 1998).

Ensuring that businesses take advantage of statistical analysis tools to make effective business decisions determines data mining success. Today, getting the most value from a data warehouse investment requires applying the analytical techniques commonly known as data mining.[2] Data mining is more a matter of designing business solutions than of "automatically finding data relationships" with the latest and greatest tools. The current emphasis on tools may cause confusion among those who do not fully understand the science of statistical analysis, for which data mining is simply another term. This chapter is an overview of statistical analysis. Without good data, statistical analysis is neither meaningful nor accurate.

## CHAPTER OVERVIEW

This chapter defines data mining and describes current data mining techniques. It also discusses appropriate (and inappropriate) ways to use data mining in business.

## WHAT IS DATA MINING?

Data mining is commonly defined as the exploration and analysis of data in order to discover meaningful pat erns and relationships.[3] This definition is often misunderstood as suggesting that something magical will happen if you decide to do data mining. A definition less likely to be misinterpreted is: Data mining is the analysis of data and the application of statistical techniques on data to solve specified, defined business problems.

In this chapter the terms data mining and statistical analysis are used interchangeably. Successful statistical analysis is not passive and it is not magical. With increasing focus on the consumer, more companies are using statistical analysis to drive their businesses. Unfortunately, they often rely on inexperienced analysts to implement it, with lost opportunity and high resource consumption the result.

Data mining techniques vary in complexity from simple descriptive techniques to complex regression modeling. The simplest include frequencies, cross tabulations, and descriptive statistical techniques such as averages and variances. The most complex are the regression "family" of statistical techniques, including neural networks, the most advanced regression technique (see Appendix I).

Although *data mining* is a relatively new term, most data mining techniques are not new. The revolving credit industry, for example, has used

---

2  Andy Frawley, "Marketing Warehouse ROI," *DM Review,* Vol. 7, No. 6 (June 1997).
3  Michael J.A. Berry and Gordon Linoff, *Data Mining Techniques* (New York: John Wiley & Sons), 1997.

data mining in the form of credit scoring for more than 50 years.[4] In that industry, score modeling is so commonplace that it has become a commodity.[5] With such intensive use of data for scoring applications, many businesses saw a need for a ready supply of "raw materials" in the form of data for statistical analysis in solving business problems. Other industries that use these techniques are the mortgage, insurance, consumer goods, retail, and medical fields.

Some data mining definitions include the term "automatic," implying that answers will magically appear when a mining tool is applied to a data warehouse. However, there is nothing "automatic" about data mining. Developing successful applications requires careful, focused problem specification, statistical model design, data analysis, and sophisticated analysis. Statistical analysis begins with a descriptive summary of the data and ends with prediction and explanation regression techniques that predict future behavior, identify customers who have desired business characteristics, or explain customer behavior. To help businesses derive economic value from their data, statistical analysts must:

- Define the business problem.
- Design an analysis to predict, explain, or answer a well-posed business question.
- Select a superset of data variables and create any new or derived variables that might apply to the business problem.
- Summarize data using queries and descriptive techniques such as frequencies, averages, and cluster analysis.
- Reduce the number of variables using techniques such as factor analysis and trained human judgment.
- Select the appropriate statistical technique.
- Decide whether the objective is to predict outcomes, identify accounts, or explain behavior.
- Define the outcome desired and gain consensus for it.
- Build the statistical model.
- Profile the identified customers using descriptive techniques and cluster analysis to determine model performance, describe accounts, and report results.
- Implement the model in production or operations.
- Track model performance to ensure it works as expected.

4 D. Durand, *Risk Elements in Consumer Installment Lending* (Washington: National Bureau of Economic Research, Inc.), 1941.
5 Jesse Snyder, "Opportunity Knocks at Scoring Door," *Collections and Credit Risk* (April 1997).

## TABLE 8–1
### Cross Tabulation Frequency Table—Occupation by Education

| Occupation | Education | | |
|---|---|---|---|
| | BS | MS | Ph.D. |
| Software | 40% | 20% | 40% |
| Banking | 20% | 70% | 10% |
| Telecom | 60% | 30% | 10% |

## DATA MINING TECHNIQUES

All good data mining applications enable users to solve business problems and transform information and behavior characteristics into activities that provide a high return on investment. Some of the basic processes are described below.

### Data Summary Techniques

Data summarization and description are the foundation of a data mining application. They help establish the validity of the data ("cleaning" the data) and reveal simple data relationships. However, these techniques are not sufficient for optimal solution of business problems. Data summarization is only one of many steps and options in statistical analysis.

Frequencies, means, other measures of central tendency and dispersion, and cross tabulations, decision trees and cluster analysis are the most fundamental descriptive statistical analysis techniques.

Queries and descriptive tools summarize both continuous (age, income, balance amount, etc.) and categorical data (gender, home ownership, occupation, etc.). Descriptive statistics for continuous data include indices, averages, and variances. For example, if the average age of a customer file is 45 years and the standard deviation is 2 years, we know that most of the customers are about 45. However, if the standard deviation is 20 rather than 2 years (a large variance), we know that the customers have a wide range in age.

Categorical descriptive techniques include one-way frequencies and cross tabulations. Table 8–1 shows the distribution of occupation by education level. It shows the percent distribution, by education level, for three different occupations.

Rather than use the mean and standard deviation, some analysts categorize continuous variables in order to report frequencies. Age, for example, may be grouped. If the customer file includes accounts between ages 18 and 65—a continuous variable—an analyst may group these accounts as:

1. 35 and younger (young)
2. 36 to 50 (middle-aged)
3. 51 and older (old)

The analyst then uses frequencies and cross tabulations to summarize the characteristics of the categorical age variable.

Categorization of continuous variables, often termed "binning", is typically done for two reasons: (1) it is easier for most people to understand a simple one-way or two-way frequency table with three or four categories than to understand the significance of the mean and standard deviation, and (2) traditional modeling techniques, such as linear and logistic regression, do not handle non-linear data relationships unless the data are first transformed. Categorization is one form of data transformation that many consider acceptable for use with traditional statistical modeling. In a given scoring model, for example, the continuous variable time on job might include zero points for less than 3 years, 15 points for 3 to 8 years, and 40 points for more than 8. Binning created the categories and the regression model determined the number of points for each time category.

Although binning helps the analyst build a scoring model to deal with non-linear data:

1. *It is labor-intensive.* Although analysts have spent a great deal of time automating this process, it still consumes a disproportionate amount of time and energy. If a data file has 1,000 variables and half of them are continuous, 500 must be binned. A human, or a computer program, must decide on every category on every one of the 500 variables. Then the performance of every category must be compared to the overall average based on the dependent variable.

2. *It is resource intensive.* Binning requires multiple iterations through the database in order to determine the best categories for each variable. This requires substantial computer investment, especially for large data files with many variables.

3. *It can be subjective.* Determining the cut-off values for each categories requires human judgment. In the time-on-job example, the first cut-off could easily have been 2-1/2 years instead of 3.

4. *Information gets lost.* Some information is "thrown away" when variables are binned. Instead of detecting small changes in the data for each month or year for the time-on-job variable, for instance, a model would detect only large discrete jumps in the data. Categorization thus gives an individual who is on the job for 3 years the same number of points as one on the job for 8 years. However, an individual on the job for 8 years and 1 month gets 25 more points than one on the job for 8 years. The information con-

## TABLE 8–2
### Database with six observations (rows) and seven variables (columns)

| Observation Number | Name | Age | Income | Gender | Rent/ Own | Monthly Payment | Credit Limit |
|---|---|---|---|---|---|---|---|
| 1 | Bill | 28 | 47,000 | M | O | 2350 | 5000 |
| 2 | Jan | 41 | 49,000 | F | O | 2450 | 6000 |
| 3 | Fred | 28 | 23,000 | M | R | 1300 | 1500 |
| 4 | Sue | 43 | 26,000 | F | R | 1450 | 2500 |
| 5 | Sara | 40 | 24,000 | F | R | 1400 | 2000 |
| 6 | Sam | 45 | 48,000 | M | O | 2400 | 5500 |

tained in the continuous small monthly increments of the variable is lost when categories are created.

5. *It is time-consuming and expensive to implement.* When models are implemented, binning requires additional programming to duplicate the categorization process. This not only costs time and money, it delays implementation.

If your analysts consistently create categories for continuous variables, it may be a warning that they are not using appropriate data mining procedures (see below, pp. 143–144). One of the benefits of newer technology, such as neural networks, is that variable binning is not necessary.

### Variable Reduction Techniques

A data warehouse is a two-dimensional table with the rows called *observations* and the columns known as *variables* (because the value varies). It is not unusual to have a customer file with a thousand variables and millions of observations. Table 8–2 shows a data file with seven variables. (Although name and observation number are labeled as variables in the table, they would not be used in score modeling data mining applications because they identify unique records in the database).

Variable reduction is necessary for data mining on large databases. A database with 1,000 variables must be reduced if analysis is to be meaningful. In order to make any sense of a data mining model—or even to develop a proposal to solve a business problem—an analyst must reduce the number of variables to a manageable subset. Typically, a final scoring model will include between 10 an 40 variables. It is important to select the smallest subset of variables that will represent underlying dimensions of the data. In a financial database, for example, one underlying dimension might be short-term delinquency history, but it might be represented by many variables, such as number of 30-day delinquencies in the last 3 months, number of 60-day delinquencies in the last 3 months, or number of 60-day delinquencies in the last 6 months.

The ultimate objective of most data mining activities is to create a scoring model. Scoring models predict the probability of a particular outcome or explain a specified event or customer behavior. The analyst uses three variable reduction techniques to reduce the number of variables in the model:

1. Human and business judgment.
3. Factor or principal components analysis.
2. Stepwise regression variable selection

Each technique varies considerably in terms of its applicability, performance, effectiveness, sophistication, complexity, and practicality.

*Human and Business Judgment*   Human judgment can play an important role in selecting variables. Marketing analysts, for example, may use human judgment to select the final set of candidate variables for predictive or explanatory models. (For a discussion of predictive and explanatory models, see p. 154.) In databases with hundreds of variables, many can be used interchangeably. A marketer may choose one over another because it offers a better "story" for advertising purposes. In credit scoring models, some variables are selected over others because they meet regulatory requirements or they have validity when used as reasons for adverse actions.

*Factor Analysis*   A mathematical extension of human judgment, factor analysis is one of the most sophisticated ways to reduce the number of variables in a large file. Factor analysis detects relationships, or correlations, among variables (very good techniques take into consideration both linear and non-linear variable relationships). Factor-analytic techniques group related variables; an analyst can then select one representative variable from each group.

Note that factor analysis deals only with predictor variables. The outcome, or dependent, variable, is not included.

Factor analytic groups are often called dimensions. Generally the variable with the strongest relationship to the outcome is chosen to represent a dimension. Of course, inclusion in the model must also make sense from a business perspective. For example, the data in Table 8–2 offers three possible dimensions:

1. Financial capacity dimensions (includes income and credit limit variables)
2. Shelter dimension (includes own/rent and monthly shelter payment)
3. Physical/demographic characteristics dimension (includes age and gender)

A marketing analyst wanting to build a model using a subset of the variables in Table 8–2 might choose income from the first dimension, own/rent from the second dimension, and age from the third.

For all its sophistication, factor analysis is by no means an exact science. For example, a variable in the shelter dimension such as monthly payment might also overlap with variables in the financial dimension, which could cause this analyst to determine that there are only two data dimensions, financial and physical characteristics, instead of three. However, in spite of its subjectivity and dependence on human judgment, factor analysis lends guidance and structure to the task of reducing many variables to a smaller, more manageable subset.

*Stepwise Variable Selection*   This statistical technique measures the correlation between each predictor variable and, unlike factor analysis, the outcome variable. Stepwise selection techniques compare each variable to its ability to predict or explain the desired outcome. Forward Stepwise variable selection starts with the one variable that has the highest relationship with the outcome variable, then selects those with the next strongest relationships. Backward Stepwise selection can start with all the variables and sequentially drop those with the weakest correlation to the outcome, retaining only those with the highest correlation.

Analysts must be careful to avoid correlated predictor variables when using stepwise regression. Too many correlated variables in a scoring model can cause problems if an analyst wishes to make judgments about the relative importance of the predictor variables used in the model.

## Observation Clustering Techniques

Just as factor analysis organizes database variables into a smaller number of dimensions, cluster analysis organizes *observations* into relatively homogeneous groups, called *clusters*. Like factor analysis, cluster analysis combines statistical analysis with human judgment. Businesses perform simple, one variable, clustering nearly every day, as in:

1. Cluster 1: Accounts that are not delinquent; Cluster 2: Accounts that are 30 days past due; and Cluster 3: Accounts that are 60+ days past due.
2. Cluster 1: Gold card accounts, and Cluster 2: Classic card accounts.
3. Cluster 1: Fixed rate mortgage accounts, and Cluster 2: Variable rate mortgage accounts.

Most complex, statistically-derived, clusters are calculated in much the same way. The major difference, aside from the mathematical calcula-

## TABLE 8–3
### Observations in Cluster One and Cluster Two

| Observation Number | Name | Age | Income | Gender | Rent/ Own | Monthly Payment | Credit Limit | Cluster |
|---|---|---|---|---|---|---|---|---|
| 1 | Bill | 28 | 47,000 | M | O | 2350 | 5000 | 1 |
| 2 | Jan | 41 | 49,000 | F | O | 2450 | 6000 | 1 |
| 3 | Fred | 28 | 23,000 | M | R | 1300 | 1500 | 2 |
| 4 | Sue | 43 | 26,000 | F | R | 1450 | 2500 | 2 |
| 5 | Sara | 40 | 24,000 | F | R | 1400 | 2000 | 2 |
| 6 | Sam | 45 | 48,000 | M | O | 2400 | 5500 | 1 |

tions, is that the complex clusters use between 10 and 20 variables, which might include product type, customer tenure, delinquency status, age, occupation, homeownership, or income. There is no optimal number of statistically-derived clusters in a database. It is the analyst's responsibility to determine the appropriate number for each modeling project.

Clustering is generally used as a hierarchical technique. For example, in a world made up of all human beings as the observations, the most narrowly focused or smallest cluster level might be families. Additional or higher cluster levels in the hierarchy—neighborhoods, cities, states, nations, etc.—become increasingly broader. The analyst determines at what level cluster analysis stops. Though the family level has the advantage of being a well-defined homogeneous group, for example, there are two many families in the United States to include them in most statistical models.

Table 8–3 shows a data set with six observations, from which the analyst defined two clusters. The first includes observations 1, 2, and 6, the second observations 3, 4, and 5. As shown in Table 8–4, Cluster 1 is made up of high-income (avg. $48,000) people with high shelter payments (avg. $2,400) and high credit limits (avg. $5,500). Cluster 2 is lower-income (avg. $24,333) renters, with lower monthly payments (avg. $1,383) and

## TABLE 8–4
### Cluster One and Cluster Two Averages

| Cluster | Age | Income | Monthly Payment | Credit Limit |
|---|---|---|---|---|
| 1 | 38 | 48,000 | 2400 | 5500 |
| 2 | 37 | 24,333 | 1383 | 2000 |

## TABLE 8–5
### Gender and Ownership frequency distribution by Cluster

| Cluster | % Male | % Own |
|---|---|---|
| 1 | 66% | 100% |
| 2 | 34% | 0% |

lower credit limits ($2,000). For both clusters the average age is 37-38, so there is no differentiation on this variable. Table 8–5 shows the frequency distribution for the clusters: Cluster 1 is predominantly male (66%) and includes 100% homeowners; Cluster 2 is predominantly female and is 100% renters.

*Putting Cluster Analysis to Work*    There are several ways cluster analysis is used in data mining. First, it can be used to segment a database into account groups that share similar key characteristics. In the credit card industry, a common application is to cluster a portfolio into 5 to 10 different segments based on 5 to 20 key variables. Separate scoring models are then built for each segment.[6] One cluster may include new accounts that are not delinquent, while another may include new accounts that are delinquent.

Another use for cluster analysis is to describe a particular group of customers. For example, suppose a scoring model is being built using a customer file. The analyst wants to summarize the top scoring 20 percent of the accounts on 11 important variables. Using cluster analysis, the analyst groups the accounts, analyzes the 11 characteristics for the high-scoring ones, and summarizes them as in Tables 8–4 and 8–5. The result is a good sense of the characteristics for this group that can be used to write advertising copy or promote a new product to them.

Clustering, which is primarily a descriptive statistical technique, is sometimes inappropriately used instead of regression score modeling for database segmentation. Using clustering for scoring by segmenting observations results in uneven data segments, with large numbers of observations for some groups and small numbers for others. For example, most clustering analysis projects result in between 10 and 25 clusters. In a database of a million accounts, a cluster might have any number from a few hundred to hundreds of thousands of individual records, a range that is too broad to allow meaningful conclusions as a scoring model or to create results that promote action for the different cluster segments.

# PREDICTION AND EXPLANATION TECHNIQUES

Predictive and explanatory scoring models are the focal point of most data mining activities because they provide the most valuable and productive solutions to business problems. Although the data analysis procedures already discussed are important to data mining, it is the prediction and explanation techniques that deliver models that result in productive actionable activities.

---

6 Fran Lyons, "Using Segmentation Analysis," *Credit World* (May-June 1993).

The same statistical techniques and tools are used in the development of both prediction and explanation scoring models. The difference is in how the data are used for each model. In prediction, the objective is to forecast future performance of behavior based on prior information and behavior. The outcome variable is measured across time. For example a new account is observed for 6 to 24 months to determine if the customer pays as agreed. If so, that customer is labeled a "good" account when a new customer prediction scoring model is being built. If not, the account is labeled "bad." The "good" and "bad" labels are used as the outcome variable in the score model development.

In explanation modeling, there is no requirement for a prediction or forecast. These models explain behavior, replacing traditional cross tabulation analysis. Explanation models have several important advantages over simple cross tabulations. They are capable of more complex analysis with many more variables. They also enable immediate action. For example, an explanation score can provide a list of accounts, rank-ordered on the strength of their relationship to the explanatory variable, that exhibit a certain behavior or that have a specified characteristic.

Prediction and explanation tools include multiple linear regression, logistic regression, multiple discriminant analysis, CART, CHAID, linear programming, decision trees, and neural networks, all of which belong to the regression family of statistical procedures. They all can be used for both prediction and explanation. Neural network technology is the most sophisticated and modern of these (see Appendix I).

### Prediction Example (Behavior Scoring - Credit Risk)

Predictive scoring models, such as the new account and behavior scoring models, have been used in the revolving credit, direct mail, and retail and personal installment loan businesses for more than 50 years. Recently other businesses, like the mortgage industry, have begun to adopt them. These statistical techniques are well understood in the financial industry, with numerous publications describing the model building process.[7] In these models, a customer (for behavior models) or prospect (for new account models) is scored in order to predict the likelihood of certain performance, desired or undesired, in the future.

When building a scoring model, an analyst uses historical data for each individual in the development sample. In the simplest case, a point in time

---

7 See, for example, Edward M. Lewis, *An Introduction to Credit Scoring,* 2d ed. (San Rafael, CA: Fair, Isaacs & Co., Inc.), 1992 or Gary Chandler and John Coffman, "Applications of perform-ance Scoring," *Journal of Retail Banking,* Vol. V, No. 4 (Winter 1983-84).

# FIGURE 8–1

| Sept 1995 | Oct | Nov | Dec | Jan 1996 | Feb | Mar | Apr | May | Jun | Jul | Aug | Sept | Oct | Nov | Dec | Jan 1997 | Feb | Mar |
|---|---|---|---|---|---|---|---|---|---|---|---|---|---|---|---|---|---|---|
| 1 | 2 | 3 | 4 | 5 | 6 | 7 | 8 | 9 | 10 | 11 | 12 | 13 | 14 | 15 | 16 | 17 | 18 | 19 |

12   11   10   9   8   7   6   5   4   3   2   1   1   2   3   4   5   6   7
Months from observation point

— History Building Period ————————————————⇧———— Outcome Period ————

19   18   17   16   15   14   13   12   11   10   9   8   7   6   5   4   3   2   1
Months from date model score building starts ("today")                                                today

or *observation point* from six months to two years ago is selected. The information known about the individual at that point is used to predict future performance. Because the observation point is in the past, the "future" performance, called the outcome period, is used to evaluate the performance of the scoring model. Figure 8–1 shows, the observation point, the performance (historical) period, and the outcome (measurement) period. The outcome period is the dependent variable in the score model. The History Building Period is used to develop the predictor variables in the score model.

Defining the outcome is a very important part of building a score model. If a lender, for example, wants to predict credit risk, a possible definition of a "good" customer may be an account that has never been more than 30 days past due during the outcome period, and a bad customer one whose account has been 90 days past due or worse. One problem with outcome definition is that most models in the financial industry use only binary outcomes, such as "good" and "bad," or "respond" and "not respond," to make it easy to measure the relationship between binned predictor variables and the outcomes. Good statistical techniques, like neural networks, can accommodate multiple category outcome models, such as current, delinquent, bankrupt, and charge-off.

Once a credit model is built, the accounts are scored "today," as they apply for credit. The score is a proxy that estimates the account's future performance. In the revolving and installment credit industries scores built to evaluate new accounts are called *application* scores and those built to predict how existing accounts will perform are termed *behavior* scores. If in model development "good" customers are coded "1" and "bad" customers "0," then a high-scoring individual looks like a good or low-risk account and a low-scoring individual like a bad or high-risk account. The score development sample is used to determine a profitable cutoff score, with all accounts scoring above it approved as creditworthy and those scoring below rejected as unacceptable risks.

## Explanation Example (Segmentation - Marketing)

Explanatory modeling uses statistical techniques to identify customers who exhibit a characteristic—the dependent variable—based on other characteristics—the "predictor" variables. Once identified, accounts can be described based on important characteristics. Descriptive statistical techniques such as averages, frequencies, and cluster analysis provide valuable information about the nature and behavior of the identified accounts. Explanation modeling is thus the advanced statistical equivalent of complex cross-tabulation analysis.

Explanation data analysis is rare in business today, partly because simple analysis procedures like cross-tabulations and frequencies imitate human judgmental methods; the tendency is thus to use the simpler techniques because they are more familiar. The judgmental process starts when management or analysts ask a question, such as "What do my most profitable customers look like?" In most businesses today, the profitable customers are identified by descriptive characteristics such as age (older), income (higher), and housing (homeowners). But an analyst's ultimate goal should not be to determine what these customers look like; instead, the analyst must reverse the process, identifying the accounts using an explanatory scoring model first and then describing them using cluster analysis and other simple statistical tools.

The initial request from management should guide the process. The initial charge should be: "Give me a list of customers, ranked from most likely to least likely, that either are or have the potential to be my most profitable customers." The analyst then builds an explanatory scoring model to do that. From the ranked list, an analyst can then describe the customers using simple descriptive and cluster analysis. For example, the analyst can select all customers or a subgroup, perhaps the top 20 percent, that are identified by the explanatory model and then summarize those identified using descriptive statistics.

For instance, suppose that the Chief Executive Officer (CEO) of a company instructs her staff to "increase revenue" (not uncommon!). The Chief Marketing Officer (CMO) postulates that one way to do this is to sell more products to current customers, but recognizes that if they have all already bought all the company's current products, the company should instead solicit new customers. So the CMO asks the Director of Marketing Research (DMR) for a count of current customers who have

## TABLE 8–6
### Frequency Distribution of Customers by Number of Products

| | |
|---|---|
| Single Product | 80% |
| Multiple Products | 20% |

bought only one product and those who have bought more than one. The DMO performs a legitimate query on a sample of the database to calculate a percentage frequency table comparing the two groups (Table 8–6). If 80 percent of current customers have bought only one product, there is a potential to sell them more. Note that so far, there has only been one pass through the database on a single variable, number of products.

At this point data mining usually deteriorates into a series of undirected, descriptive, "slice and dice" exercises. These inappropriate techniques generate hundreds of ad hoc database queries. For example, one analyst might speculate that older customers buy more products, so he sets up three age categories: young (18-34), middle-aged (35-55), and old (56-74). To do so, he creates a new variable, age_category, and then cross tabulates age groups by number of products. The result is a frequency table of age_category by single- and multiple-product customers.

When data mining is focused solely on simple descriptive techniques, analysts can lose sight of the original goal. In order to reach the goal, they should build an explanatory regression model, selecting a sample of customers and a number of the most important variables, say, 20, determined by using business and statistical methods. They can then code multiple-product customers "1" and single-product customers "0." The 20 variables are the explanatory variables in the regression model and the 1 and 0 the dependent variable (this model can be thought of as a 21-variable cross-tabulation). An analyst can then calculate the traditional regression or neural network model just like a predictive scoring model.

The resulting model yields scores for all the accounts in the customer file. When the single-product customers are ranked by score from highest to lowest, the highest-scoring accounts look much like multiple product customers, and obviously many of them will be prospects for this group. This model will also reveal multiple-product customers with low scores. These customers who do *not* look like other multiple-product accounts deserve special attention, because, for example, they may be likely to cease being customers.

After all customers are scored and ranked, it is beneficial and often necessary to describe the accounts using simple descriptive statistical techniques and cluster analysis. For example, the analyst can provide descriptive statistics for the top 20 percent of the accounts, including the single-product customers who "look like" multiple-product customers.

Cluster analysis is a good technique for this; it gives the marketing department the information it needs to target these accounts with appropriate promotions and advertising copy.

Suppose, for example, that a cluster analysis yields two clusters in the top 20 percent, both professionals who are heads of households, but one made up of older high-income telemarketing-responsive females and the other of younger middle-income direct-mail responsive males. Marketing will telemarket to the first group and send direct mail to the second group, targeting both with tailored advertising copy.

Explanatory modeling presents a great opportunity to increase the power of data warehouses and reduce human and computer processing costs. Unfortunately, very few businesses take advantage of it. Using explanatory scoring instead of undirected cross tabulation and slice-and-dice analysis provides the following business benefits:

1.  Access to information that can be acted upon
2.  Reduced human and computer resource demands for data mining projects
3.  Faster turn-around for analysis and implementation of data mining projects
4.  Ability to focus on outcomes and results rather than queries and categorizing data
5.  Maximum use of the data warehouse
6.  An environment in which analysts function not as computer programmers but as true business support professionals

## ARE YOUR ANALYSTS USING THE RIGHT TECHNIQUES?

The primary concerns in solving a business problem with data mining applications are asking the right question and developing the right score model. Asking the right question leads to developing the right score model: Questions posed with an action-driven objective are best. Posing "curiosity" questions encourages time-consuming, nonproductive queries and "slice and dice" data mining. Statistical and problem-solving model design determines the data mining techniques and their order of execution. If management simply wants a description of a group of accounts to create advertising copy, for example, the appropriate question is "What do the accounts look like?" However, if the objective is to stimulate further action, the appropriate question is "Can you give me a list of accounts, ranked from highest probability to lowest, that have the desired characteristic?"

There are certain warning signs that can alert you if management is not asking the right questions or analysts are not using the right data mining techniques to answer business questions. You should be concerned if analysts:

1. Slice and dice the data with queries, frequencies, and other descriptive statistics in response to business questions that require account identification (techniques for describing accounts are seldom the same as those used to identify them.) You know there is system inefficiency if there is an unusually high demand for human and computer resources but low production of usable output.
2. Provide information that cannot be effectively acted upon in answer to a well-phrased business question. The proper response is a list of the highest-scoring accounts that meet the criteria required to answer the business question.
3. Categorize continuous variables without compelling business reasons.
4. Always use the entire data warehouse, never samples.
5. Use cluster analysis rather than score models for prediction or explanation. Some analysts segment data with descriptive techniques rather than building regression models to identify accounts.
6. Think and act like data processors, not business analysts.
7. Perform a disproportionate amount of trial and error and "human in the loop" data analysis.
8. Force every categorical dependent variable model design into binary outcomes, e.g., good/bad or respond/not respond. Good statistical practices accommodate multiple category outcome models.
9. Do not use business knowledge and a statistical technique, like factor analysis, to reduce the number of variables eligible for a final model.
10. Do not account for nonlinear data relationships, including interactions among the variables.
11. Use a large number of correlated (related) variables to describe or identify a group of customers.

Many analysts who use data mining technology are continually searching for the next "magical" tool in the hope that it will instantly solve complex business analysis problems. At the same time, they often fail to take full advantage of existing statistical tools. Many companies continue to rely on 1920s statistical technology (e.g., cross tabulation), 1950s technology (e.g., categorization of continuous variables), and inappropriate techniques (over-use of descriptive statistics) to manage their businesses.

## WHAT NEXT?

Significant advances in statistical technology occur about every 20 to 40 years. Karl Pearson developed the Pearson Correlation

## FIGURE 8–2
### Traditional Scoring Example

> John Doe    Behavior Trend Assessment
>
>
> 1. Summary
>    Data Scoring

## FIGURE 8–3
### Traditional Scoring and Transaction Scoring Contrast

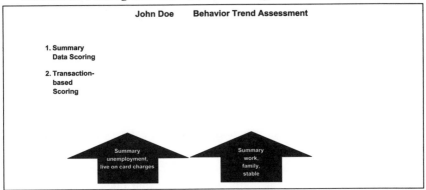

> John Doe    Behavior Trend Assessment
>
> 1. Summary
>    Data Scoring
>
> 2. Transaction-
>    based
>    Scoring
>
> Summary                Summary
> unemployment,          work,
> live on card charges   family,
>                        stable

Coefficient in the early 1900s. In the 1930s Sir Ronald Fisher made multiple regression popular. About 20 years later, logistic regression came to the fore. In the past ten years, neural network applications have demonstrated that their advanced statistical properties add to predictive and model-building performance. However, we cannot count on new tools promising significant advantages in statistical modeling to arrive at a rate that delivers acceptable business returns.

Next to making their current modeling process more efficient with clean, modeling-ready, warehouse data, businesses can significantly increase predictive model performance by getting more information from the existing data. "Clean" data is often described as edited data. Before data warehouses, it was not unusual to perform data edits every time an analyst developed a statistical model. For example, if year of birth is a field on the customer master file and age is a variable used in a marketing model, the analyst would subtract year of birth from current year. However, if age is entered by mistake in the year of birth field, the age calculation results in an impossible age value. Before data warehouses and strict editing requirements, it was not unusual to find customer ages of 1950 years.

Recent scoring models using detailed transaction information rather than summarized monthly data have shown strong positive predictive modeling improvements over summarized data. Figures 8–2 and 8–3 show the contrast between the information content of summarized data and detailed transaction information. Figure 8–2 shows a simple scoring model using one summarized variable, monthly balance. If this is $1,000 for both last month and this month, there is no change in the risk score. Figure 8–3 shows the same data but details the transactions making up the two monthly balances. The transactions from last month indicate stability, family orientation—good creditworthy behavior. Those for this month suggest that the customer is living on credit. The cash and other "risky" transactions suggest a change in the customer's behavior and spending patterns.

This example demonstrates how much more economic value credit scoring professionals can get from the same data by amplifying the detail. While it is true that building models with detailed transaction information increases demand on computing resources, any increased costs are usually more than offset by the increase in savings from credit losses and the gain in marketing opportunity.

Another recent score technology enhancement, one successfully applied to the medical insurance and product warranties claims businesses, is to build a score model that does not have a dependent variable. In these industries, while there is likelihood of fraud or abuse, there are few if any examples of "bad" accounts. Modeling that does not use an outcome value works extremely well in situations where there is no history of score modeling or collecting data with designated outcomes. The technique finds "outliers," observations that do not conform to expected behavior patterns. Once these accounts are identified, risk analysts investigate. If they are confirmed as fraudulent, they are flagged and used later for traditional score modeling.

Finally, one company is now using text information in statistical models. Text data can include customer service notes, text on a Web page, collector's notes, or text in a transaction authorization record. The company groups the text into categories using both supervised and unsupervised clustering techniques. These categories are then used as predictor variables in neural network models.

Analysis of the text data enables discovery of relationships between the text and traditional numerical data. The technique is not dependent on language rules. As a consequence, it discovers relationships among symbols, including part or account numbers, merchant identification information, stock keeping unit (sku) numbers, phone numbers, etc. Text data can be used to analyze credit card transaction information, to monitor Web behavior, and to analyze purchasing behavior. Work is now also being done to include pictures and images. This is a significant enhancement in model performance because it uses business data that can be readily accessed but was not previously available for score modeling.

# CONCLUSION

This chapter is an overview of the statistical analysis process. The underlying hypothesis is that predictive and explanatory score modeling techniques are good examples of data mining, but traditional cross tabulation analysis is not. If your statistical analysts are concentrating on cross tabulations rather than more advanced techniques, you are not taking full advantage of existing technology and your business will suffer.

The proper statistical techniques can provide tremendous insights for managing a business. After all, data mining is simply another term for statistical data analysis. Businesses that understand data mining are well positioned to understand changing customer behavior and patterns. They can also adopt new technology and processes, such as neural networks and transaction scoring, more easily.

## APPENDIX I

### FIGURE 8A–1
Multiple linear regression architecture

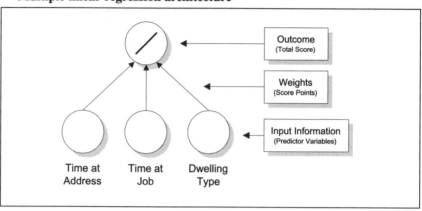

## NEURAL NETWORKS
### Neural Networks as Statistical Techniques

The neural network technique is an advanced form of the traditional regression model currently used to develop many business score models. A neural network calculates weights (score points) for predictor characteristics (e.g., age, income, time on job) from data examples (e.g., good or bad loans). This weighting is done off line just as a traditional score model is updated or "rebuilt."

The most common type of neural network, the multi-layer perception (MLP) or feedforward backpropagation network, is actually an enhanced version of traditional multiple regression. In fact, when MLP neural network architecture is configured without a middle layer, it reduces to the mathematical equivalent of a multiple regression algorithm. This concept is described below, with pictures in the first example and with a simple mathematical formula in the second.

Figure 8A–1 shows the architecture of a multiple regression model. This is how a neural network would look without a middle layer. The circles at the bottom are the predictor variables, the one at the top represents the outcome or dependent variables, which might be a "good" or "bad" credit risk or a "yes" or "no" response to a direct mail solicitation. The arrows represent the weights assigned by the regression model.

Figure 8A–2 shows a neural network architecture with a middle layer. The circles on the bottom represent the predictor variables in a scoring model, which are the same as those in a regression model. The circles in

## FIGURE 8A-2
### Neural Network Structure

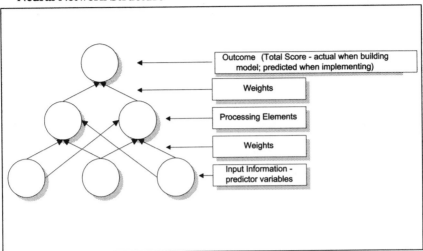

the middle represent the "magical" middle layer processing elements. This middle layer is one of the most significant differences between neural networks and traditional regression models. The top circle represents the score, or outcome, of the model, just as in the regression model.

Figure 8A-3 shows a three-layer neural network with its three separate "regression components" highlighted. Each highlighted section is, in a sense, a regression model of its own. The middle layer processing elements can be viewed as intermediate or derived variables that pass information on to the next layer. These elements are therefore "inputs" or "predictors" for the next layer, which is the outcome or score.

The following mathematical comparison also demonstrates that neural networks are a form of "nested" regression. Consider a regression mod-

## FIGURE 8A-3
### Regression Components of Neural Network

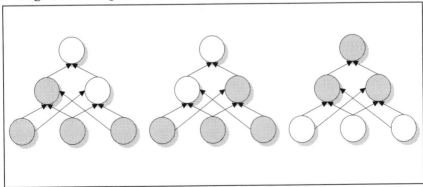

eling problem with a single outcome variable, Y, and two predictor variables, X1 and X2. The regression model can be expressed mathematically as:

1.  $Y_i = \alpha_0 + \alpha_1 X_{1i} + \alpha_2 X_{2i}$

The formula for a feedforward backpropagation neural network is:

2.  $Y_i = \alpha_0 + \alpha_1 F(\beta_{10} + \beta_{11} X_{1i}) + \alpha_2 F (\beta_{20} + \beta_{21} X_{2i})$

where

3.  $F(I) = \dfrac{1}{1 + e^{-I}}$

is the unipolar sigmoid function.

If we assume that the simplest case of a sigmoid function is a straight line, we can eliminate the "F" function in the neural network equation. We can then define two new variables, $Z_1$ and $Z_2$ as:

4.  $Z_{1i} = \beta_{10} + \beta_{11} X_{1i}$
5.  $Z_{2i} = \beta_{20} + \beta_{21} X_{2i}$

Notice that both these new variables have the same functional form as the multiple regression equation (1). Using these new variables we can write the neural network equation as:

6.  $Y_i = \alpha_0 + \alpha_1 Z_{1i} + \alpha_2 Z_{2i}$

This "simplified" neural network formula also has the same functional form as equation (1). Since the variables $Z_1$ and $Z_2$ are themselves defined as regression equations, the concept of a neural network as a "nested" regression equation is understandable.

The neural network architecture, with its middle layer, allows for the kind of complex non-linear data relationship modeling that is not easily accomplished with traditional regression techniques. At the same time, the model yields a score in the same way as the traditional regression scoring model, one that has the same characteristics and utility as the regression score. The neural network system can also generate explanations for how it arrived at the score, a capability that is extremely useful for generating turn-down reasons, directing account verification, and assisting with customer management.

## How Neural Networks Work

Back propagation neural networks typically have at least three interconnected levels. The first layer is made up of network inputs. Though they are the same as those used in traditional regression models, they are now called predictor variables. The middle layer contains processing ele-

## FIGURE 8A–4
### Training a Neural Network

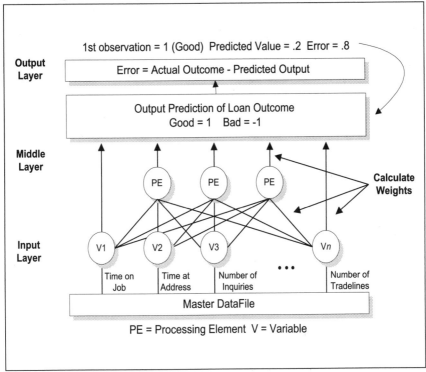

1st observation = 1 (Good)  Predicted Value = .2  Error = .8

**Output Layer**

Error = Actual Outcome - Predicted Output

Output Prediction of Loan Outcome
Good = 1    Bad = -1

**Middle Layer**

PE    PE    PE

Calculate Weights

**Input Layer**

V1    V2    V3    •••    Vn

Time on Job | Time at Address | Number of Inquiries | Number of Tradelines

Master DataFile

PE = Processing Element  V = Variable

ments that include transfer functions allowing neural networks to model non-linear data. The third layer produces the neural network output, the predicted outcome—better known as the score.

While traditional regression models use matrix inversion to calculate weights, neural networks use a mathematically-based trial and error method. Using the input information contained in the predictor variables, the neural network mathematically estimates an outcome (e.g., good or bad loan). During this score model development phase, the network continually adjusts its estimate of the outcome based on the accuracy of the previous estimate. When the network can no longer improve on its estimate of the outcome, the calculation of the weights, and therefore the score model development, is completed. Once development is finished, the network saves its weights and the score model is ready for deployment. When the score is deployed, the weight values do not change. The following is a more detailed description of the neural network weight calculation process.

Figure 8A–4 shows the structure of a three-layer neural network during the model development process. The input layer shows predictor characteristics; there can be any number of these. There also can be any

## FIGURE 8A–5
### Implementing a Neural Network

number of middle-layer processing elements. The output layer is the outcome, or objective, that is to be predicted; this outcome, when the model is put into production, will produce the neural network score.

The outcome is often binary (e.g., good/bad loan or response/nonresponse). However, a neural network can also model multiple category outcomes (e.g., good, delinquent, bankrupt, and charge-off) or a continuous valued outcome (e.g., sales volume). Regardless of the type of outcome, however, a neural network score is a continuous value. In the case of categorical outcomes, whether single or multiple, the network output represents the probability that the outcome will occur for each category. In the case of a continuous outcome, the neural network output is an estimate of the outcome, given the particular predictors.

During model development the neural network calculates weight values for all the interconnections among the processing elements. These weights are in turn used to calculate the score. The weight values do not change when the score is displayed in production.

When training a network on credit lending applicants, for example, good loans are assigned a value of +1 and bad loans a value of -1. The objective is to make a network outcome (the sum of the weight calculations) for each applicant that is as close as possible to +1 for good loans and -1 for bad loans. If during development the network output for an individual good loan is 0.2, the error for that loan is 0.8 (1.0 - 0.2 = 0.8). The network sends *(propagates)* the error information back through the interconnections to adjust the weight values to reduce the error. The process continues until the network can no longer change the weights to reduce error in the estimates. When all the training examples result in the minimum prediction error, the network is fully trained.

Figure 8A–5 shows a neural network during implementation. Neural networks are used to score new applicants because the lender does not know how the prospect will perform on a loan. The score, therefore, is a prediction of how the applicant will perform in the future, based on previous experience with similar applicants. The model scores new individuals with unknown outcomes.

There are only two differences between this implementation neural network and the development network shown in Figure 8A-4. First, during implementation, the weight values are fixed—they do not change when the model is used in production because model development is complete. One of the most common misconceptions about neural networks is that "continuously learn" while in production; this is not so. The best-trained model has been installed into the operational processing system. Second, there is no known actual outcome in implementation. The score is simply a prediction, the best estimate of the unknown future outcome.

## REFERENCES

Berry, Michael J.A., and Gordon Linoff. "Data Mining Techniques. New York: John Wiley and Sons, 1997.

Chandler, Gary, and John Coffman. "Applications of Performance Scoring," *Journal of Retail Banking*, Vol. V, No. 4 (Winter 1983-84).

Cremer, Richard E. "Consumer Credit Program Key to Montgomery Ward's Growth," *Direct Marketing* (December 1972).

Durand, D. *Risk Elements in Consumer Installment Lending*. Washington: National Bureau of Economic Research, Inc., 1941.

English, Larry P. "The High Costs of Low Quality Data," *DM Review*, Vol. 8, No. 1 (January 1988).

Frawley, Andy. "Marketing Warehouse ROI," *DM Review*, Vol. 7, No. 6 (June 1997).

Lewis, Edward M. *An Introduction to Credit Scoring*. 2d ed. San Rafael, CA: Fair, Isaacs & Co., Inc., 1992.

Lyons, Fran. "Using Segmentation Analysis," *Credit World* (May-June 1993).

Snyder, Jesse. "Opportunity Knocks at Scoring Door," *Collections and Credit Risk* (April 1997).

# 9

# INCORPORATING ECONOMIC INFORMATION INTO CREDIT RISK UNDERWRITING

**Mark Zandi**
*Chief Economist and Co-Founder*
*Regional Financial Associates, Inc.*

Signs of a near perfect economy abound. The economy is expanding strongly, with unemployment and inflation at generational lows. As a result, confidence is surging. Most surveys of consumer sentiment are near all-time record highs. Investors are also rejoicing as stock prices have tripled in just the past three years.

Yet despite the stellar economy, household credit quality has deteriorated dramatically. The American Bankers Association reports that this past fall delinquency (30 days and over) for eight different types of closed-end consumer loans rose to its highest rate since the wake of the 1990-91 recession. At 5.5 percent bank credit card delinquencies are at a record high. Bankruptcy filings also continue to break new records, rising beyond an estimated 1.35 million in 1997 (see Figure 9–1).

**FIGURE 9–1**

**Bankruptcies and Delinquencies Have Soared**

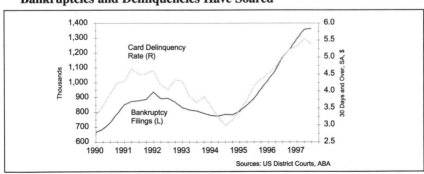

Sources: US District Courts, ABA

## FIGURE 9–2
### VISA Accounts Soar in the 1990's

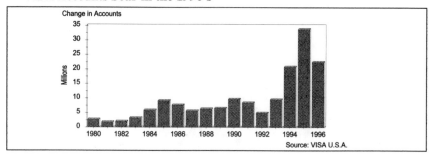

Source: VISA U.S.A.

Close to 6 percent of all U.S. households have filed for bankruptcy in the current economic expansion.

Does the deterioration in credit quality in the midst of what appears to be a near perfect economy suggest that economic conditions do not influence credit conditions? Can economic conditions thus be ignored in credit risk underwriting? This chapter identifies reasons for the recent deterioration in credit conditions and makes the case that the economy is a key determinant of credit quality. If the economy had not performed as well as it has, the current deterioration in credit quality would have been substantially worse than it is. This is illustrated by considering the impact the next economic recession is likely to have on credit card delinquencies and personal bankruptcies.

Not accounting for economic information in the credit risk underwriting process will result in significant losses for many consumer lenders. How to incorporate economic data into credit risk modeling in preparation for the next recession is discussed.

## CREDIT QUALITY IN THE SHORT RUN

The reasons behind the currently poor credit conditions can be determined using regression analysis. Regression results explaining personal bankruptcy filings during the past decade are shown in Table 9–1.

Today's bankruptcies and delinquencies are in large part the result of the substantial lowering of loan standards between early 1993 and late 1995. Changing loan standards, which are proxied by the loan-to-value (LTV) ratio on conventional mortgage loans, affect filings with an average lag of two and a half years. The standards that were in place in late 1995 thus continue to influence credit conditions.

Symptomatic of the lowering in standards during that period was the surge in new credit card solicitations and originations. In 1995 alone, close to 35 million VISA cards were originated. Throughout all of the 1980s, in contrast, only about 5 million VISA cards were issued annually, regardless of the economic conditions (see Figure 9–2).

# TABLE 9-1
## Explaining Personal Bankruptcy Filings

|  | Coefficient | T-statistic |
|---|---|---|
| **Household Consumer Debt Service Burden** | | |
| Lag 0 | -29.7 | -2.6 |
| Lag 1 | -7.4 | -1.0 |
| Lag 2 | 10.9 | 2.7 |
| Lag 3 | 25.0 | 7.8 |
| Lag 4 | 34.9 | 8.8 |
| Lag 5 | 40.6 | 8.4 |
| Lag 6 | 42.2 | 7.7 |
| Lag 7 | 39.7 | 6.5 |
| Lag 8 | 33.0 | 4.4 |
| Lag 9 | 22.1 | 2.2 |
| *Mean Lag = 7 quarters* | | |
| **Conventional Mortgage Loan-to-Value Ratio** | | |
| Lag 0 | -5.2 | -4.2 |
| Lag 1 | -3.1 | -2.4 |
| Lag 2 | -1.2 | -0.8 |
| Lag 3 | 0.6 | 0.3 |
| Lag 4 | 2.2 | 1.1 |
| Lag 5 | 3.5 | 1.8 |
| Lag 6 | 4.7 | 2.4 |
| Lag 7 | 5.7 | 3.2 |
| Lag 8 | 6.6 | 4.3 |
| Lag 9 | 7.2 | 6.2 |
| Lag 10 | 7.7 | 9.0 |
| Lag 11 | 7.9 | 8.5 |
| *Mean Lag = 10 quarters* | | |
| **Unemployment Insurance Claims** | | |
| Lag 0 | 0.032 | 6.2 |
| Lag 1 | 0.014 | 4.9 |
| Lag 2 | 0.005 | 1.3 |
| Lag 3 | 0.004 | 1.2 |
| Lag 4 | 0.012 | 4.8 |
| Lag 5 | 0.029 | 5.8 |
| *Mean Lag = 2 quarters* | | |
| **Number of Households** | 52.3 | 7.7 |
| **Constant** | -9537.4 | -13.6 |

R-Bar Squared = .998          **Notes:**
Durbin-Watson = 1.793         Dependent variable is bankrupcty filings, SAAR, Ths.
Range: 1987Q1-1997Q3          The almon lags are a second degree polynominal with no constraints

*Sources: US District Courts, BLS, FRB, FHFB, BOC, RFA*

## FIGURE 9–3
### Lower Mortgage Credit Standards

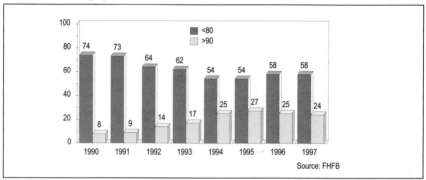

Source: FHFB

The lowering in credit standards was not unique to credit card lending; standards fell for most other types of consumer loans and for residential mortgages as well. Rising LTV ratios—or lower downpayments—indicate lower standards in residential mortgage lending. Less than one-tenth of conventional mortgage loans had LTVs of more than 90 percent at the start of the decade. At their peak of popularity in mid-1995, loans of more than 90 percent LTV were approaching one-third of conventional mortgage loan originations (see Figure 9–3).

Mortgage loans equal to 125 percent or even 150 percent of house values have become increasingly common. Such loans generally wrap most of the borrower's debt, including mortgage and secured and unsecured consumer installment debt, into one large secured and tax-deductible mortgage loan. So-called sub-prime mortgage and automobile lending—loans to borrowers with blemished credit histories—have similarly burgeoned in the 1990s.

Recently lenders have responded to their mounting credit problems by tightening their standards for extending credit. The most significant tightening has been by credit card lenders, who have experienced the most serious credit losses. In a late 1997 Federal Reserve Board survey of senior loan officers of major credit card lenders, almost one-fourth more said they were tightening than said they were easing their standards compared to the standards they had in place three months before. Credit card lenders have been progressively tightening since early 1996 (see Figure 9–4).

Tighter standards have resulted in slower consumer debt growth. Consumer installment credit growth has weakened to below 5 percent year-over-year growth, less than one-third of the growth experienced at its peak in mid-1995 and about equal to current personal income growth. The growth in credit card debt has decelerated even more sharply, falling from close to 25 percent at its peak to near 8 percent more recently.

**FIGURE 9–4**

**Banks are Less Willing to Make Credit Card Loans**

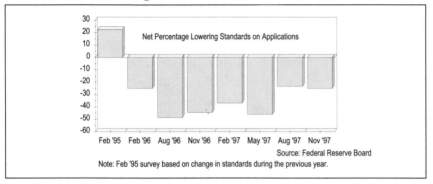

Household debt service burdens have stabilized as a result, albeit at a relatively high 17 percent of after-tax income.

More conservative underwriting practices will soon result in more stable credit conditions. Consumer loan delinquencies have already peaked and bankruptcies and creditor's net losses will stabilize and may even fall slightly in 1998.[1]

Other factors will ensure that delinquencies and bankruptcies do not fall substantially, however. Most important is the continuing erosion in the social stigma attached to bankruptcy, increased gambling, and the increased use of personal credit for business use. The change in the bankruptcy laws in late 1994—often cited as a contributing factor to greater bankruptcy—has not been important in the recent credit problems.[2]

## LENDER COMPETITION

While household credit quality is expected to stabilize soon, lenders face substantial credit risks early in the next century. These risks will become more apparent as the credit environment improves through 1998 and lenders begin to reevaluate their currently tight loan standards. Lenders

---

1 Delinquencies are peaking well before bankruptcies and creditor's losses, since a significant and rising proportion of bankruptcies are by households—known as straights—that never go delinquent. This phenomenon can be explained in part by households that played a Ponzi game with their debt—servicing their ever-increasing debt load with new credit—when credit standards were loose but could not continue to play the game in the currently tighter credit environment.

2 These factors are captured in the regression analysis through the number-of-households variable. This variable, like a time trend, will not only capture the impact of a rising number of households on the number of filings, but also long-run factors such as increasing willingness and ability to file. That the late 1994 change in the bankruptcy law has not materially affected subsequent filing behavior is evident from a very similar rise in bankruptcy filings in Canada during the same period, though there have been no significant changes to Canadian bankruptcy laws. The possible impact of a change in the bankruptcy laws on filings was also tested statistically through the regression analysis. It was not found to be significant.

## FIGURE 9–5
### Lenders Will be Able to Extend Credit

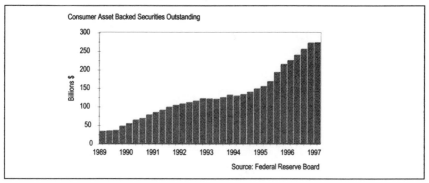

Source: Federal Reserve Board

will find it difficult not to ease those standards in the face of still fierce competition.

Fueling competition are the relatively wide profit margins in consumer lending despite record credit losses. The return on credit card assets is still nearly double the return on all other commercial bank assets. Banks will thus continue to devote a significant amount of marketing and development resources to support the growth of such a profitable line of business.

The explosive growth of the asset-backed securities market in the past decade has also broken down barriers to entry in the household lending industry as creditors are able to quickly start and expand their operations. Everything from credit cards to home equity loans to auto loans is being securitized and sold to pension funds, life insurance companies and foreign institutions. Since its beginnings in the late 1980s, the consumer asset-backed market has ballooned to nearly $300 billion outstanding (see Figure 9–5). This is roughly equal in size to the so-called junk corporate bond market and to one-third of the investment grade corporate bond market. Indicating the popularity of asset-backed debt among investors is the rapid narrowing of interest rate spreads, which are as thin as they have been since their introduction.

Consumer lenders are not likely to compete by significantly lowering loan rates. Despite competitive pressures, lenders are loath to lower their rates, because such a strategy results in significant adverse selection. Though lowering rates would increase market share and entice loan growth, lower loan rates would be most attractive to the least creditworthy borrowers. The lender's riskiest current customers would also be enticed to borrow more. A recent Boston Federal Reserve study of the credit card industry shows that lower loan rates result in lower bank income; the greater income generated from larger outstandings is more

## FIGURE 9–6
### Low-income Households will Demand Credit

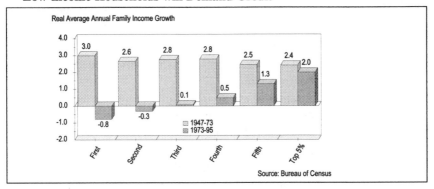

Source: Bureau of Census

than offset by the loss of income from the lower loan rates and higher credit losses.[3]

Lenders are more likely to compete by offering credit to riskier borrowers using increasingly sophisticated credit scoring and solicitation technologies. According to a late 1996 Federal Reserve survey, 85 percent of bank credit card lenders used credit scoring models in their solicitation efforts and almost all use such models in underwriting applications. These models, which numerically weigh or "score" some or all of the factors considered in the loan underwriting process, suggest the relative risk posed by each potential borrower. An accurate scoring model holds the promise of increasing the speed, accuracy, and consistency of the credit evaluation process while reducing costs. Scoring technology allows lenders to more effectively control the risks they take compared to the risks of other competitive strategies, such as lowering loan rates. So far this decade the use of scoring technology has indeed fostered the rapid expansion of available credit. It will likely be used even more intensively in the future.[4]

## BORROWER QUALITY

While lenders are bending to competitive forces and easing their credit standards, the most avid borrowers will increasingly be the least creditworthy. Growth in consumer borrowing has been strongest among rela-

---

3 This study, entitled "Can Demand Elasticities Explain Sticky Credit Card Rates," is in the Boston Federal Reserve's *New England Economic Review* (July/August 1996).

4 Scoring models are only as good as the borrower information used to develop them. The accuracy of borrower information from credit bureaus is often a concern, particularly given the rapid growth in credit alternatives in recent years. Score models are also based on the questionable assumption that the relationship between borrower characteristics and payment behavior is relatively stable. The reliance on less than accurate scoring models may be a contributing factor in the recent deterioration in credit quality.

tively low-income households that have seen their real incomes fall during the past quarter century. Since the early 1970s, real average family incomes have fallen for the bottom two quintiles of the income distribution and remained largely unchanged for the middle quintile (see Figure 9–6).

Only those families at the very top of the income distribution ladder have experienced rising incomes similar to that experienced in the first quarter century after World War II.[5]

In an attempt to maintain their living standards in the face of falling incomes, lower income households have been avid borrowers. According to the Survey of Consumer Finance, last conducted by the Federal Reserve in 1995, debt burdens—equal to the proportion of after-tax income devoted to principal and interest and consumer installment and mortgage debt— are relatively high and rising for families with incomes of less than $50,000 annually. In contrast, debt burdens are relatively low and falling for those families with greater incomes. Families with the highest annual incomes of over $100,000 had debt burdens in 1995 that were approximately half those of families making less than $10,000.

Lower-income families already have the most serious difficulty making payments on their debt. More than one-fifth of families with annual incomes of less than $50,000 experienced at least one period of delinquency greater than 60 days in 1995, according to the Survey of Consumer Finance. This compares to less than 5 percent of families with annual incomes greater than $50,000. Bankruptcy filers are also relatively poor. The Center for Credit Research found in a recent survey of filers that the median income of Chapter 7 filers was less than $18,000 annually and that of Chapter 13 filers was less than $24,000. This compares to national median household income of $36,000.

The strongly expanding economy and low unemployment have recently lifted incomes across all income groups. This will not continue longer term, however. The factors that have constrained incomes of low-income households and have made them voracious but precarious borrowers will remain in place through early in the next century at least. Globalization, deregulation, technological change, and more recently Medicaid and welfare reforms will continue to limit the incomes of households with relatively little education and training. These households will borrow as much as lenders are willing to provide in an effort to maintain their living standards in the face of shrinking incomes.

---

5 The upper income for families in the bottom quintile is approximately $13,000, the second quintile $25,000, the third $39,000, the fourth $60,000, and the top 5 percent over $105,000. Median household income is $35,000 and average income is $55,000. The erosion in real incomes for low income families during this period may be overstated, as single parent households have grown quickly and family size has shrunk.

The increasing volatility of household incomes also presents greater risks to household lenders. During the 1990s, employers have raised the flexibility of the work force through the use of contingent workers, including independent contractors, those who work for temporary help agencies and contract firms, and the self-employed. Employers are also asking workers to change the number of hours they work to meet changing demand for the goods and services they produce. Employees benefit because they are less likely to lose their jobs when demand is soft. Employers benefit because, although overtime hours are costly, the costs and time involved with hiring and firing workers is even more significant.

Changing incomes, however, make it increasingly difficult for households to manage their debt loads even when they have jobs. Households that make borrowing decisions when they are working more overtime hours and their incomes are strong may find it difficult to repay their debt when the hours disappear and their incomes are weaker.[6]

Households have also become riskier borrowers as personal credit is increasingly being used for business purposes. As the number and size of credit lines have increased, the borrowing capacity of many households has become large enough to help finance small business activities. The surge in new business formations, prompted by the strong economy and perhaps the rash of corporate downsizing in recent years, is now leading to rising business bankruptcies. During the past five years, over 3.5 million businesses have been incorporated, according to Dun & Bradstreet. A high proportion of new firms fail, however, regardless of how well the economy is doing. Business failures have indeed been on the rise for much of the past two years, forcing owners who have mingled their personal and business finances into personal bankruptcy as well.

## THE NEXT RECESSION

The possibility that lenders will ease loan standards in response to the more stable credit conditions expected this year, particularly to hard-pressed lower income groups, will limit any improvement in credit quality. Delinquencies, bankruptcies, and creditor's losses will be lower by year's end, but they are not expected to fall substantially. Moreover, there is a significant risk of an unprecedented deterioration in credit quality when the economy eventually experiences a full-blown recession.

---

6 The recent deterioration in credit quality may in part be related to the increased volatility of incomes. Households were borrowing strongly in 1994 and early 1995 when the economy was very strong and many were working long high-paying hours in manufacturing and construction. When the economy weakened in late 1995 and early 1996, however, though these households did not lose their jobs, their incomes were no longer sufficient to service their larger debt loads.

## FIGURE 9–7

### Does the Economy Matter?

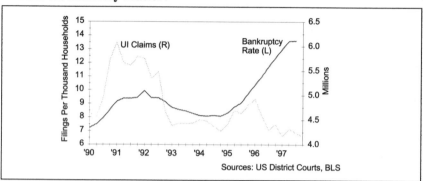

Sources: US District Courts, BLS

This view appears incongruous with recent events, however. The currently poor credit environment has occurred despite near perfect economic conditions. That the relationship between the economy and credit quality appears to have broken down is illustrated by examining the relationship between unemployment insurance (UI) claims and the number of bankruptcy filings.

UI claims are a very timely and accurate barometer of economic conditions since they are an actual count of the number of people who have lost their jobs and are in need of government assistance. During the 1990-91 recession, UI claims rose; so did filings. When the economy recovered in the mid-1990s and UI claims fell, so did filings. Since 1996, however, though UI claims have fallen to their lowest levels since the late 1980s, filings have soared (see Figure 9–7).

The economy is an important influence on credit quality despite the recent divergence in UI claims and bankruptcy filings. The important influence the economy has on credit quality is illustrated clearly in the regression results shown in Table 9–1. What cannot be accounted for in a two-dimensional chart are all the other factors that influence the number of filings; these have changed dramatically in recent years. The most important is the shifting loan standards just discussed..

After controlling for shifting loan standards, household debt burdens, the number of households, and the increasing willingness and ability of households to file, UI claims remain a highly significant factor in explaining the number of filings. Indeed, if the economy had not improved over the past two years with UI claims falling from 4.9 million in early 1996 to 4.2 million at year's end 1997, annual filings would currently be some 60,000 higher.

The next recession presents a particularly significant threat to lenders since credit is so much more widely available than at any time in the past.

## FIGURE 9–8
### Credit Card Lines Continue to Soar

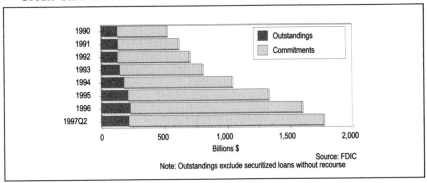

According to the Survey of Consumer Finance, almost half of all households had some credit card debt, up from 44 percent in 1992 and 37 percent in 1983. The increase in credit card usage is even greater for lower-income households. The share of families earning less than $10,000 a year with credit card debt, for example, more than doubled, to one-fourth of all families, in 1995.

Credit is not only more widely available, but households have access to greater amounts of credit. Households not only have close to $500 billion in credit card debt outstanding currently, they have access to over $1.5 trillion in unused credit lines that can be borrowed at their discretion (see Figure 9–8).

At the start of the decade, by comparison, there was approximately $200 billion in credit card debt outstanding and only $400 billion in unused credit lines. Unused home equity lines of credit have also grown quickly, doubling in the 1990s to nearly $100 billion. Households will most likely use these credit lines when their incomes are disrupted due to rising unemployment in a weak economy.

RFA's model of the economy and household credit quality has been used to assess the potential impact of the next recession on filings. It is assumed that the next recession begins in mid-1999—the earliest a recession is likely given the currently strong and well balanced economy—and is similar in length and severity to the last recession in 1990-1991. The jobless rate peaks at just over 7 percent by late 2000, up from 5 percent currently. Lenders are assumed in this scenario to lower their loan standards from mid-1998 up to when the recession begins.[7] Under this recession scenario, the bank card delinquency rate peaks at 7 percent and bank-

---

7 To generate a recession scenario a number of other assumptions are also made, including but not limited to rising interest rates later this year as the economy expands quickly enough to generate inflationary fears and monetary tightening.

## FIGURE 9–9

**Household Credit Conditions in the Next Recession**

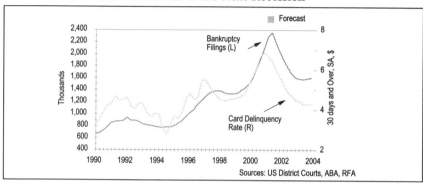

Sources: US District Courts, ABA, RFA

ruptcy filings soar to 2.4 million (see Figure 9–9). The near 1.4 million personal bankruptcy filings expected for 1998 could turn out to be only a happy memory in the next recession.

## INCORPORATING ECONOMIC DATA INTO CREDIT RISK MODELING

The need to incorporate economic information into the credit risk underwriting process is evident. This can be done quantitatively by augmenting the credit scoring models currently used by lenders with economic data. Credit scoring models predict the risk behavior of individuals by accounting for their past credit history. Credit performance as predicted by credit scoring models is therefore influenced by the economic conditions that prevailed leading up to the development of the credit scores. Since economic conditions change quickly and are often different from those that prevailed historically, credit decisions based on credit scores developed using historical information thus do not fully account for all the information available to lenders.

Economic data can be brought into the credit score process by including leading economic indicators (LEIs) as an additional variable to explain customer credit performance, along with traditionally constructed credit scores. The LEI is a weighted average of a number of economic variables that tend to lead contemporaneous economic activity by approximately six to twelve months. Such variables include, but are not limited to, unemployment insurance claims, help-wanted advertising, building permits issued, and consumer confidence. Since economic conditions lead credit quality performance by six to twelve months, the LEIs will lead changes in credit quality by as much as twelve to twenty-four months.

LEIs can be constructed at a metropolitan area level because timely, consistent and reliable economic information is available. Metro area economies are also very distinct and can perform very differently. For example, employment in the Los Angeles metro area economy is still down approximately 6 percent from its early 1990s peak, while employment in Orange County, CA just south of Los Angeles has more than fully recovered. Metro area economies are also relatively large, with the smallest having populations of over 75,000, thus reducing concerns that the use of regional economic data could violate CRA requirements.

The specification of economic augmented credit score models can be simply represented by the following equation:

$Pit = a + b1*Sito + b2*LEIit_0$

Where: Pit = Probability of Default by Customer i during period t,

$Sit_0$ = Credit Score for Customer i at time $t_0$,

$LEIit_0$ = Leading Economic Indicator for Customer i at time t₀, and

a, b1 and b2 are estimated parameters.

The probability that a customer will default at some point in the future is determined by the risk scorecard currently used by the lender and a variable that serves as a leading economic indicator.

As shown in the specification, LEIs are not included as part of the credit score; the scores currently used by lenders are not affected by the introduction of economic information through the LEIs. The augmented score model therefore does not interfere with any requirements, such as Regulation B, to inform applicants of the reasons for an adverse action. The results do allow the lender to adjust credit policy, however, by adjusting cutoff scores to maintain an acceptable level of risk given a changing economic environment as measured by the LEIs. For example, a 600 cutoff score may be sufficient to maintain a 3 percent bad rate—meaning that 3 out of every 100 loans approved meet some definition of delinquency—in a modestly expanding economy. This may be consistent with an approval rate of 35 percent. If the economy weakens or falls into recession, however, then the cutoff score may need to be raised to 650 to maintain the same 3 percent bad rate. This would result in an approval rating of only 30 percent as loan volume is sacrificed as the lender becomes more conservative. In a strongly expanding economy, in contrast, a 500 cutoff score may be adequate to maintain a 3 percent bad rate, resulting in an approval rating of 40 percent.

## CONCLUSION

After steadily deteriorating during the past three years, the outlook for credit conditions is relatively positive through the remainder of the decade. Chances that the current economic expansion will falter any time soon are small. The sound economy and tighter loan standards will also soon result in more stable credit conditions.

The long-term outlook is rife with risk, however. Pressures on lenders to again lower their lending standards in an effort to maintain market share will reappear as credit conditions stabilize. The households most likely to want credit, however, will be the least able to service it. Household credit conditions will likely deteriorate to an unprecedented level in the next recession. Lenders should take the opportunity now to incorporate economic information into their credit risk underwriting processes in preparation for that time.

# 10

# CASE STUDIES IN CREDIT RISK MODEL DEVELOPMENT

**Hollis Fishelson-Holstine**
*Senior Vice President, North American Markets*
*Fair, Isaac and Company, Inc.*
© *1998 Fair, Isaac and Company, Inc. All rights reserved.*

To improve their decision-making, many credit grantors are turning to predictive modeling technologies. Frequently, the decision on when and how to build a model turns into a consideration solely of technologies and computer results. Yet developing credit risk models depends on far more than technology. It depends upon reviewing a wide array of issues before, during, and after development. Addressing these issues will result in a model uniquely suited to your marketplace and business environment.

In this chapter we demonstrate, with the help of four case studies, some of the issues that should be considered in developing risk models (see Figure 10–1 on the following page).

## UNDERSTAND YOUR OBJECTIVE

The first consideration in model development is understanding your business objectives. For example, does the objective support far-reaching corporate policy, such as improving the overall profitability of a portfolio? Or is the objective to improve day-to-day tactics by, for instance, identifying the best credit line for a segment of accounts? What performance do you wish to measure—losses? revenue? profit? And over what time frame?

Once you thoroughly understand the business problem, decide whether the model required should be predictive or descriptive. A predictive model seeks to identify and mathematically represent underlying rela-

## FIGURE 10–1

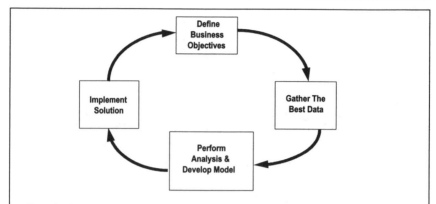

Developing a credit risk model involves a series of steps, illustrated here:
1. Define your business objectives and ascertain whether they are attainable through a predictive model.
2. If a model is the answer, determine if data exist for model development or whether you need to gather more from external and internal sources.
3. Analyze which modeling technology will work best to meet your objectives, and develop a preliminary model that, through additional analysis, will enable you to test how it will handle any identifiable implementation constraints.
4. Align implementation with your stated objectives to ensure that it meshes with in-house practices and personnel.

tionships in the data that are not simply temporary anomalies, whereas the benefit of descriptive models is the insight they provide. By contributing valuable information about the portfolio, descriptive models can influence the types of decisions to be made.

Sometimes neither a predictive nor a descriptive model is needed. Instead, one or more pieces of information can be used to achieve the desired results. For example, suppose after thorough analysis you determine that although you are targeting potentially profitable customers, your current application scoring model is rejecting too many respondents. Rather than adding or developing a model, you might change the score cutoff and implement a new set of policy rules so that you increase the acceptance rate from the same model.

The following case study presents the objective of improving portfolio profitability and its solution—a descriptive model.

## CASE STUDY 1—PROFILING INCREASES
## RESPONSE FROM PROFITABLE CUSTOMERS

*Problem*    A US bank issued a private label credit card for a national retailer. The retailer knew that credit card customers generated more sales than non-cardholders. To boost overall sales, the retailer therefore wanted to send a pre-approved credit card offer to non-cardholders. Since the customer base was large and the retailer had a limited marketing budget, it was necessary to select a sample of non-cardholders to solicit.

Just as the retailer was interested in generating more sales, the bank was interested in generating more profit by financing the purchases made on the retailer's credit cards. The question was thus: For a pre-approved mailing, could the retailer's non-cardholders be segmented to maximize sales for the retailer while simultaneously maximizing profitability for the bank?

*Solution*   The bank chose cluster codes developed by Fair, Isaac in conjunction with a provider of consumer data and mailing services. These codes are a demographic-based segmentation tool built from census data and household level demographic data from a database that contains 77 million mailable names.

Using the cluster codes to analyze the masterfile data of existing cardholders and the retailer's sale data, the bank was able to define the most profitable customers for both bank and retailer. After appending the cluster codes to some 2.1 million prescreened names, the bank could identify the highest-potential prospects.

The cluster code profile of current cardholders showed the profitable demographic group to be high school-educated service and blue collar workers with low-to-moderate incomes and a house valued at under $50,000—a group very different from the professional and managerial workers that the retailer had targeted in the past. That upscale, white collar group, even with higher credit risk scores, was actually shown to be least profitable.

Approximately 1 million names were selected from the prescreened population. In addition, a small control group of prospects was selected at random. The mailing was dropped in September for the Christmas season, with all prospects tracked by the cluster codes.

*Results*   Using the response rate of the randomly selected non-cardholder customers, and projecting it to a mailing of 1 million, the bank estimated total sales would have been $10 million without using the cluster codes. The optimum cluster code group had total sales of $14 million—an improvement of 40 percent. The same held true for response: The control group had a response rate of 2.8 percent, the optimum code group had a 3.7 percent response rate—a 32 percent increase. The descriptive cluster codes not only added insight, they significantly increased sales and profit.

## GATHER AND USE THE BEST DATA

An important aspect of developing the optimal model is to access data from a variety of sources, both internal and external, and then clean and organize it. An effective model starts from a development sample that is representative of the future population desired. Since it is not uncommon to identify a business problem for which the required data is unavailable or inaccessible, it is critical to determine if the data to be used for developing the model will be available—and affordable—over the long term.

Data used in assessing prospect or customer risk can come from a variety of sources. Typically, credit bureau, masterfile, application, and a combination of application and demographic data are used. However, new types of scores can assess customer performance more often, making it possible to consider very recent data in designing strategies for different customer segments.

One relatively new source is transaction data, which is predictive for certain applications. Behavior models use masterfile data to score customers on a monthly basis; transaction models enable credit grantors to score customers dynamically. With transaction models, lenders can react quickly to changes in customer profiles and change customer treatment as required.

The following case study shows how one telecommunications company used transaction data to advantage.

## CASE STUDY 2—TRANSACTION AND EVENT-DRIVEN DATA IDENTIFIES BAD ACCOUNTS

*Problem*   A long-distance telecommunications provider wanted to be able to identify high-risk customers as quickly as possible. The problem? A high percentage of losses came from new accounts that used the product quickly, with either no intent to pay or inability to continue payment. Although a good assortment of credit risk tools was being used, early risk identification practices had not been successful at stopping account abuse quickly.

To improve its early stage account management the company sought a predictive model that would rank new customers by their likelihood of payment. There was no way to develop behavior scores before the first billing cycle, as no payment or delinquency information was available.

The company already had an early warning "high-toll" monitoring system based on judgmental criteria to determine which accounts required action. The objective of model development was to replace these judgmental criteria with a more objective, empirically derived model.

*Solution*   Fair, Isaac explored the predictiveness of application and early usage characteristics. To build the risk model, standard characteristics such as applicant age, time at address/employer, and income were combined with non-standard indicators, including credit bureau scores and demographic information derived from processing the application.

Since the telecommunications company kept daily tabs on such factors as usage (transaction) types and frequency and length of calls placed, it had an additional source of data. Model development efforts focused on the first 30 days of account activity, where early transactional data provided the first indications of account performance. The model predicted likelihood of repayment of the charges incurred. The model also considered all transactions each day and provided an end-of-day score to be used in the company's early warning high-toll monitoring system to determine which accounts required action.

**Results**   Comparing the two approaches, using the development database showed that a score-based system could result in a 38 percent increase in dollars saved (under the assumption that the high-toll system immediately blocked all accounts from further usage) when using a score cutoff that maintained the same percentage of bad accounts as the high-toll method. Similarly, a 41 percent increase in dollars saved could be attained by adjusting the score cutoff to match the approximate percentage of accounts reviewed in the high-toll approach.

## MODEL DEVELOPMENT

After defining the problem and addressing data considerations comes determining the best modeling technique. This requires decisions about the performance definition (or outcome) and sampling window, testing whether assumptions of the modeling technique hold true, performing data reduction or transformation, selecting the variables to be used, and determining the number of models to be developed. After preliminary models are constructed, they must be tested to see how they will handle any identifiable implementation constraints.

One key consideration is performance definition. Performance definitions help clarify the outcome desired from a predictive model. Standard performance definitions are not possible. Instead, a definition grows from the nature of the products and a mix of business and statistical considerations.

For example, if you want to predict the likelihood of an event (e.g. response to an offer vs. non-response; propensity to revolve vs. transact; or payment vs. failure to pay), the model should have a dichotomous or categorical outcome—that is, the customer or prospect falls into one category or the other. (This could also be generalized to multiple categories.) If you want to determine where your accounts or prospects fall on a continuum, such as likely amount to be repaid or revenue earned, the model would be built for a continuous outcome. Depending on the shape of the outcome, various techniques can be applied, such as logistic regression, CART, or linear regression. The choice of which to use will depend on the nature of the underlying data as well as the proposed implementation.

Once you have determined whether the outcome is categorical or continuous, ascertain the appropriate outcome to predict; this depends on the business application. The following case study addresses a collection model developed with a continuous performance outcome (dollars outstanding that collections efforts might recover).

## CASE STUDY 3—CONTINUOUS OUTCOME IN COLLECTIONS

*Problem*  A bank vice president in charge of risk management wanted to determine if the use of collection scores might improve results for the collection department. He decided to run his own validation test to examine how well collection scores could rank order repayment on delinquent accounts. Specifically, he wanted to know whether collection scores could help the bank assign accounts for early outplacement. In addition, he wanted to discover any "soft" benefits that could be derived from using the scores and how those might improve operational efficiency, thereby reducing the expense of collection operations.

*Solution*  5,000 accounts, 60 or more days delinquent, were chosen at random and scored with Fair, Isaac collection scores from Trans Union. The bank was able to obtain scores on 87 percent of the accounts. Account balances were typically in the $400 range no matter what the collection score. Over the next six months, the risk manager observed payment amounts at the account level, by score.

*Results*  After six months of observation, the scores proved they worked to rank order payment amounts. The lower scoring accounts paid significantly fewer dollars over the six-month period than those in the mid-to-higher ranges. The collection score successfully ranked accounts by repayment amount (from less than $100 to $600) even though the outstanding balances, like the account balances, were similar throughout the sample (approximately $720 to $760).

The study also found that the scores could be used to rank the likelihood of subsequent charge-off.

## IMPLEMENTATION ISSUES

A final consideration in model development is implementation. Align implementation with your stated objectives and ensure that it is support-

**FIGURE 10-2**

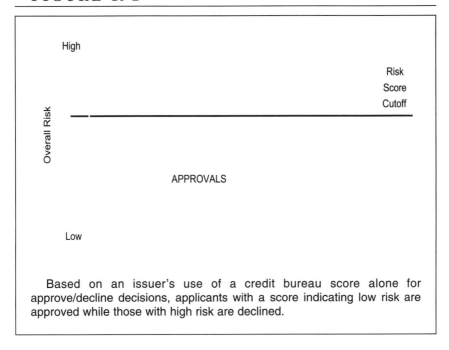

Based on an issuer's use of a credit bureau score alone for approve/decline decisions, applicants with a score indicating low risk are approved while those with high risk are declined.

ed by in-house practices and personnel. Is the system flexible, user friendly, and credible to the people who will use its results? Is the system capable of tracking and testing results? Also address the legal implications of how the model will be used before implementation. A thorough evaluation will afford seamless implementation of a system that will change and grow with the business.

One example of an implementation issue is the need to use more than one score to achieve a desired outcome.

## CASE STUDY 4—IMPLEMENTING A DUAL SCORE STRATEGY

**Problem**    A credit card issuer wanted to reduce bankruptcy losses among new customers. The goal was to design acquisition strategies that would boost portfolio revenues without increasing current losses due to bankruptcy. For this approach to succeed, the issuer needed to separate probable bankrupt accounts from profitable accounts that look like bankrupts.

**Solution**    The issuer's current ("champion") strategy was to use credit bureau-based risk scores to evaluate applicants. Applicants scoring within acceptable score ranges indicating low risk were approved and those with unacceptable scores were declined (see Figure 10–2).

## FIGURE 10–3

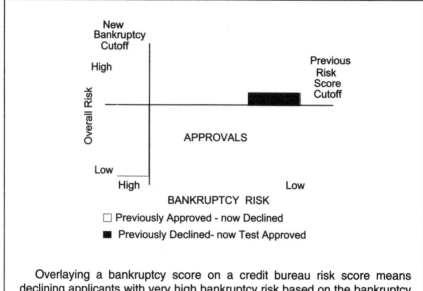

Overlaying a bankruptcy score on a credit bureau risk score means declining applicants with very high bankruptcy risk based on the bankruptcy score, even when they pass the risk score cutoff. To compensate for the decline in approvals, picking up a small test group with very good bankruptcy risk but marginal overall risk can increase portfolio revenues without impacting quality.

In order to analyze the benefits of incorporating bankruptcy-specific tools into existing strategies, the lender performed a retrospective analysis for a credit bureau bankruptcy score. Results of the retrospective validation were used to design and implement new strategies.

To limit bankruptcy losses but boost portfolio revenues, the lender implemented a "challenger" strategy in which a credit bureau bankruptcy score was used in conjunction with a credit bureau risk score to eliminate applicants likely to file for bankruptcy. Using this approach alone, however, would reduce the approval rate and thus revenues.

To avoid this, the issuer then looked for a "swap set" to compensate for the drop in approval rate as the overlay of the bankruptcy score eliminated additional potential approvals (see Figure 10–3).

The issuer decided to test approving applicants who were slightly more risky according to the credit bureau risk score when the bankruptcy score indicated low bankruptcy risk.

*Results*    The issuer gained insight into how the bankruptcy score could be incorporated along with risk measures to identify potential bankrupts and not approve them, while identifying a small test group with much less bankruptcy risk and more revenue potential. Adding a credit bureau bankruptcy score raised the approval rate by 2.3 percent—and revenues by 3.4 percent, with no increase in bankruptcy losses and only a negligible increase in non-bankrupt charge-offs.

## SUMMARY

There are myriad ways to approach model development—no one factor plays a more important role than another. But if we were to select the most important criterion in the success or failure of model development, it would be the quality of the decisions. Whatever path you take, whatever model you develop, whatever system you choose, it should allow you to make better decisions. These decisions could encompass which prospects to solicit, for what products, at what time, for how much credit, and at what price.

To achieve this optimal decision-making, look first to your data. If it does not meet your requirements, acquire additional data from a reputable source. Then employ a developer with domain expertise who can glean the essentials from the data and guide you in technology selection, analysis, and implementation. The result will be the optimal credit risk model for today's—and tomorrow's—business challenges.

## APPENDIX I

## CHOOSING THE APPROPRIATE
## MODELING TECHNOLOGY

A wide variety of predictive technologies can be used, including scoring models, neural networks, classification and regression trees, and other more remote technologies and applications such as genetic algorithms, expert systems, or fuzzy logic.

In choosing a suitable modeling technology, a review of the types of predictive models is only the first step. Once one or more possible techniques have been chosen, both the end-user and the developer should do a thorough evaluation. These checklists may prove helpful.

### Developer Checklist

Developers should evaluate the strengths and weaknesses of a technology for a particular modeling application based on desired results. Ask the following questions when evaluating technologies.

*Performance*   Does this approach:
- Demand restrictive data assumptions?
- Require a reasonable sample size?
- Handle missing or dubious data?
- Handle sample weighting?
- Handle performance inference?
- Feature constrained optimization and goal programming?
- Recognize rare events?

*Confidence*   Does this technique:
- Make complete use of data? Does the technology exhaust predictiveness of given information and does it examine the residual contribution of alternative predictors?
- Allow easy what-if scrutiny? Can you easily modify a given solution and create a new solution?
- Provide insight to test data structure assumptions and identify relationships among predictors?

*Cost-Effectiveness*   Does it:
- Require reasonable skill levels? Is the staff familiar with both the technology and problem areas?
- Require only reasonable amounts of computing resources?

## End-User Checklist

*Performance*   Does the technology:

- Replicate results? Is the solution appropriate for the problem and does it give acceptable performance in practice?
- Provide fault tolerance? Is the solution robust over time and in operation?
- Exhibit explanatory capability? Can the solution be "sold" to operations staff and does it meet legal requirements (e.g., give reasons for decline)?
- Provide an empirically derived solution, based on historical data?

*Confidence*   Is it:

- Innovative? Does adopting the technology create a competitive advantage or will it improve corporate image?
- Supported with a proven track record in a related or unrelated field?
- Easily understood? Are both the mechanics of obtaining a solution and the theoretical foundation of the technology clear?

*Operational Effectiveness*   Is it:

- Usable by staff of varying skill levels?
- Compatible with existing computing platforms, whether multiple personal computers or a single mainframe computer?
- Compatible with existing technologies, such as data pre-processing systems and tracking and feedback systems?

*Strategic Control*   Does the technology:

- Provide information to aid strategic decisions such as projection of population profile and population performance?
- Offer a high degree of management control (i.e., are there many knobs to turn or many settings per knob)?
- Allow for consistent scaling schemes, such as scaling over time or across populations?
- Enable tracking for population profile and performance?

# 11

# REJECT INFERENCE IN CREDIT OPERATIONS

**David J. Hand**
*Department of Statistics*
*The Open University, Milton Keynes, UK*

## INTRODUCTION

This chapter is concerned with the problem of "reject inference" in the credit granting process—the issue of how to take proper account of people rejected for a loan, since one does not know whether they would have been good or bad customers. This matters particularly in assessing how well a scorecard is performing and in constructing a new scorecard.

Because a given scorecard will gradually deteriorate over time (as the applicant population evolves, new marketing initiatives take effect, types of competing products change, and so on), it will eventually have to be replaced. However, the data available for constructing the new scorecard are incomplete. There will be application or behavioral data or both for all applicants, but outcome data only for those who were granted a loan —those who scored above some threshold on the previous scorecard. (For convenience we are ignoring issues such as customers who decline offered loans, though the ideas can be extended to cope with these.) Quite clearly, and as several studies have shown, constructing scorecards based only on those who were previously granted a loan is likely to lead to inaccuracies when the scorecards are applied to the entire population of applicants. On the other hand, since applications previously rejected do not have information about their good/bad class, they do not contain information about the relationship between the items comprising the scorecard and the value of good/bad status. This is a dilemma that can easily have serious consequences. In what follows, we describe methods that have been proposed for overcoming this problem. We begin with discussion of models have been used for credit scoring and the nature of the data to which they are applied.

## THE MODELS

The basic model underlying the decision of whether or not to grant credit is, in principle at least, straightforward: One compares the information available on application forms or in records of past behavior with similar information from previous customers whose outcome is known. Typically, the information from previous customers is summarized into a predictive statistical model or "scorecard.". Applying the model to the known information about potential customers yields a prediction of their probability of being a good risk. A decision is made by comparing this estimated 'creditworthiness' score with some threshold.[1]

Many statistical methods have been used for the purpose, from classical linear discriminant analysis, multiple linear regression, and logistic regression to the newer neural networks, recursive partitioning methods (tree-based methods), and nonparametric nearest neighbor methods. Results of comparative studies have occasionally been published, although commercial constraints hint that many more have been carried out than have been published. The published studies, as well as our own practical experience in comparing credit scoring models, suggests that the more sophisticated and flexible modern methods do not generally have much of an advantage over the older methods—though this generalization does not always apply in contexts other than credit scoring. Some studies do suggest that more powerful methods do better, but others suggest the opposite. Such results raise the question of what it is about credit scoring data that detracts from the apparent theoretical advantages of modern (typically computer-based) tools.

There appear to be several explanations. One is that in many problems it is simply not possible to get clear separation between the "good" and "bad" risks. Unless the behavior is quite extreme, the customer could often easily fall into either class. Another partial explanation is that people have been working with credit data for many years. Characteristics

---

1 Reviews of such methods in general are given in D.J. Hand, *Construction and Assessment of Classification Rules* (Chichester: Wiley, 1997) and in the context of credit scoring in E. Rosenberg and A. Gleit, "Quantitative Methods in Credit Management: A Survey," *Operations Research* 42:589-613 (1994); D.J. Hand and W.E. Henley, "Inference about Rejected Cases in Discriminant Analysis," in *New Approaches in Classification and Data Analysis,* ed. E. Diday et al. (Berlin: Springer-Verlag, 1994), pp. 292-99; and L.C. Thomas, "Methodologies for Classifying Applicants for Credit," in *Statistics in Finance,* ed. D.J. Hand and S.D. Jacka (London: Arnold, 1998), pp. 83-103.

and combinations of characteristics likely to distinguish between the two groups are well known, so that there is relatively little new knowledge about the separation for more sophisticated methods to discover. Again, of course, there are exceptions. In a context where a small improvement in predictive ability can translate into a large absolute sum of money, it is important that experimentation continue.

## THE DATA

So much for the models used in credit scoring. What about the data?

Much classical statistical work is based on an ideal model that assumes small, clean, static data sets obtained by random selection. Credit data typically do not conform to this ideal. The data sets are often large, involving hundreds of thousands or millions of records. Large data sets introduce new kinds of problems. Some are housekeeping issues, such as how to store and access data conveniently, but there can be more fundamental problems, such as how to obtain estimates if the data will not all fit into the computer's memory and what to make of highly significant effects that are nonetheless very small.

Of perhaps greater concern is the fact that credit data sets are often not clean. They often include anomalous values or patterns that are difficult to explain. For example, we came across a situation in which a characteristic featured in the scorecard that had not been noted for any of the applicants in a particular year was being recorded as "not given." It is difficult to believe that all the applicants that year simply refused to give this value! The error led to a difference of several points on the scorecard values for applicants in that year, a difference regarded as important by those who used it, and that must have led to some applicants being rejected for a loan they should properly have received.

Credit data are also rarely static. More often, they extend over time, evolving as new customers enter the data set and old ones exit. Most predictive modeling takes it as a premise that the aim is to predict properties (in this case creditworthiness) of new subjects drawn from the same distribution (and drawn independently, as well). In credit work, however, the aim is to predict properties of subjects obtained in the future. As distributions evolve over time, the models will degrade unless this is taken into account. This introduces higher order and dynamic complications that are rarely considered in the statistical models. More work needs to be done in this area.

Finally, credit data sets are rarely obtained by random sampling of a well-defined population of customers or potential customers. Often an entire population is used—all those who applied for a loan during a given time period, for example. This raises questions about the nature of the model building process. No longer is the problem one of inference from a sample to a population (and to individuals within that population), it is now one of forecasting. Perhaps even worse, however, is the fact that the data sets available for analysis may have been obtained by a complex and non-random selection process from the population to which an inference is required. For example, Hand, McConway, and Stanghellini[2] describe a study in which a population of potential customers is solicited by mail. Some reply and some do not. Those who reply are assessed for credit-worthiness. Those who score highly are offered a loan. Some accept and some decline. Those who take out a loan are (naturally) followed up. Some turn out to be good customers, paying the installments on time, some do not. And so on. At each step, a subset—and a nonrandom one at that—is taken. The difficulty arises when one wants to base an inference from the data at hand to the larger set from which the data were taken.

This is precisely the problem of reject inference. In particular, reject inference describes the problem of inferring the good/bad properties of those customers who have not been granted a loan (that is, those customers who have been 'rejected'). If this inference is successful, one has a description of the overall population of people who apply for a loan, and one can then construct statistical models of this population.

The next three sections examine methods that have been proposed for overcoming this problem.

## ACCEPTING SOME REJECTS

There is one ideal solution to the problem, a solution in tune with scientific philosophy but that has not always found favor in practical credit scoring because of commercial constraints. That is to take a random sample from the rejects, grant them loans, and monitor their repayment behavior. These applicants, appropriately weighted and combined with those who would have been accepted by the original scoring rule (or a random sample of them) will yield an overall (stratified) random sample from the population of applicants, which can then be used to construct a new scorecard.

Of course, the reason that this is unappealing in a banking context is that these applicants are thought to be poor risks; they were thought likely to lose the bank money, which is precisely why they were rejected. The point is, however, that by accepting some of them, the longer term profit of the bank could be increased by building a more predictive scorecard.

2 "Graphical Models of Applicants for Credit," *IMA Journal of Mathematics Applied in Business and Industry*, 8:143-45 (1997).

In any case, the bank's profits need not suffer much at all if the sample of apparent poor risk applicants who are accepted is selected carefully. To see this, let us first examine exactly what it is that our models seek to predict.

So far we have glossed over precisely what the scorecard has been constructed to predict. This is partly because it varies from situation to situation, from product to product, and partly because the response variable is often a proxy for another variable. A common ideal response variable would be the profit that a potential customer is likely to earn for the bank, but this is typically very difficult to calculate, depending, as it does, on many factors—the customer's pattern of repayment, the interest rate, the term, the cost of the marketing that brought the customer in, the cost of support facilities for customers, and so on. That is why simple "repayment default risk" is often adopted as an easily defined proxy. Because it is thought to be strongly related to profitability, its ease of measurement makes it an appealing variable to use. Moreover, if the bank is prepared to accept default risk as a proxy for profitability when constructing the scorecard, it should also be prepared to accept it when measuring the likely loss from accepting a poor customer.

The sample from the rejected subgroup can be chosen so that one samples less heavily from amongst those thought to be at greatest risk. The likely extra loss from accepting some applicants who are thought more likely to perform less well than others can thus be kept to a minimum. The expected proportion good for any particular pattern $x$ of applicant characteristics can then be calculated as an appropriately weighted sum of (1) the expected proportion good at $x$ amongst those who scored above the acceptance threshold on the original scorecard and (2) the expected proportion good at $x$ amongst those who scored below the acceptance threshold on the original scorecard. The weights will depend on the relative probabilities falling above and below the acceptance threshold, as well as the probability of being included in the sample given that the original score was not acceptable.

This approach to coping with the problem of reject inference deserves to be considered more widely. The apparent extra loss can be kept to a minimum, and it will improve long term predictive ability, and hence reduce loss overall. Of course, it needs to be planned in advance. It cannot be applied retrospectively, when no rejects have been accepted. And there may be practical (legal) constraints because it implies the possibility of treating differently people who are apparently identical in terms of their creditworthiness. For example, two applicants may have identical patterns of characteristics, leading both of them to be classified as bad risks, but the strategy may lead to one being accepted for a loan and the other not.

# MIXTURE DECOMPOSITION

There is a method for estimating the sizes of each of the two classes in a single population without having any information whatsoever about the probability that any pattern of characteristics belongs to each class. In credit scoring terms this means that one could estimate the proportions good and bad in the population without even knowing the outcomes of those accepted, let alone those rejected. Of course, this apparently magical trick cannot be performed free of charge. The cost is an assumption—a strong one at that—about the distribution of patterns of characteristics among the goods and, separately, among the bads. In particular, one must assume that these distributions are known up to the value of some parameters, which can be estimated from the data.

The trick is performed simply by matching the distribution of the observed data with the overall distribution formed as the weighted sum of the assumed distribution of the goods and the assumed distribution of the bads. The weights—the proportions of goods and bads—and the parameters of the two component distributions, are estimated by optimizing some goodness-of-fit measure between the data and the theoretical combined distribution. Maximum likelihood methods are the most popular. The overall distribution of the goods and bads is called, reasonably enough, a *mixture distribution,* and methods for carrying out such exercises have been described.[3]

Extensions of the basic ideas permit one to take advantage of anything that is known about the component distributions. In this case, one knows the true good/bad classes of some applicants, namely those previously accepted (as well as some previously rejected if the strategy outlined in the preceding section is adopted).

The drawback of this, clearly very attractive, approach is that the assumed forms of the distributions for the goods and bads must be reasonably accurate. Unfortunately, the nature of credit data, which involves categorical characteristics often defined in terms of fairly complex underlying concepts, means that no distributions spring to mind as obvious.

# EXTRAPOLATION AND BIAS

Let $X$ denote the set of characteristics used in the original scorecard—the one used to make the original accept/reject decisions and responsible for the true good/bad classes being known for the accepts but not for the rejects. Let $Y$ denote the characteristics to be used in a proposed new

---

3 See, for example, B.S. Everitt and D.J. Hand, *Finite Mixture Distributions* (London: Chapman & Hall, 1981).

scorecard. We can now distinguish between two situations: (1) $X$ is a subset of $Y$, meaning that the new set of characteristics includes all those in the original set; it may be the same as this set, though it may include more characteristics. (2) $X$ is not a subset of $Y$, meaning that the original set had characteristics not included in $Y$. For example, *age* might have featured in the original scorecard, but not in the new one.

The scorecard based on the original set of characteristics $X$ led to a classification rule that partitioned possible patterns of characteristics into two classes, the "accepts" and the "rejects." When $X$ is a not subset of $Y$, the set of possible patterns for the characteristics used by the new scorecard will also be partitioned. In the second situation, however, it is possible that every pattern defined by the set of new characteristics is associated with some accepts and some rejects. That is, in the first situation we have *no information at all* about the proportion of goods and bads for some $Y$ patterns (those corresponding to the previous rejects), while for the second situation we may have information about the proportion of goods and bads for all possible $Y$ patterns, but only for the accepts—with nothing known about the proportion of goods and bads for any of the patterns for the rejects.

In the first of these situations there is no alternative to extrapolation from the accept patterns over the reject patterns. That is, one fits a model for the probability of being good for the accept patterns and extends this model over reject patterns. How effective such extrapolation will be will depend on a number of factors. Extrapolation methods are based on the untestable assumption that the form of the model where it can be observed also extends over the other regions. If there are few reject patterns—if relatively few applicants have sets of characteristics that will lead them to be rejected—then the extrapolation might be reasonably accurate. If the data set is small, so that even over the accept patterns one can only construct a rather inaccurate model, there is little hope for accurate extrapolation over the reject patterns.

Depending upon the purpose to which the inferred good/bad status of the rejects is to be put, it might be helpful to define confidence bounds on the extrapolation. For a given reject pattern, such bounds would tell us the lowest and highest likely proportions of bads.

The second situation, the one where $X$ is a subset of $Y$, is conceptually more demanding. We have information, possibly for *all* response patterns, about the proportions of goods and bads. But we only have this information for those who were accepted; for any particular pattern we have no indication of the relative proportion of goods and bads amongst those rejected. Those who were rejected may have entirely different proportions of goods and bads from those who were accepted—indeed, one might expect the proportion of goods amongst the rejects to be quite different, since the original scorecard was constructed precisely with this aim in mind. That is, it is entirely likely that the characteristics in $X$ not included in $Y$ contain some power to separate the goods from the bads.

Some reject inference implementations fail to take this into account.[4] They assume that the proportion of goods is the same for the rejects as it is for the accepts. Given this assumption, since the number of applicants with any given response pattern is known, the number of goods can be determined simply by scaling up the proportion of goods among the accepts appropriately. However, if the assumption is false, which is likely, this will produce biased, possibly highly inaccurate, results. Hand and Henley[5] give an example of how the proportions of goods among the accepts differs from the proportions of goods among the entire population (accepts plus rejects) for each pattern of $Y$. They also show that the ratio between these two proportions varies substantially across patterns of characteristics. This means that bias is inevitable if one simply assumes that the proportion of goods is the same for the accepts and rejects.

## CONCLUSIONS

Various other strategies have also been adopted for reject inference. Sometimes scorecard developers ignore the issue, treating the accepts as if they were a random sample from the population of potential applicants. This assumption is not justifiable if the original scorecard had any predictive validity.

Sometimes scorecard developers assume that all rejected applicants are bad risks—that the original scorecard was correct in rejecting them, though not in its classification of accepts as good (if it were, there would be no point in constructing a new scorecard). This strategy can sometimes be appropriate. If, for example, a more demanding definition of 'good' is to be applied, then all those previously classified as bad will remain bad and some of those classified as good will now become bad.

Some rejected applicants find alternative lenders. The growth of databases and the interchange of records means that the repayment behavior of these can perhaps be followed up. Of course, great care is needed in the statistical inference in view of the possibilities of subtle bias in the samples—it is likely that not *everyone* who was rejected will find an alternative supplier, and in any case the conditions associated with their new loan

---

4 See, for example, the *augmentation* method described by D. C. Hsia, "Credit Scoring and the
   Equal Credit Opportunity Act," *Hastings Law Journal* 30:371-405 (1978).
5 Hand and Henley, *supra,* note 1.

are likely to differ from those of the one for which they were rejected, so that their behavior (and subsequent good/bad status) may differ.

Reject inference is just one of many problems arising from incomplete, missing, or partial data. Indeed, it might be regarded as one of the more straightforward problems, since the cause is clear and well understood, even if the solution is difficult. Other such problems are less well understood. Data may be missing for many reasons other than the deliberate selection process arising from application of a previous scorecard. Sometimes values are missing for structural reasons—a spouse's income can only be given if one has a spouse. Sometimes the probability that a value is missing is related to the unknown value itself, making inference particularly subtle.[6] Hand[7] describes a data set of 25 characteristics recorded for 3883 applicants in which only 66 applicants had no missing values and one applicant had 16 missing values.

In other contexts, such as medicine, great store is placed on the quality of the data, and great efforts are expended to ensure high quality. In part this is due to regulatory monitoring of data quality. Data arising from clinical trials often have to be deposited in a database so that it can be reanalysed should questions arise. Of course, one important difference between clinical trial datasets and credit scoring data sets is size, with the latter typically being much larger than the former. This means that automated methods of maintaining data quality are more relevant for the latter. Traditionally data verification and cleaning has generally been handled by a constraint-based approach, in which missing values are imputed and errors corrected on the basis of logical relationships between characteristics and information on the range of possible values they can take. This might be characterized as the computer scientist's approach. In contrast the statistician might be concerned with relationships that are unlikely but possible. More work in this area is needed. Methods of multiple imputation for incomplete data might be a step in this direction.

The problems of biased samples arising from selection processes pervade credit data. Ignoring them can lead to distorted models and markedly suboptimal scorecards. One general strategy for overcoming such problems is to try to reconstruct the full population distribution, so that standard scorecard construction methods can be applied. Reject inference, in particular, seeks to do this when the distortion is due to an accept/reject decision resulting from applying an earlier scorecard. Several methods have been proposed and are used; while some of them

---

6 Id.
7 D. J. Hand, "Consumer Credit and Statistics," in *Statistics in Finance,* ed. D.J. Hand and S.D.
   Jacka (London: Arnold, 1998), pp. 69-81.

are clearly poor and should never be recommended, there is no unique best method of universal applicability.

## REFERENCES

Everitt, B.S., and D. J. Hand. 1981. *Finite Mixture Distributions.* London: Chapman & Hall.

Hand D.J., and W.E. Henley. 1994. "Inference about rejected cases in discriminant analysis." In *New Approaches in Classification and Data Analysis,* Ed. E. Diday et al. Springer-Verlag. 292-299.

Hand, D.J. 1997. *Construction and Assessment of Classification Rules.* Chichester: Wiley.

Hand, D.J. 1998. "Consumer Credit and Statistics." In *Statistics in Finance,* ed. D.J. Hand and S.D. Jacka. London: Arnold. 69-81.

Hand, D.J., and W.E. Henley. 1997. "Statistical Classification Methods in Consumer Credit Scoring: A Review". *Journal of the Royal Statistical Society,* Series A, 160, 523-541.

Hand D.J., K.J. McConway, and E. Stanghellini. 1997. "Graphical models of applicants for credit." *IMA Journal of Mathematics Applied in Business and Industry,* 8, 143-155.

Hsia, D.C. 1978. "Credit Scoring and the Equal Credit Opportunity Act." *The Hastings Law Journal,* 30, 371-405.

Rosenberg, E., and A. Gleit. 1994. "Quantitative Methods in Credit Management: A Survey." *Operations Research,* 42, 589-613.

Thomas, L.C. 1998. "Methodologies for Classifying Applicants for Credit." In *Statistics in Finance,* ed. D.J. Hand and S.D. Jacka. London: Arnold. 83-103.

# 12

# EVALUATING AND MONITORING YOUR MODEL

**Richard Schiffman**
*Production Manager*
*Fair, Isaac and Company, Inc.*

## INTRODUCTION

You've just completed development and implementation of a new credit risk model. Time to sit back, relax, and let the model do its job. Suddenly an alarm sounds in the distance. You wake up and realize it's Monday, and you've got a very busy day ahead of you.

Your manager just received a copy of an OCC bulletin discussing several bank practices that resulted in improper use of scoring models. Specifically it mentioned "deficient bank management information systems that impede tracking, monitoring, validating the credit scoring model at development, and revalidating the model over time." You've been handed the job of ensuring that all appropriate reports are produced, and that the information is used appropriately to help meet regulatory requirements and business goals.

The underlying assumption of credit risk models is that past performance can be used to predict future behavior. Since the predictions are based on the behavior of groups of similar accounts, the model can tell you which groups of accounts are more likely to perform satisfactorily compared to other groups, but it cannot give you an absolute performance measure for an individual account. Many factors will affect the observed performance of the model, such as excessive overrides, a changing applicant population, and the economy. Tracking how the model performs helps you identify and measure many of these factors. Tracking is critical to ensuring that the model continues to serve the organization effectively.

## TABLE 12–1
### A Credit Scorecard

| Characteristic | Attribute Score Points | | | |
|---|---|---|---|---|
| Residential Status | Owns/Buying 42 | Rents 25 | All Other 19 | |
| Time at Address | < 1 year 8 | 1-4 Years 14 | 5-9 Years 23 | 10+ Years 37 |
| Marital Status | Married 35 | Divorced 21 | Widowed 30 | Single 24 |

Simulated characteristics, attributes, and weights for demonstration purposes only.

In this chapter we discuss factors that can affect the performance of the model and describe a set of reports that can help measure these effects. We will focus on front-end scoring models, those used by lenders as part of the original decision making process. Credit scoring is a process whereby a numerical weight is assigned to each predictive variable (characteristic) on a credit application. The score for each characteristic is determined by the value (attribute) the characteristic has for the application. The individual weights are then totaled, with the total score representing the risk of the applicant. Applications scoring above a certain total (the cutoff score) are recommended for approval. In practice you may have information in addition to the credit score that is used in the decision making process. This information is sometimes used to override the score model's recommendation to accept or decline.

The information used in the scoring model can come from a variety of sources, including the credit application, a credit bureau file, and customer information files. The score itself may also be used in areas other than the accept/decline decision. Tiered pricing, credit line assignment, counter-offers, and cross-selling can be done based on credit scores. Table 12–1 is an example of a credit scorecard.

## WHEN SHOULD YOU TRACK YOUR MODEL?

Begin monitoring your scoring model as soon as you start using it and continue throughout the model's life. First ensure that the model has been installed in your application processing system correctly and that applications are being accurately scored. Re-score a sample of accounts manually and compare the results to the original scores. Investigate any discrepancies to determine the cause.

The most common sources of scoring errors are operator entry error, and programming errors in the setting up of the scorecard in the application processor. Minimizing these errors early is extremely important. If they go undetected, the reports you produce will be of less value, and the predictive value of future models will be diminished. Periodically, this audit process should be repeated to ensure that operators are continuing to enter applications accurately.

Soon after implementation you'll begin producing a standard set of front-end reports to measure model stability. Front-end reports are based on information available at time of application; some of them can be produced by the application processing system. They include the Population Stability, Characteristic Analysis, and Final Score Reports.

In general, you can begin producing reports about a month after implementing the model. You'll want to review them at least quarterly, monthly if application volume is sufficiently high. The goal of these reports is to give you a picture of what your "through-the-door" population looks like, and to tell you how often the recommended scorecard decision is being overridden.

Back-end reports measure how the model is performing and the quality of the portfolio. Production of back-end reports should begin as soon as accounts have begun to show performance, typically about three months after model implementation. These reports should also be produced quarterly or monthly if an organization has sufficient volumes. The goal of these reports is to verify that the scorecard is correctly rank-ordering the risk of accounts (i.e., higher scoring accounts are performing better than lower scoring accounts), and to measure portfolio quality. These reports can also provide a "benchmark" level of delinquency against which the performance of new accounts can be compared.

## WHY TRACK YOUR MODEL?

### Regulatory Compliance

The United States government requires model tracking. According to OCC Bulletin 97-24 (May 20, 1997), bank management is responsible for ensuring that credit scoring models are used appropriately. As part of this process, the organization is required to revalidate the model on a regular basis to ensure that it continues to be a valid predictor of applicant risk. In addition, the organization must review the performance of overrides—accounts that scored below the model cutoff score but were approved. Banks must also take appropriate action when the credit score model shows signs of degradation.

Among bank practices OCC examiners have identified as having resulted in improper use of the scoring models are:

- Bank staff inadequately trained to effectively monitor performance of the scoring model
- Deficient management information systems (MIS) that prevent tracking, monitoring and validation of the model over time
- Excessive overriding

## Feedback

By producing a standard set of tracking reports on a regular basis you obtain important feedback about the performance of the model, your applicant population, the data entry staff, and the credit analysts. This feedback is essential, as it helps you determine what needs to be modified to ensure that your business goals are met. For example, you may notice from the reports that the percentage of accounts overridden (rejecting accounts that scored above the cutoff score or accepting accounts that scored below the cutoff score) has been increasing. If performance reports show that low-side overrides (accounts scoring below cutoff that are approved) are performing poorly, you can modify your policies to make it more difficult for credit analysts to approve these accounts.

Reviewing reports on a regular basis can also help you identify potential problems very quickly and make modifications to reduce potential losses. For example, the bank may have recently begun a campaign to increase the number of student accounts. After three months, performance reports show that these student accounts have much higher delinquency than the benchmark for accounts that have been on the books for three months. It is reasonable to expect that if left untreated, these student accounts will continue to have higher delinquency resulting in higher charge-off rates and losses than the rest of the portfolio. By anticipating this, you can take action on the front-end, perhaps by eliminating the campaign to attract student applications, and on the accounts you have already accepted. Working collections more aggressively and keeping credit limits low can help minimize the loss ratio for this portion of your portfolio.

Similarly, standard reports can help you identify opportunities. On the heels of a campaign to send credit card applications to homeowners, the reports may indicate that recent accounts are scoring higher on average than in the past, and thus represent lower risk. Further investigation may reveal that this increase in average score is due to an increase in the percentage of homeowners applying for credit. Armed with this information, you might seek to expand the program.

## TABLE 12–2
### Population Stability Report

| Score | Standard Number of Applications | Recent % of Total | Number of Applications | % of Total | Contribution to Index |
|---|---|---|---|---|---|
| Below 180 | 1200 | 12 | 1100 | 15 | 0.005 |
| 180-199 | 950 | 10 | 900 | 12 | 0.006 |
| 200-209 | 1050 | 11 | 825 | 11 | 0.000 |
| 210-219 | 1100 | 11 | 875 | 12 | 0.000 |
| 220-229 | 1350 | 14 | 900 | 12 | 0.002 |
| 230-249 | 1300 | 13 | 850 | 11 | 0.002 |
| 250-269 | 1200 | 12 | 825 | 11 | 0.001 |
| 270-289 | 1050 | 11 | 700 | 9 | 0.001 |
| 290 & Up | 800 | 8 | 525 | 7 | 0.001 |
| Total: | 10000 | | 7500 | | PSI = 0.019 |

# STANDARD TRACKING REPORTS

### Front-End Reports

Front-end reports are based on information available at the time of application, typically information from both the credit bureau and the application itself. Performance information is not included. Front-end reports provide valuable information about your applicant population, as well as the effect of your policies for decisioning accounts, and they provide it very quickly. Often these reports can give you insight into how your portfolio may perform in the future, allowing you to make adjustments that can increase revenue or reduce losses and collection costs. A standard set of front-end reports includes:

- Population stability report
- Characteristic analysis report
- Final score report
- Override tracking report

*Population Stability Report*   The population stability report compares the score distribution of recent applications to a standard population that is usually based on your development sample. It seeks to answer the question, "How is my current population scoring in comparison to applications from the past?" Table 12–2 is a sample population stability report.

Simulated characteristics, attributes, and weights for demonstration purposes only.

Contribution to Index compares the percentage of applicants for the recent and standard populations in each score range according to the following formula:

Contribution to Index = (Recent % - Standard %)/ln(Recent %/Standard %)

The index values for the individual score ranges are added together to obtain the population stability index (PSI), which measures the shift in the applicant score distribution. Higher PSI values indicate a larger shift in the distribution.

When creating the standard distribution, try to have between 8 and 12 score ranges, each containing approximately 10 percent of the population. A PSI of less than 0.1 indicates a stable population. An index of greater than 0.1 indicates that the population has changed and further investigation is warranted. The PSI does not indicate whether recent accounts are scoring higher or lower than the development standard: the value of the index contributions (and therefore the index itself) will always be greater than zero. To determine the direction of the shift you need to look at the score distribution data. In Table 2, recent accounts are scoring lower than accounts in the development standard.

While the PSI value is useful, it is more important to look at how this index is changing over time. This will give you insight into how the population is changing, and whether the quality of applicants is improving (scoring higher on average), or declining (scoring lower on average). If in each of the last three quarters applicants have been scoring lower on average than in the previous quarter, it is reasonable to expect that scores will continue to decline unless action is taken to attract higher quality applicants.

While the population stability report will identify shifts in applicant distribution and tell us whether they are positive or negative, it does not provide insight into what is causing a shift. For this, you need the Characteristic Analysis Report.

*Characteristic Analysis Report*   Like the population stability report, the character analysis report compares the distribution of recent applications to a standard population, usually based on the development sample. However, while the population stability report compares the distribution of scores, the characteristic analysis report compares the distributions of attributes across each scorecard characteristic. It seeks to answer the question, "What is causing my current population to score differently compared to applications from the past?" Table 12–3 is a sample characteristic analysis report.

## TABLE 12–3

**Characteristic Anaysis Report**
**Scorecard Characteristic: Residential Status**

| Attribute | Score | Standard Count Points | Recent Percent | Count | Percent | Score Difference |
|-----------|-------|-----------------------|----------------|-------|---------|------------------|
| Owns | 32 | 3500 | 35 | 2925 | 45 | 3.2 |
| Rents | 23 | 4000 | 40 | 1950 | 30 | -2.3 |
| Lives with Parents | 18 | 2000 | 20 | 1463 | 23 | 0.5 |
| Miscellaneous | 20 | 500 | 5 | 162 | 2 | -0.5 |
| Total: | | 10000 | | 6500 | | 0.9 |

Simulated characteristics, attributes, and weights for demonstration purposes only.

The score difference shows how many points higher or lower, on average, the recent population is scoring compared to the development sample. These individual differences are totaled to provide the score difference for the characteristic. Positive numbers indicate that recent applicants are scoring higher on average than the development sample. Negative numbers indicate the reverse. The score difference is calculated according to the following formula:

Score Difference = (Recent % - Standard %) x Score Points

In Table 12–3, the percentage of applicants who own their home increased from 35 percent to 45 percent, resulting in an average increase of 3.2 points for this attribute {(.45-.35) x 32 = 3.2}. For the entire characteristic residential status, recent applicants are scoring almost one point higher than the development sample.

The characteristic analysis report should contain a table for each scorecard characteristic. A summary table showing the total score difference for each is useful, as it will show which characteristics are having the greatest impact on score. You can then look at the individual reports to determine which attributes are contributing most to the shift in applicant scores, so that you can decide what action to take.

In addition to looking for shifts in a given characteristic, you should also track the characteristic analysis summary reports to see how the applicant population is changing over time. Once a trend of decreasing or increasing scores is identified, corrective action can be taken before there is a significant impact on the portfolio.

*Final Score Report*  While the two previous reports focused on the composition of the through-the-door applicant population, the final score

## TABLE 12–4
### Final Score Report

| Score | Number of Applications | Approved | Declined | Acceptance Rate | Override Rate |
|---|---|---|---|---|---|
| Below 180 | 286 | 17 | 269 | 6% | 6% |
| 180-199 | 354 | 64 | 290 | 18% | 18% |
| *200-219 | 523 | 350 | 173 | 67% | 33% |
| 220-229 | 563 | 417 | 146 | 74% | 26% |
| 230-249 | 614 | 503 | 111 | 82% | 18% |
| 250-269 | 597 | 525 | 72 | 88% | 12% |
| 270-289 | 539 | 490 | 49 | 91% | 9% |
| 290 & Up | 501 | 481 | 20 | 96% | 4% |
| Total: | 3977 | 2848 | 1129 | 72% | |
| Below Cutoff | 640 | 81 | 559 | 13% | 13% |
| Above Cutoff | 3337 | 2767 | 570 | 83% | 17% |

* Indicates cutoff score of 200
Simulated characteristics, attributes, and weights for demonstration purposes only.

report looks at the decisions made based on score. It shows how often the model's recommended accept or decline decision is being overridden. An account that scores above the cutoff score but is declined is considered a high-side override. Accounts approved that scored below cutoff are low-side overrides. Excessive overriding can increase account acquisition costs and may indicate a lack of faith in the scorecard.

Note that in general, the override rate is highest in the score ranges just above and just below the cutoff score. As you move further from the cutoff score, there is less opportunity to improve on the scorecard's recommended decision and the override rate decreases. Because higher scoring applications represent lower risk, the acceptance rate should increase as score increases, as shown in Table 12–4.

Again, it is important to monitor trends. Acceptance rates may change over time, and it is important to understand why. Changes in acceptance rates within a given score range will primarily be the result of overrides. When looking at changes to the overall acceptance rate, both the override rate and a changing applicant population must be considered. If, for example, recent applicants are scoring lower on average than in the past, it is reasonable to expect the overall acceptance rate to decrease. Of course, changes in the cutoff score will affect the overall acceptance rate and will often affect the override rate within score ranges.

*Override Report*   While credit scoring theory states that all accounts that score above cutoff should be approved, and all accounts below cutoff should be declined, this rarely happens. Organizations use both policy and judgmental reasons to override the score's recommendation. Policy overrides are executed for a specific reason. For example, an organization may decline all applications that have a bankruptcy reported on the credit bureau file within the last two years. Even if an application scored well above cutoff, it would not be approved if it met a policy decline criteria. Judgmental overrides are made based on a credit analyst's experience. Since they are not the result of a documented policy, they should be minimized.

When an application is overridden, it is important to identify the reason. By keeping track of override reasons, you can periodically review the frequency with which each override reason is being used, and determine if policies need to be modified. It is important to minimize the number of applicants categorized as miscellaneous, because this provides no information about why the applicant was overridden. Table 12–5 is a basic override tracking report, which includes both policy and judgmental override reasons.

Override analysis can be taken a step further by categorizing judgmental overrides by credit analyst or loan officer. This can give you information about which loan officers are overriding most frequently. The ultimate goal is to determine the specific reason for the overrides so that decisions can be made more uniformly across loan officers. Where appropriate, new policies can be created to formalize the decision process.

It is especially important to identify reasons for low-side overrides. Because these accounts are approved, there is an opportunity to review their performance, using the information either to support continued use of this override policy, or to support modification or elimination of it. Tracking the performance of low-side overrides will be discussed in more detail below.

### Back-End Reports

Back-end reports are created based on the information about the performance of accounts in a portfolio. Among the many different types of performance reports are those that look at current delinquency, historical delinquency, current balance, profitability, and other financial informa-

### TABLE 12–5
**Override Tracking Report**

| Override Reason | Approved | Declined |
|---|---|---|
| Negative CB Information | 0 | 363 |
| Debt Ratio Too High | 0 | 117 |
| Student | 214 | 0 |
| Savings Account Balance > 5000 | 35 | 0 |
| Miscellaneous | 67 | 75 |

Simulated characteristics, attributes, and weights for demonstration purposes only.

## TABLE 12–6
### Override Performance Report

|  | # of Accounts | # Ever 60+ Days | Delinquency Rate | Good/Bad Odds |
|---|---|---|---|---|
| Student Accounts | 342 | 120 | 35% | 1.9 |
| Previous Experience | 65 | 10 | 15% | 5.7 |
| Below 180 | 214 | 79 | 37% | 1.7 |
| 180-199 | 458 | 133 | 29% | 2.4 |
| *200-219 | 1238 | 297 | 24% | 3.2 |
| 220-239 | 2490 | 423 | 17% | 4.9 |
| 240-259 | 2247 | 270 | 12% | 7.3 |
| 260 & Up | 1969 | 98 | 5% | 19.0 |
| Total Scored: | 8616 | 1301 | 15% | 5.6 |

*Indicates cutoff score of 200
Simulated characteristics, attributes, and weights for demonstration purposes only.

tion. We will focus on reports that help measure the performance of the credit score model as opposed to the health of the portfolio. Specifically, we will look at scorecard validity and effectiveness and the tracking of override performance.

*Override Performance Report*  The override performance report provides feedback on the performance of approved accounts that scored below cutoff (low-side overrides). By tracking overrides by score as well as reason you can determine if these accounts are performing better than would normally be expected for accounts in the below cutoff score ranges. In Table 6 we show overrides by both score and reason.

The delinquency rate represents the number of accounts ever delinquent 60+ days divided by the total number of accounts in that score range or override reason. The "good versus bad odds" is the number of good accounts in that score range divided by the number of bad accounts. In the score range just above cutoff (200-219) 941 accounts were never 60+ days past due (defined as good), and 297 accounts were. The good versus bad odds are 941/297=3.2, indicating that there are roughly three good accounts for each bad account in this score range. This corresponds to a delinquency rate of 24 percent, the highest level of incremental risk acceptable based on your cutoff score. A quick way to measure the performance of overrides is to compare their delinquency to accounts scoring just above cutoff. In this example, only accounts with previous experience performed better than accounts just above cutoff. It is important to note the small number of accounts (65) that fell into this category; the observed performance may not be statistically reliable.

*Scorecard Validity*  Federal law requires that credit scoring models be periodically revalidated to ensure that they are statistically valid predictors of applicant risk. Essentially you must demonstrate that higher scoring accounts perform better than lower scoring accounts. For this you must ensure that you have a sufficient number of "bad" accounts, and that all accounts in the development window have been on the books long enough to demonstrate performance. This is typically done by looking at a group of accounts with 6-17 months on the books. Accounts with less than six months on the books typically have not had sufficient time to show performance; including accounts with up to 17 months on the books allows you to view the performance of a full year's worth of accounts and eliminate the effects of seasonality. However, depending on your portfolio, you may need to look at a larger window of accounts.

The actual validation test is applied only to accounts that scored above the cutoff. Any accounts booked that scored below cutoff were approved based on criteria other than score; therefore, their performance is not indicative of the performance of the scorecard. Often, accounts that have ever been 60+ days delinquent are defined as "bad" accounts for the purpose of validation. If an organization has enough accounts that are 90+ days delinquent, this can be used as the definition of a "bad" account. Accounts ever 30+ days delinquent should only be defined as "bad" when not enough accounts have attained a delinquency status of 60+ days past due to produce statistically reliable results.

Scorecard validity can be assessed by looking at the odds versus score curve for accounts in your validation window. By plotting the ln(odds) versus score relationship you can determine whether a scorecard effectively rank orders risk. If the slope of the odds curve is greater than zero (positive slope), then the scorecard does rank order risk. In Figure 12–1, all three lines represent valid scorecards.

## FIGURE 12–1
### Odds Versus Score Relationship

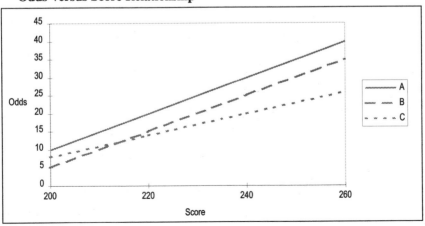

*Scorecard Effectiveness*   You can expect that over time a scoring model will degrade somewhat, losing its ability to effectively rank order applicant risk. This can be demonstrated by looking at the odds curve. Model effectiveness can be measured by the slope of the odds versus score curve. The steeper the slope, the more effectively a score model rank orders applicant risk.

Assume that line A represents the odds versus score line for the development sample, and line B represents the odds versus score line for a recent validation sample. Both lines have the same slope; therefore the effectiveness of the scorecard has not changed. Even though the observed performance for line A is better in every score range, the relative ability of the scorecard to rank order risk is the same. Line C represents a less effective scorecard. The odds versus score line has a lower slope, indicating a decrease in the ability of the scorecard to rank order risk.

A measure called the points to double the odds (PDO) can be used to measure scorecard effectiveness. This statistic indicates the increase in points required for a group of accounts to have twice the odds of another. For example, if accounts with a score of 220 had odds of 20 to 1 and accounts with a score of 260 had odds of 40 to 1, the PDO would be 40. Forty points would be required to double the odds from 20 to 40. The PDO measures how well a scorecard rank orders applicant risk. A low PDO indicates that the scorecard identifies risk very effectively, since small changes in score result in large changes in odds. A higher PDO indicates that the scorecard identifies applicant risk more broadly and therefore is less effective.

## Supplemental Reports

*Portfolio Chronology Log*   The portfolio chronology is a list of events that can affect the portfolio or the performance of the scorecard. Examples of events to include in your chronology log would be installation of new scorecards, modification of cutoff scores or approval strategies, modification of collection or account management policies, expansion of product offerings, or promotional campaigns. By maintaining a portfolio chronology log, you can better identify the causes for observed phenomena that can affect the performance of your portfolio or the profile of your applicant population.

# INTERPRETING REPORTS

Like clockwork at the beginning of each quarter a mountain of paper is delivered to your desk. Your job is to turn this mountain into a concise set of recommendations for action. While there is no magic formula for doing this, here are some general guidelines:

## Identify Objectives

Before you can begin any meaningful analysis, you must first determine what your objectives are. This chapter has focused on evaluating and monitoring credit score models. There may be additional objectives, some of which may seem to be at odds with each other. For example, you may want to increase the number of new loans being made, but also want to keep delinquency under a certain threshold. It is important to keep all your objectives in mind throughout the analysis process. While you may not be able to meet all of your goals, by keeping them all in mind you can meet or come close to as many as possible.

Knowing your objectives will also help you focus on the appropriate reports. If you are attempting to validate your model, start by looking at performance reports. If you are doing a full analysis of overrides, monitor a combination of front-end and back-end reports. As you do your analysis you may need to review additional reports.

## Produce a Set of Reports

To successfully evaluate your credit score model, you need a variety of reports. While each report is useful in isolation, rarely will a single report give you all the information you need to make a sound decision. For example, a population stability report may indicate that recent applicants are scoring higher on average than in the past. While this is important, it does not provide enough information for you to accurately evaluate the model and produce meaningful analyses. What is causing this shift, and how is it affecting your portfolio?

To answer, you would next look at the characteristic analysis reports, which may attribute the increase in average score to an increase in the percentage of homeowners applying for credit. Continuing the investigation, you may be reminded by the portfolio chronology log about a recent campaign to offer loans to existing customers who own their own homes. Lastly, you may want to look at back-end reports to see how these accounts are performing. Only after investigation of several reports, then, would you have sufficient information to make meaningful recommendations.

## Monitor Trends

In reviewing reports, it is often useful to compare current with previous reports to see how things are changing over time and to identify possible problems or potential opportunities. If a possible problem is identified, you gain additional time to make modifications before a serious problem occurs. For example, you may notice a trend of increasing delinquency over the last six months. While the current delinquency levels may still be acceptable, it is important to know that they are rising. By identifying this trend early, you can make appropriate modifications to ensure that your business goals are met. These might include changing your account management practices to work delinquent accounts more aggressively, modifying acquisition practices to attract lower risk applicants, or updating revenue and expense forecasts to reflect the changes seen in the portfolio.

On the other hand, you may notice that delinquency rates for recently booked accounts are lower than for accounts of similar time on books in the past. Further investigation may reveal that recent applicants are scoring higher than in the past due to an increase in the percentage of applicants who own their homes. Armed with this information, you may determine that the current lower delinquencies can be attributed to the increase in the percentage of applicants who are homeowners. As a result, you may expand programs to attract more higher scoring, lower risk applicants.

## SUMMARY

Using a credit risk model without monitoring is like driving without a map. It is difficult to know where you are and, equally important, where you are going. By regularly reviewing a complete set of tracking reports, you obtain the information you need to comply with federal regulations, increase profitability, and forecast more effectively.

Credit risk models are tools designed to help in the decision process of granting credit. Monitoring a credit risk model is essential to maximizing its benefits. Portfolios, populations, policies and economic conditions all change over time; by monitoring your model, you are better able to identify these changes and take appropriate action.

Effective monitoring requires you to look at a variety of reports of both application (front-end) and performance (back-end) data to obtain a complete picture of your portfolio. Individual reports rarely tell the full story, so relationships between reports must also be investigated. While the standard reports discussed in this chapter are extremely useful, you should produce supplemental (custom) reports as necessary to investigate specific phenomena or portions of your portfolio in more detail.

To gain the most benefit from monitoring your model, produce standard reports on a monthly or quarterly basis. When reviewing these standard reports, it is important to identify trends so that you know what to expect in the future. Early identification of trends gives you the time to modify your policies to take advantage of opportunities and minimize potential problems.

## REFERENCES

Rushton, Emory Wayne. *OCC Bulletin* 97-24. May 20, 1997.

Lewis, Edward M. 1992. *An Introduction to Credit Scoring.* Available from Fair, Isaac and Company, Inc.)

# 13

# ISSUES IN MODEL
# DESIGN AND VALIDATION*

**Dennis C. Glennon**
*Risk Analysis Division*
*Office of the Comptroller of the Currency*

## INTRODUCTION

Credit scoring is becoming an integral part of the underwriting and risk-management procedures of many banks. Increased productivity, lower underwriting costs, and consistent application of underwriting guidelines are benefits that make credit scoring an attractive alternative to a judgmental process. The reduction in underwriting costs particularly can be substantial and thus critical, especially for high-volume banks in highly competitive markets.

The downside lies in the uncertainty about model accuracy. This aspect of a credit scoring model (often referred to as a score card)—the primary focus of this chapter—is one of the more important concerns management should have about the safety and soundness of an automated underwriting system.

There are, unfortunately, few hard and fast rules for evaluating the validity of a model. In general, we expect models to be validated (1) when they are developed and implemented, and (2) on an on-going basis to make sure they perform as expected. Although there is no consensus about what constitutes the best modeling approach—banks and vendors may use linear regression, logit regression, discriminant analysis, artificial neural networks, and linear programming to construct scoring models—any model will perform well on the development data. All the modeling methods are designed to find the "best" combination of attributes and attribute weights to predict the performance of the development sample.

This does not insure that the model will perform well out-of-sample. A fundamental assumption about the validity of an empirically derived scoring

---

* The opinions expressed are those of the author and do not necessarily represent those of the
 Office of the Comptroller of the Currency.

model is that the relationship between the credit profiles and performance behavior of future accounts will closely resemble that of past accounts. This condition can be violated for many reasons, not all of which are within the control of the model developer or user. For example, changes in consumer behavior or shifts in market or industry conditions may cause a significant shift in the structural relationship between a consumer's profile and expected performance.

But several factors affecting out-of-sample performance that are within the control of the model developer or user are often overlooked because of limited knowledge, resources, and data. Foremost among these are sample design and model specification,[1] issues arising out of the statistical and mathematical properties of the methods used by modelers.

In this chapter, we take a closer look at the potential impact of some common sample-design and model specification issues. Concern over these issues first surfaced in reaction to the rapid decline in many credit card scoring models since 1993. Although many explanations have been put forth to explain the poor performance of the 1994-96 vintages—changes in bankruptcy laws, lower underwriting standards, poor model management, and a general shift in borrower behavior, to name a few—we believe poor model selection contributed significantly to the decline in portfolio quality.

Below we discuss censored development samples and model mis-specification, and the potential impact they have on performance. Our objective is to illustrate, given the practical problems associated with limited data and delays in measuring actual performance, that better model selection may result in models that are more robust to shocks in the market or changes in a lender's marketing strategies. Though we discuss the issues as they relate to modeling in the pre-approved credit card market, much of the discussion applies to models in markets for other products (e.g., mortgage, small business, auto finance).

## CENSORED SAMPLES

Though the quality of a bank's portfolio depends initially on the quality of the accounts booked, over time it is how the bank manages these accounts (retention, collection, renewals, etc.) that preserves the value of the portfolio. Note that a poor account-selection process, which results in new accounts of significant lower quality, will force a lender to spend more time managing the portfolio to control losses. For small deviations in actual vs. expected per-

---

1 This is clearly true for banks that develop their own models. Banks that buy models may not directly control the methods used to develop samples and specify models. However, through their choice of vendors they indirectly control these factors.

formance defensive strategies to reduce exposure to losses can be effective. Major deviations in performance, however, can swamp the bank's ability to reduce its exposure using account management techniques.

There is, then, a clear incentive to develop or purchase a model that is good at identifying the actuarial risk of *new applicants*. The conventional way to construct a scoring model is first to select a sample of applicants who are believed to represent the characteristics and performance profile of the bank's targeted market. In practice, a sample of recently booked accounts is used to represent the targeted market. Since performance is measured in terms of delinquencies (e.g., 60+ days past due or worse), the sample will include only accounts that have seasoned at least 12 months—possibly longer, depending on the period used to define performance—in order to generate a steady-state representation of the population's performance history.

Under this design, however, the development sample is censored. That is, the sample does not reflect the performance behavior of full applicant pool, but only the performance of applicants who *were approved*. Since the intended purpose of the model is to assess the expected performance of *all* applicants, a model developed on a sample that excludes declined applicants will underestimate the risk quality (the likelihood of becoming delinquent) of an applicant drawn from the full population. Most model builders address this well-known modeling problem[2] using one of several methods of augmenting the sample data with files drawn from the rejected pool of applicants (reject-inference analysis). Although the best approach would be to generate actual performance data that reflects the behavior of the pool of rejected applicants, this approach would be expensive. In practice, many model developers use statistical methods to infer the performance of rejected applicants—an approach that seems adequate currently.[3]

---

2 See G.S. Maddala, *Limited-Dependent and Qualitative Variables in Econometrics* (NY: Cambridge University Press), 1983; W. J. Boyes et al., "An Econometric Analysis of the Bank Credit Scoring Problem," Journal of Econometrics, 40:3-14 (1989); and W.H. Greene, "A Statistic Model for Credit Scoring," NYU Working Paper EC-92-29 (1992).

3 To illustrate the potential impact of using a censored data set, suppose a soft drink company surveying consumers who buy the product at movie theaters and pizza parlors finds that they prefer a sweeter formula. Since movie theaters and pizza parlors attract a disproportionately larger number of young customers relative to the population as a whole (or soft-drink consumers in general), the sample is censored. If, in fact, the soft drink company re-formulates the drink to reflect the survey results, when it markets the new formula drink in grocery stores, cafeterias, and hospitals (where the customers are more likely prefer a less sweet formula — a taste generally associated with older costumers), total sales may fall. If the soft drink company solicits information across a more representative sample of the full market (customers at movie theaters, pizza parlors, grocery stores, restaurants, etc. including those who buy the product often, only occasionally, and never), a more accurate model of consumer behavior would likely emerge. Similarly, if a specific marketing strategy attracts a group of applicants who are not representative of the whole population, building a risk model based on the behavior of this subgroup would not necessarily generalize across other segments of the population.

In addition to the reject-inference issue, other forms of censoring may surface. For example, in the credit card industry low introductory rates are often used to increase response rates to pre-approved solicitations. However, account attrition due to re-pricing within the first year can be quite high. In the mortgage industry, interest rate cycles have increased the frequency of re-financing—a result that decreases the percentage of accounts that maintain a relationship over the full performance period. If the development sample includes only those accounts that remain active during the origination and performance period (perhaps 12 to 24 months for credit cards and 4 to 5 years for mortgages), a large early-attrition rate—a form of censoring—is likely to skew the results of the model. This is more likely if the underlying relationship between performance and an applicant's credit profile differs across accounts that attrite and those that do not.

A potentially serious censoring problem may exist in pre-approved lending markets, where response rates are generally below 3 percent of the solicited population and response rates below 1.5 percent are not uncommon. Moreover, response rates tend to be sensitive to pricing and terms-of-credit strategies. A given marketing strategy may, depending on industry and market conditions, increase the response rate by 50-100 percent. Risk models developed using accounts booked under a different marketing environment are likely to perform poorly in evaluating the performance of a more recent targeted population.

We illustrate this concept more formally, and discuss the potential impact on model performance, using the example illustrated in Figures 13–1 and 13–2. If the areas of the outer circles represent the relative size of the pool for each type of applicant (good and bad) and the inner circles represent applicants with a specific mix of performance characteristics, then within the population (the larger circles), the area (combining shaded and unshaded areas) of the "good" applicants is about four times larger than that of the bad. This implies that there are about four good accounts for every bad account in the population as a whole — though this information is unknown to the lender. Let the vertical line that cuts the circles represent a credit score cutoff derived from an analysis of the full population. The cutoff line partitions the population of good and bad accounts into two groups of applicants based on their credit profile. The applicants to the right of the cutoff line are identified by the model as high-risk borrowers and those to the left as low-risk with scores that reflect risk outside (right) or within (left) the limits of the bank's tolerance for risk. Applicants in shaded areas would be declined under the population-based model cutoff.

Because we assumed that population-based credit score accurately ranks risk over the full population, the percentage of good applicants that

## FIGURE 13–1

**Selection Bias**

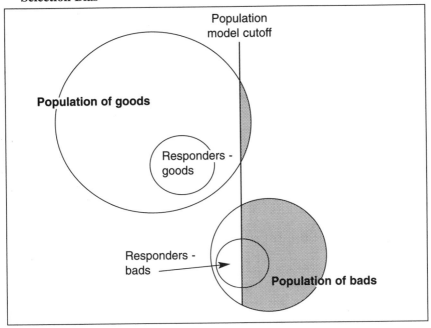

## FIGURE 13–2

**Selection Bias**

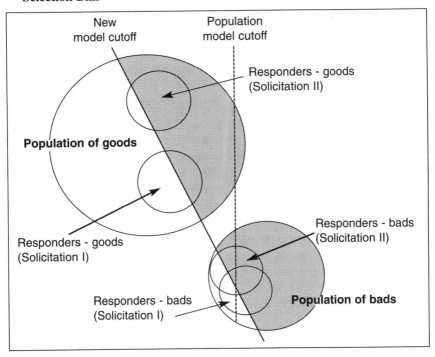

are excluded based on low credit scores is small (the small shaded area in the goods circle), and the percentage of bad applicants excluded is relatively large (the shaded area in the bads circle). Thus, the number of good applicants booked, based on the information content of the credit score only, would be roughly 10 for every 1 bad applicant approved if the response rate was 100 percent and credit scores are accurate measures of risk. The credit score in this example clearly leads to an improvement in the quality of the bank's portfolio over a naive rule of approving all applicants—the goods to bad ratio increases from about 4 to 1 with no scoring (i.e., the population odds) to 10 to 1 when the credit score cutoff rule is used).

If, however, the marketing strategy chosen results in less than a 100 percent response rate, say a rate in the 10 percent range (as reflected by the area of the smaller circles within the population circles in Figure 13–1), the performance distribution of the applicants is likely to be quite different. The smaller circles represent subsets of the population that have, as a group, different performance characteristics than the population as a whole.[4] This is reflected in the distribution of bad applicants above the population-based scorecard cutoff in the sample. For example, in Figure 13–1, there is roughly one bad with a score above the cutoff for every three below (i.e., a 1:3 ratio of unshaded to shaded area inside the bads circle) in the full population-of-bads. However, the distribution of bads for responders (as reflected by the smaller circle inside the population-of-bads circle in Figure 13–1) suggests there is roughly one bad above the cutoff for every one bad below (i.e., a 1:1 ratio of unshaded to shaded area in the response bads circle).

In addition, because there are relatively few accounts from the larger population of good applicants responding, the actual number of good applicants booked relative to bad accounts is much lower than the 10:1 ratio for the population. In fact, it appears to be closer to 2 goods for every 1 bad. The large decrease in the relative areas of the "booked" good and bad applicants from those that responded to the mailing (from 10:1 to 2:1) illustrates how censoring due to small response rates can influence the performance distribution.

The potential impact is even greater if a bank uses only the data from responders to previous solicitations to develop its risk model (i.e., the smaller circles) instead of the entire population (i.e., the larger circles). In general, the various methods used to develop the model would generate adequate performance statistics. The models would successfully partition

---

4 Under this construct, we would represent a sub-group of responders with the same performance characteristics as the population using a less dense, but similarly sized, circle. The difference in performance characteristics between the responders' sub-population and the population as a whole is reflected in the size and location of the smaller circle within the larger, suggesting that the smaller groups are not representative of the full population.

the development sample into separate credit-quality groups. Based on the characteristics of these groups, a cutoff score could be used to grant credit to the first group, and deny credit to the second. In this way, the overall odds of good accounts to bad should rise.

Suppose we assume a scoring model developed using the responders in Figure 13–1 (responders to solicitation I; the smaller circles in Figure 13–1) is represented by the "new model cutoff" line in Figure 13–2. The improvement in the ability of the new model to accurately predict the performance of the responders' data (i.e., using data from the responders, solicitation I, sample only, not the population) is reflected in the new cutoff line that partitions both the good and bad responders, so that the odds of good to bad increase from the 2:1 ratio observed in Figure 13–1 to roughly 3:1.

If a bank maintains the same pricing and marketing strategies over time, and lending terms in the industry are relatively constant, the profile of responders is likely to remain stable over time. The actual performance of more recent solicitation campaigns would likely rise to the 3:1 reflected by the new model cutoff line. If, however, there is a change in either marketing strategy or behavior of competitors that results in a different sub-sample of the population responding (e.g., the responders circles labeled solicitation II in Figure 13–2), actual performance will likely differ significantly from expected levels. In this example the ratio of actual goods to actual bads would be far lower (roughly 1:1 as reflected by the ratio of the unshaded areas of the circles for good and bad responders goods to solicitation II) than the expected 3:1 ratio. Had the bank maintained the original cutoff score— the vertical, dashed line—based on the population distributions (and thus reflecting the potential behavior of both responders and non-responders), the ratio of actual goods to bads would have been much higher, around 2:1, since a much larger number of good accounts that responded to the second solicitation were rejected under the new cutoff rule than bad accounts.

This example illustrates that developing a model on a censored sample (responders only) may lead to one that is more likely to perform poorly during periods of rapid changes in the market.[5] From a modeling perspective, developing a model that incorporates the potential behavior of non-responders with that of actual responders is a more desirable strategy under these circumstances.

Developing a model that is based on a sample of the full population is difficult, however. The biggest impediment is the lack of data on the larger segment of the market made up of non-responders. A number of statistical and

---

5 The Venn-diagram-based argument is a nice pedagogic device, but the outcomes depend on where the circles are placed. In Figures 13–1 and 13–2, the circles are strategically placed to emphasize the potential problem.

econometrics techniques have been developed specifically to address the problem of censored samples by introducing information on the censored data into the model. An alternative approach would be to build a research data base made up of a representative group of applicants from the full population. The population data set could then be used to define a broader scoring model that should be, on average, more robust to shifts in the market.

The issues that emerge from a censored development sample are often misunderstood due to the apparent modeling paradox that it creates. Conventional model-building techniques rely on goodness-of-fit measures to identify the "best" model. A model developed on a censored data set is likely to fit the censored data better than a model developed on a broader set of data that reflects the full population. The model developed on the censored sample is likely to capture more of the idiosyncratic behavior of development sample data and therefore appear to be a better model.

However, the objective of the modeling process is not to fit the performance of *past accounts* but to predict the expected performance of *future applicants*. Past performance is useful only insofar as it represents future behavior. The factor that is most influential in determining the "goodness-of-fit" of a model developed on the censored data—capturing idiosyncratic behavior—is likely to lead to its ruin as a predictor of risk.

Although a model developed on a censored data set should outperform a model generated on the full population in fitting performance of the censored data, a model developed on the population data will be more robust to shifts in the market or marketing strategies that attract applicants from different segments of the population. This conclusion suggests that a model-replacement policy in which a bank modifies or redevelops its models before each solicitation is an ineffective strategy to combat the shift in the population. A more effective strategy would begin with models that reflect the population, not just the idiosyncratic behavior of a sub-sample of the population.

## MODEL MIS-SPECIFICATION

Designing a sample that reflects the full population of the targeted market is only the first step in generating a scoring model that is robust to shifts in the market or marketing strategies.[6] The next step in the modeling process is to identify factors that both are closely correlated with performance and *maintain a stable relationship with the performance meas-*

---

6 Models developed on poorly designed samples may still perform well over time if the market is stable. However, stability is observed after the fact (i.e., an ex post concept); a model must be used in an environment in which information on the future stability of the market is unknown (ex ante). For this reason, sample design issues should be explicitly addressed instead of relying on luck.

*ure over time.* The former condition is relatively easy to satisfy; the latter is not.[7] Moreover, the method used to satisfy the former may make it harder to fulfill the latter.

Though several of the data search (or reduction) methods discussed in the statistics literature are useful in identifying factors that are highly correlated with performance, stepwise regression analysis is the most common technique. This approach performs a sequence of regressions, adding or deleting factors based on the relative statistical significance of the factors that enter into each regression.[8] An F-test of the hypothesis that the factor weight is zero is used as the inclusion criterion. For each regression the F-statistic:

$$F_i = [\frac{b_i}{s(b_i)}]^2 = t^2 \tag{1}$$

is generated. The factors with the largest F-statistics (that also exceed a minimum, predetermined critical level) are candidates for inclusion in the model.

This approach is not, however, without its critics.[9] Foremost among the criticisms is the inflated risk of overfitting the sample data.

There is, however, an additional concern that the diagnostic statistics used to identify the "best" model specification may also be distorted by the correlation among the factors. This problem involves the overstatement of the statistical significance of some included variables that, in fact, may have no predictive power in their own right. The estimation procedure may inadvertently identify a spurious statistical relationship between an included variable and performance that will not hold out-of-sample.

To illustrate, let y represent the performance variable (i.e., good/bad), and x, w, and z represent factors that define the profile of the applicant pool. Suppose the correct, but unknown, model is:

$$y = \pi_0 + \pi_1 x + \pi_2 w + \varepsilon_{y|xw}. \tag{2}$$

where the $\pi i$'s are factor weights and $\varepsilon_{y|xw}$ is an error term with $E(\varepsilon^2_{y|xw}) = \sigma^2 I$. The factor z is, by design, assumed to be unrelated to

---

7 It is common for modelers to focus exclusively on the issue of correlation. Datamining methods are used to find the specification that fits the data "best." If the "stable relationship" condition is not addressed, the resulting model is likely to "overfit" the sample data by reflecting idiosyncratic behavior in the data. This form of model mis-specification will result in poor out-of-sample performance. The difficulty in satisfying the stability condition is due (once again) to the uncertainty of the future relationship between performance and applicants' characteristics profiles.

8 See J. Neter and N. Wasserman, *Applied Linear Statistical Model* (Homewood, IL: Richard D. Irwin, Inc., 1974).

9 See S. Derksen and J.H. Keselman, "Backward, Forward, and Stepwise Automated Subset Selection Algorithms: Frequency of Obtaining Authentic and Noise Variables," *British Journal of Mathematical and Statistical Psychology,* 45:265-82 (1992).

y. Suppose, also, that the modelers are sure that x should be included in the model, but because the true model is unknown, they are not sure that z should be included. Using stepwise regression, the modelers would specify the following model

$$y = \gamma_0 + \gamma_1 x + \gamma_2 z + \varepsilon_{y|xw}, \tag{3}$$

and then test the hypothesis that the coefficient on z is zero (i.e., $H_0$: $\gamma_2 = 0$). Note, however, that by design, equation (3) incorrectly excludes w and incorrectly includes z. Based on the relationship between the F- and t-statistics in equation (1), a t-test of the hypothesis $H_0$: $\gamma_2 = 0$ can be used. By design, we should find $t_{\gamma_2} < t_c$ — the predetermined critical value — and conclude that, based on the data, z is in fact statistically unrelated to y.

However, it can be shown using equations (2) and (3) that the expression for the t-statistic used to test the null hypothesis that $\gamma_2 = 0$ can be written as

$$t_{\gamma_2} = \frac{\sum_t (y_t - \gamma_1 x_t)\, z}{s(\sum_t \rho^2_t\, (z|x))^{1/2}}$$

where s is the standard error from the regression of equation (3) and $\rho_t$ is the $t^{th}$ residual from the regression of z on x and a constant term (see MacKinnon, 1992). The interesting feature of this statistic is that, when the true model is given in equation (2), the numerator will be non-zero when $\pi_2$ is non-zero and the residuals from the regression of w on x are asymptotically correlated with z. Moreover, the denominator tends to zero as the number of observations increases. Since credit bureau data (x, w, and z in this example) are likely to be correlated—especially if the data are pre-tested to identify variables that are correlated with y—and the number of observations used in developing a scoring model is quite large, it is possible that the t-statistic $t_{\gamma_2}$ will exceed any pre-specified critical level. Hence the hypothesis that $\gamma_2 = 0$ is rejected even though z should not be included in the model. In this case, the data reduction technique itself produces a mis-specified model.

These results demonstrate that data-reduction methods that allow the data to find the "best" model may in fact generate poorly specified *prediction* models, though the model will appear to perform well on the *development* sample. The mis-specification will surely reduce the effectiveness of the model on the targeted population—future applicants.

These results suggest that the choice of model specification should be based on more than the results of a stepwise regression or other method of searching through the data for the "best" fit. Instead, modelers should use their product-, market-, and industry-specific knowledge to define broad underwriting categories to guide the selection of factors to include in the model. In addition, they might also use a selection process to choose among specific factors that fall within the same broad categories.

Model mis-specification may also result from data limitation problems. For example, the debt-to-income ratio of the borrower is often used as an indicator of ability to pay—higher ratios would tend to reflect weaker credit. Until recently, it was common for lenders to discard (or fail to retrieve from the credit report) data on total debt. Risk models were developed omitting information on debt coverage ratios.[10] The models were developed on a partial list of factors known to be predictive of performance and therefore systematically omitted factors that are conceptually related to performance. Omitting such factors will bias the estimates of the factor weights, the direction and magnitude of the bias depending on the correlation among the factors.

To illustrate, if we assume again that the true specification is given in equation (2) then

$$y = \pi_0 + \pi_1 x + \pi_2 w + \varepsilon_{y|xw}. \tag{4}$$

If the model is mistakenly specified as

$$y = \alpha_0 + \alpha_1 x + \varepsilon_{y|x} \tag{5}$$

then $\alpha_1 = \pi_1$ (an unbiased estimator) if x and w are uncorrelated. That is, if in the regression

$$w = \delta_0 + \delta_1 x + \varepsilon_{w|x}, \tag{6}$$

$\delta_1 = 0$. If x and w are correlated (i.e., $\delta_1 \neq 0$) then equation (4) can be rewritten using equation (6):

$$y = \pi_0 + \pi_1 x + \pi_2(\delta_0 + \delta_1 x) + \varepsilon_{y|x,w}$$
$$= (\pi_0 + \pi_2 \delta_0) + (\pi_1 + \pi_2 \delta_1) x + \varepsilon_{y|x,w} \tag{7}$$

From equations (5) and (7), it is easy to show that the parameter estimates from the regression of equation (5) are $\alpha_0 = \pi_0 + \pi_2 \delta_0$ and $\alpha_1 = \pi_1 + \pi_2 \delta_1$.[11] The omitted variable bias is reflected in the second term on the

---

10 The common argument then was that the informational content of the debt ratios was captured implicitly through correlation with other included factors.

11 See E. E. Leamer, "False Models and Post-Data Model Construction," *Journal of the American Statistical Association,* 69: (1974).

right hand side of equation (7) for $\alpha_1$ (i.e., $\pi_2\delta_1$). The direction and magnitude depends on the sign and size of both $\pi_2$ and $\delta_1$. Since $\delta_1$ is a measure of the correlation between x and w, the stronger the correlation, the larger the impact. Moreover, the bias is positive if $\pi_2$ and $\delta_1$ are of the same sign (i.e., either both positive or both negative).

The relationship between $\alpha_2$ in equation (5) and $(\pi_0 + \pi_2\delta_0)$ in equation (7) also shows that if the relationships between x and y and between x and w are stable (i.e., that $\delta_{1,t} = \delta_{1,t+i}$ for all i; i = 1,2,...) then the misspecified model - equation (6) - will perform well relative to the development sample over time (t). However, if changes in the market disproportionately affect the excluded variable, w, equation (5) will fail to accurately capture these changes; model accuracy will deteriorate. The deterioration in model performance could be especially great if the relationship between the included and excluded factors implicit in the model's factor weights (i.e., $\delta_{1,t} \neq \delta_{1,t+i}$) is no longer valid; equation (6) will fail to be robust to shifts in the market.

While the issue of omitted variable bias is always present in empirical analysis, it is especially worrisome in credit scoring given the pervasive problems of incomplete data on borrowers' financial status, competitors' strategies, and shifts in market/industry conditions over the business cycle. Validation analyses at the time of model implementation can be useful in identifying potentially harmful omitted variable problems. In-sample validation analysis on the development and hold-out sample is useful in identifying models that overfitted the development data. Out-of-sample validation analysis (on data generated in periods other than that used for the development sample) is especially useful in identifying the potential effects of changes in omitted variables on model performance. These analyses, combined with a process of selecting factors using a hierarchical evaluation procedure provides the best protection against omitted variable bias.

Although there is no guarantee this approach will generate stable models, this broad method of developing and validating the model at time of implementation is more likely to produce models that are robust to changes in the market or marketing strategies over time than is simple stepwise regression. Even the best specified model is susceptible to shifts in the behavior of borrowers and competitors. For this reason, users must continue to monitor and track their models for shifts that undermine model performance and to manage their models to maintain the overall quality of their portfolio.

## ISSUES IN MODEL VALIDATION

The previous discussion may have given the impression that with vigilance modeling error can be completely eliminated. This is not true; all

## TABLE 13-1

### Validation Reports

- Population Stability Report
- Characteristics Analysis Report
- Final Score Report
- Delinquency Distribution Report
  - Ever Delinquent
  - Currently Delinquent
  - Vintage Analysis Table
- Portfolio Chronology Log

models will have prediction errors. In fact, forecast errors can sometimes be large even if the model performs well on all diagnostic tests at time of development. However, if the model is correctly specified, the errors are likely to average out over large samples—a very useful result when developing models in which accurate performance data is not available for up to 18 months after loan origination.

It is common for users to rely on their ability to manage their models over time to maintain accuracy and reliability. This involves identifying shifts in the data over time and applying new criteria (e.g., cutoff values) or modifying existing models to counter deterioration. In this section, we discuss several potential issues that arise in post-implementation validation analysis.

There is no single report or set of reports that determines the overall reliability of a score card over time. The monitoring analyses recommended by vendors are designed to provide the user with a tool-box of diagnostic reports to determine if a model is performing as *expected* (irrespective of the user's tolerance for risk). However, because of the rather long period—12 to 18 months or longer—required before accurate statistics on performance are available, the monitoring reports are designed to provide early warning of possible shifts in both the population and trends in behavior that may reflect poor model performance (see Table 1 for list of recommended reports). It is difficult to interpret the results summarized in these reports because it is not always clear that a shift in, say, the population or the delinquency distribution reflects random variation around stable values, or permanent deterioration in the model. If those reports are generated on a regular schedule, however, they provide a history from which trends can be analyzed—an accumulation of information that can be evaluated to determine if the changes are temporary or permanent.[12]

---

12 Ad hoc reports are likely to provide similar information; however, by their very nature of being ad hoc, they lose or leave to chance "early-warning" benefits. Except for sudden, large shocks in the market or shifts in the population, deterioration in a score card will not be observed until the accounts mature—a problem made worse during periods of rapid growth when the portfolio is dominated by unseasoned accounts that have yet to reveal their true performance. Thus, an ad hoc approach ignores loss of reliability due to a slow but steady shift in consumers' behavior.

In addition to trend analysis a model should be back-tested periodically to determine its ability to predict performance under more recent market and industry conditions. Back-testing—the comparison of expected performance (as predicted by the model using current information) to actual performance after accounts have seasoned beyond the model's performance window—is a way to test the continuing accuracy and stability of a model. This approach is similar to a vintage or delinquency distribution analysis. However, a vintage analysis evaluates the performance of booked accounts by scores generated at time of origination. In contrast, a back-testing method would evaluate performance by scores generated on current information. This type of validation analysis increases the likelihood of identifying shifts in the market that adversely affect model performance.[13]

Back-testing also may be less sensitive to account attrition, an event that may skew the results of conventional delinquency and vintage analyses. Account attrition in some portfolios may reach levels of 30 to 40 percent within 18 months of origination, especially on accounts solicited under a relatively low introductory rate. Depending on the nature of the attrition, performance statistics alone (e.g., delinquency or loss distributions) may lead to spurious conclusions about the ability of the model to accurately predict absolute losses.

For example, if attrition is relatively low and spread evenly across good and bad accounts, the distribution of losses over score ranges will not be affected. That is, the actual performance of the portfolio would most likely correspond to expectations. However, if the attrition is the result of, say, changes in competitive offers that disproportionately targeted better-quality accounts, the higher attrition rates could mask a larger than expected runoff of *good* accounts. Though the model may still be valid, the observed performance, which reflects the actuarial behavior of the attrition-adjusted pool of accounts, is likely to be much different (and possibly worse) than expected. Thus, during periods of high attrition, it would be difficult to determine if deterioration in the quality of a portfolio is the result of degradation in the model or of poor retention/account management strategies. Back-testing would be useful in differentiating a shift in quality due to model deterioration or shifts in the quality of accounts due to attrition.

---

13 A corresponding test should be used when several score cards are used together in a "dual-card" system; however, the analysis should be modified to compare predicted and actual performance by joint score ranges (sometimes referred to as score cells). Though independent test of each model may confirm the reliability of each, validity of the joint decision model should be assessed based on a statistically-valid joint analysis.

Because the issues surrounding account attrition on model development and validation are still unresolved, it is unclear how attrition should be treated. Only through additional research will we better understand what, if anything, should be done to improve our modeling techniques to address these issues.

# CONCLUSION

Modeling and validation issues that could affect the ability of scoring models to predict performance out-of-sample are often overlooked by modelers, who concentrate their efforts on generating the "best" model on the development sample. Given that future conditions will almost surely differ from those of the development sample, models should be developed using techniques that improve their chances of performing well even during periods of moderate change in market conditions or marketing strategies.

# REFERENCES

Boyes, W.J., D.L. Hoffman, and S.A. Low. 1989. "An Econometric Analysis of the Bank Credit Scoring Problem," Journal of Econometrics, Vol. 40, pp. 3-14.

Derksen, S..and H.J. Keselman. 1992. "Backward, Forward and Stepwise Automated Subset Selection Algorithms: Frequency of Obtaining Authentic and Noise Variables," British Journal of Mathematical and Statistical Psychology, Vol. 45, pp. 265-82.

Greene, W.H. 1992. "A Statistical Model for Credit Scoring." NYU Working Paper, EC-92-29.

Henderson, H.V., and P.F. Velleman. 1981. "Building Multiple Regression Models Interactively," Biometrics, Vol. 37, pp. 391-411.

Leamer, E. E. 1974. "False Models and Post-Data Model Construction," Journal of the American Statistical Association. Vol. 69, pp. 122–31.

Maddala, G. S. 1983. Limited-Dependent and Qualitative Variables in Econometrics. New York: Cambridge University Press.

MacKinnon, J. G. 1992. "Model Specification Tests and Artificial Regression," Journal of Economic Literature, Vol. 30, pp. 102-45.

Neter, J., and W. Wasserman. 1974. Applied Linear Statistical Model. Homewood, IL: Richard D. Irwin, Inc.

# 14

# A SYSTEMATIC APPROACH FOR MANAGING CREDIT SCORE OVERRIDES

**Balvinder S. Sangha**
*Senior Economist*
*Ernst & Young LLP*

## INTRODUCTION

Credit scoring models provide an efficient way to automate and expedite the underwriting of loans without jeopardizing the bank's credit standards and portfolio quality. Scoring models are based on the premise that historical indicators of consumer credit behavior will continue to be predictive in the future, and that these historical factors have been identified by a valid statistically rigorous process (scorecard development). The factors used in the scorecard typically include loan and borrower attributes. By rank-ordering borrowers by risk, credit scoring models are an efficient tool for banks to process loan applications, price approved loans, set credit line limits and manage the on-going portfolio risk of booked loans consistently and objectively.

Banks can maximize the benefits of using a scorecard by establishing clear scorecard policies and procedures, and developing adequate management information systems support to monitor scorecard usage. A well-specified and monitored override strategy can provide benefits beyond the statistical predictive ability of the scorecard. Some implementation issues such as establishing score cut-offs, validation reports, etc. are discussed in other chapters of this book. This chapter focuses on managing scorecard usage to increase volume, reduce default risk, and increase portfolio profitability, without increasing the credit and fair lending risk exposure of the bank.

Specifically, the chapter discusses operational issues relating to effective management of credit score overrides. It explains credit score over-

## FIGURE 14-1
### Override Frequency by Credit Score

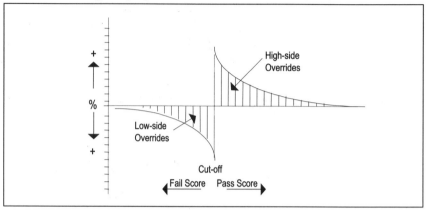

rides, identifies the implications of overrides on credit quality and fair lending, discusses best practices in development of policies and procedures and requirements for storing override data. Finally, it presents a framework for systematically monitoring how override policy is applied. A short appendix illustrates the development of risk-based pricing.

## CREDIT SCORE OVERRIDES
### Underwriting Overrides

Adopting a scoring system reduces the need for judgmental assessment in making credit decisions. However as a practical matter, some risk assessment decisions in the lending environment will be contrary to the scorecard recommendation. For the application scorecard, these "overrides" of the scorecard can be classified as high-side and low-side overrides. The high-side overrides represent a decision to deny the loan although the scorecard recommends approval, and the low-side overrides represent a judgmental decision to approve scorecard recommended denials.

Figure 14-1 shows the pattern of high-side and low-side overrides by credit score in a typical scorecard lending environment. The heaviest concentration of high-sides (judgmental denials) is above and close to the score cut-off, while the incidence of low-side overrides is below and close to the score cut-off. These override patterns in the use of scorecards reflect the judgmental evaluation of marginal applicants by underwriters for adverse credit on compensating factors not incorporated in the scorecard.

Although most credit score model users and developers agree on an intuitive definition of what constitutes an override, analysts differ about how to measure override rates. One way to measure the rate over a given period is simply the ratio of overrides (both high-side and low-side) over total applicants. This aggregate measure is useful in understanding the proportion of judgmental versus automated underwriting decisions. However, this definition does not distinguish between the two override types. Their incidence can be better analyzed by using the following definitions:

- **High-side override rate**  Ratio of denied applicants with a passing score to total number of applicants with a passing score.
- **Low-side override rate**  Ratio of approved applicants with a failing score to total number of applicants with a failing score.

Rather than evaluating all applicants, these definitions measure the override incidence relative only to those applicants who could potentially have been overridden.

The definition of override rates may also get blurred by variations in the actual implementation of scorecards such as borrower or policy dependant cut-offs. Instead of a specific cut-off threshold for distinguishing between approvals and denials, some banks use a score range to identify loans requiring judgmental review. For example, loan applications with scores between 175 and 195 may require additional underwriter review before a decision can be made. Clearly any approvals scoring below the lower bound of this range should be classified as low-side overrides, and similarly denials above the upper bound of this range should be classified as high-side overrides. However, it is not clear how the loans identified for judgmental review should be categorized.

Other banks use a third category to evaluate the credit risk implications of this group of applicants separately, while still others use the top of the cut-off range and classify any approvals falling below it as low-side overrides.[1] In any case, it is important that banks develop a consistent policy in defining overrides, with the flexibility to evaluate loans falling in the judgmental review range in multiple ways for regulatory and credit risk evaluation purposes.

In order to extend credit to under-served markets in accordance with the intent of the Community Reinvestment Act (CRA), some banks offer a lower cut-off for low-income applicants. For example, a bank may require all applicants to have credit scores in excess of 195 for approval, but allow a threshold of 175 for low-income applicants. In developing such policies, it is imperative that bank management consider the implications of decisions on override definitions, as well as their impact on credit quality of the portfolio. From a credit quality perspective, it is recommended that in this situation the score cut-off of 195 be used for defining overrides with a sep-

---

1 OCC guidelines recommend that the upper bound of the range be used as the cut-off for defining overrides (see OCC Bulletin No. OCC 97-24 Credit Scoring Models — Examination Guidance, *Appendix, Safety and Soundness and Compliance Issues on Credit Scoring Models*).

arate low-side override code for identifying low-income applicants that scored below this cut-off but were approved. A separate override code would also help the bank track applicants benefiting from this CRA policy.

These cases also illustrate why banks authorize overrides in the first place. There are two primary reasons for instituting an override policy:

1.  To further the bank's stated policies on credit extension. These may include restrictions such as not making loans on collateral located outside the bank's lending territory (high-side), or a liberalized cut-off for under-served markets for CRA purposes (low-side). These *policy overrides* must be applied consistently across all applicants. Most banks allow flexibility in the application of policy overrides (i.e., permit override of an override) under certain circumstances; such files are classified as *policy exceptions.*

2.  To use additional information to "improve" upon the scorecard-recommended decision. Most scorecards use a limited number of variables, found to be statistically predictive during model development, to compute the score. Critical underwriting factors may not have been included in the scorecard because of a statistically limited number of files with that attribute. For example, the scorecard may group all applicants with three or more major derogatories into one category and assign them the same score because few, if any, applicants in the developmental sample had more than three derogatories. Therefore, the scorecard will fail to distinguish between an applicant with ten major derogatories who presents a greater credit risk to the bank than an applicant with only three. If an applicant with ten derogatories were to pass the score (although this is unlikely because of correlation across negative credit factors), a high-side denial override indicating severe credit history is appropriate. These *informational overrides* are based on additional information used to improve the lending system. However, care should be exercised in authorizing the use of specific informational overrides because some factors may be indirectly included in the scorecard, causing double-counting of that attribute.

## Pricing Overrides

Another aspect of overrides that is often overlooked by bank management is the impact of pricing overrides in a risk-based pricing environment. As banks begin to use credit scoring models to determine the appropriate risk-based or tiered pricing, they need to consider the implications of pricing overrides on portfolio valuation. In order to appreciate their impact, it is instructive to examine the theory and application of risk-based or tiered pricing.

## TABLE 14-1
### Anybank Risk-Based Pricing Matrix

| Recommended Rates based on Credit Score, Debt Capacity, and Loan-to-value | | | | | | | | |
|---|---|---|---|---|---|---|---|---|
| Region: East | | | | Effective dates: 1/1/97 to 1/31/97 | | | | |
| DI -> | 35 | 35 | 35 | 45 | 45 | 45 | 45+ | 45+ | 45+ |
| LTV -> | 80 | 90 | 95 | 80 | 90 | 95 | 80 | 90 | 95 |
| Score | | | | | | | | |
| 190-200 | 9.25 | 9.50 | 9.65 | 9.80 | 10.00 | 10.30 | 11.00 | 11.75 | 12.80 |
| 201-225 | 8.75 | 9.00 | 9.25 | 9.50 | 9.75 | 10.00 | 10.75 | 11.50 | 12.00 |
| 226-250 | 8.50 | 8.65 | 8.80 | 9.50 | 9.65 | 9.80 | 10.00 | 10.25 | 10.50 |
| 251-275 | 7.50 | 7.65 | 7.80 | 8.25 | 8.40 | 8.55 | 9.00 | 9.15 | 9.30 |
| 276 + | 7.00 | 7.15 | 7.30 | 7.50 | 7.65 | 7.80 | 8.00 | 8.15 | 8.30 |

In the most general sense, risk-based pricing entails a higher price for higher-risk borrowers and a lower price for lower-risk borrowers. For example, higher LTV borrowers represent a higher risk for the lender relative to lower LTV borrowers; in a risk-based pricing framework, these borrowers should pay a premium over the price charged to low LTV borrowers. Most financial institutions deploying a tiered pricing structure rely primarily on the applicant credit score to determine pricing premiums to offset the additional risk borne by the lender. The appendix to this chapter presents an analytical framework that can be used to determine appropriate pricing premiums.

Tiered pricing guidelines are based on profitability and marketing analyses that consider the marginal cost and revenue estimates by groups. As lenders become more sophisticated in their use of risk-based pricing systems, they can retain their best customers by offering them competitive prices while accurately estimating the value of their portfolio. The cross-subsidization implied in the traditional pricing approach requires low-risk borrowers to subsidize the loan costs of high-risk borrowers. This practice is increasingly being phased-out as borrowers become more cost conscious and banks compete on loan pricing to increase their market share.

Table 14-1 shows a typical risk-based pricing structure driven by applicant and loan attributes for AnyBank, USA.

The table shows hypothetical loan interest rates by credit score, loan-to-value, and debt-to-income ratio offered by a lender during January 1997. The loan prices range from a low of 7 percent for the lowest-risk borrower to 12.8 percent for a high risk applicant.

Because the pricing discipline in a risk-based system can be undermined by lending officer overrides, it is important for senior management to develop a pricing override monitoring system to protect portfolio profitability. Pricing overrides may lower the actual price relative to the recommended price *(below-par override)* or increase it above the recommended rate *(above-par override)*. An additional dimension of pricing overrides is the magnitude of deviation of the actual price from recommended price. Like underwriting overrides, pricing overrides can be classified as:

1. *Policy overrides* that represent a higher or lower price than the price bank policy would recommend for borrowers with certain attributes. For example, lending officers may have the authority to offer a below-par override amounting to a 25 basis point reduction for existing bank customers, or assign an above-par pricing override of 50 basis points for customers requesting loan maturity beyond bank guidelines.

2. *Informational overrides* represent deviations from the recommended prices using information available to the lending officer but not specifically considered in the risk-based pricing structure. It is not possible to provide pricing guidance for all possible combinations of borrower attributes; some judgment is necessary in determining appropriate loan price using information available to the loan officer. For example, the pricing grid may recommend the same interest rate for all applicants with debt-to-income ratio in excess of 50 percent, not differentiating between those with a debt ratio of 52 percent and those with a debt ratio above 70 percent. A loan officer might require an above-par pricing override for a borrower with the significantly higher debt ratio because of the additional risk to the bank.

## IMPLICATIONS OF OVERRIDES

Credit scoring gives lenders an objective and powerful set of tools for making credit extension, pricing, and risk management decisions. However, subjective overrides of the credit scoring system can have severe negative credit quality, profitability, and regulatory compliance implications for the lender.

Bank management may use the estimated good to bads ratio by score intervals and points to double odds (PDO) to develop a credit risk strategy using a credit scoring model. The approval and credit line extension cut-offs are set to reflect the product risk tolerance established by senior bank management. The product-by-product credit risk tolerance levels in turn form the building blocks for the enterprise-wide credit risk management strategy. In this lending environment, unmonitored scorecard model overrides can undermine the assumptions on which the bank's risk management strategy is built. A higher than expected rate of low-side over-

**FIGURE  14–2**

**Override Frequency by Credit Score**

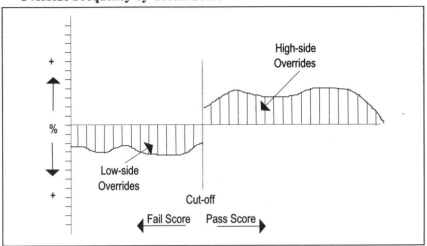

rides indicates a significant drop in the expected portfolio credit quality. How the overrides are distributed is equally important.

Figure 14-2 shows the possible consequences of lack of discipline in the use of override codes. The override distribution suggests a more random pattern in assignment of overrides than those in Figure 14–1. Instead of low-side and high-side overrides concentrated around the score cut-off, the figure shows an almost uniform distribution of overrides across all score intervals. Unless these overrides are a result of bank policies that affect borrowers at all credit score levels, this pattern suggests a significant number of subjective risk assessment decisions made contrary to model recommendations not only around the cut-off but uniformly across all scores. By approving loans significantly below the cut-off, these overrides may have significantly eroded the credit quality of the portfolio. Similarly, by not approving loans for high-scoring applicants, the portfolio mix of borrowers is skewed towards applicants who have been demonstrated by the scoring model to generate higher risk for the bank.

Pricing overrides can similarly impact expected portfolio profitability if they systematically reduce expected yield. A combination of unfettered underwriting and pricing overrides can significantly reduce the advantages offered by the scoring system. For example, a combination of low-side overrides with below-par pricing for the same borrowers implies that: (a) loans are made to unqualified borrowers, and (b) those borrowers are paying a lower price relative to their risk characteristics. Table 14–2 illustrates the significance of pricing overrides on portfolio returns for AnyBank, USA.

## TABLE 14–2
**Impact of Pricing Overrides on ROA of a Risk-Based Priced Portfolio for AnyBanks Loans Booked during 1st Quarter, 1997**

| Pricing | Number | Amount (000's) | Pricing Impact in Basis Points[1] |
|---|---|---|---|
| On-par (risk-based) | 6,782 | 33,900 | - |
| Below-par overrides | 4,165 | 33,200 | (0.40) |
| Above-par overrides | 593 | 2,075 | 0.31 |
| Total/Net Impact | 11,540 | 69,175 | (0.18) |

1The pricing impact can be computed either by using average loan amount, prepayment, and default assumptions, or by a simulation model that allows for interaction of various factors. A simulation model was used here.

Table 14-2 is based on a $70 million portfolio comprised of 11,500 loans where a significant number of borrowers received below-par pricing due to competitive pressures. Larger loans benefited from a lower price than required under the risk-based matrix, and smaller loans were charged a higher price. The net annualized impact of pricing overrides over the full portfolio (not just overridden loans) is presented in the last column.

The cumulative impact of both above-par and below-par overrides is a net reduction in return on assets by 18 basis points, which translates into a reduction in income of approximately $125,000 per year. Obviously, the impact of overrides when measured in return on equity is more pronounced. Therefore, while a risk-based pricing structure provides a significant competitive opportunity for banks to profitably expand their market share, its unmonitored implementation can have severe adverse implications. If scoring models are to be implemented successfully, underwriters and loan officers must be disciplined to conform to them.

Another significant risk presented by credit scoring models is that of regulatory compliance particularly as it relates to fair lending laws (see Box 14–1). The two compliance issues that need to be addressed in a scoring environment are disparate impact and disparate treatment.

*Disparate Impact*   Federal regulators and consumer advocacy groups have often expressed concerns about a potential for disparate impact across applicant groups due to the choice of characteristics used in the scoring model. For example, the use of "personal finance company references" may be viewed by some critics as inherently discriminatory if inner-city residents are more likely to use a personal finance company, not because they have credit problems but due to the lack of bank offices and branches in their community. Therefore, the use in the scoring model

## TABLE 14–3
### Summary of AnyBank Overrides By Race
### Home-Improvement Loans, January, 1997

|  | Non-Minority | Minority | Total |
|---|---|---|---|
| Low Side Overrides: |  |  |  |
| Number | 322 | 194 | 516 |
| Percent | 10% | 10% | 10% |
| High Side Overrides: |  |  |  |
| Number | 162 | 198 | 360 |
| Percent | 5% | 10% | 7% |
| Total Applicants | 3079 | 1952 | 5031 |

of explicitly prohibited factors (or close proxies) that impact one segment of applicants must be carefully screened, and less discriminatory variables evaluated as alternatives.

*Disparate Treatment*   A more serious risk is that of disparate treatment of similarly situated applicants. Although the judgment involved in underwriting and pricing decisions is significantly reduced if the scoring systems are used for lending and risk-based pricing decisions, credit scoring models are not a panacea for fair lending compliance. So long as there is judgment involved in the credit scoring environment, there is potential for discrimination. With an automated scorecard, the fair lending compliance risk is concentrated in the judgmental decision to override the model recommendations.

Banks using a credit scoring system need to closely monitor compliance with fair lending laws by periodically analyzing the incidence of underwriting and pricing overrides. Table 14-3 illustrates the pattern of overrides by race for Home Mortgage Disclosures Act (HMDA) reportable loans processed by AnyBank, USA. The incidence of low-side overrides (approving with failing credit scores) is roughly the same between minorities and non-minorities, but the incidence of high-side overrides (denying with passing credit scores) is twice that for minority applicants. This may present a compliance concern.

The data presented in Table 14-3 would be sufficient to reach inferences about disparate treatment at AnyBank if minority and non-minority applicants at the bank have identical credit and financial attributes. However, in practice the two populations are generally very different. A more refined analysis beyond aggregate override counts is required to fully answer the fair lending questions.

Similar fair lending implications are also present in the assignment of pricing overrides. Pricing overrides usually represent a downward price

## TABLE 14-4
**Summary of AnyBank Overrides By Race**
**Home-Improvement Loans, February 1997**

| Override Type | Non-Minority | Minority | Total |
|---|---|---|---|
| Depository Relationship (0.25 Price Reduction): | | | |
| Number | 146 | 22 | 168 |
| Percent | 10% | 2% | 7% |
| Total Borrowers | 1,520 | 960 | 2,480 |

adjustment from the risk-based pricing grid to account for specific borrower attributes. Table 14-4 shows the potential fair lending implications from the use of one below-par pricing override code (depository relationship) for AnyBank.

The table indicates that 10 percent of non-minority borrowers but only 2 percent of minority borrowers benefited from this override code. Although on its face the data appear to suggest a pattern of disparate treatment, this information is insufficient to make any conclusions about AnyBank pricing practices. A conclusive inference requires an understanding of not only the number of overrides but also the number of borrowers by race who had a banking relationship in the first place.

Although credit score overrides can be used effectively by banks to improve credit quality in using additional information not captured in the scorecard, Figure 14-2 and Table 14-2 show the adverse impact of overrides on credit quality and profitability that can result from unchecked override usage. Tables 14-3 and 14-4 demonstrate the fair lending implications of both underwriting and pricing overrides, and how such information can be used by regulators and advocacy groups to support a finding of disparate treatment. The next section provides guidance on policies and procedures about overrides that a bank can implement to mitigate these risks.

## IMPLEMENTING SCORECARD POLICIES

A clear override strategy is necessary to maximize the benefits of using a scorecard. Effective use of overrides can enhance credit quality and potentially increase portfolio return while controlling for compliance risks. The implementation strategy should establish scorecard policies and procedures, and provide adequate management information systems support to monitor its usage.

### Policies and Procedures
The first step to successful implementation of the scorecard is understanding its purpose and the needs of the end-users. For example, differ-

## BOX 14–1

### The Fair Lending Laws and Their Enforcement

A number of fair lending laws insure equal access to credit for all applicants: the Fair Housing Act (FHAct) of 1968, the Equal Credit Opportunity Act (ECOA) of 1974, the Home Mortgage Disclosure Act (HMDA) of 1975, and the Community Reinvestment Act (CRA) of 1977. The FHAct and the Equal Credit Opportunity Act (ECOA), are known collectively as the "fair lending laws."

The Fair Housing Act, Title VIII of the Civil Rights Act, prohibits discrimination on the basis of race, color, religion, sex, handicap, familial status or national origin in any housing-related activity. The law accordingly bans discrimination in the making of loans, purchasing or selling of loans, or imposition of different terms and conditions on loans. The Equal Credit Opportunity Act, is implemented through Regulation B by the Federal Reserve Board. ECOA expands upon the Fair Housing Act by prohibiting all commercial lenders from discriminating against applicants on the basis of their race, color, religion, national origin, sex, marital status, age, or other specified grounds.

The HMDA requires financial institutions to report mortgage application data, including the race and gender of each applicant, to federal regulatory agencies. The law does not prohibit discrimination in lending but serves, among other purposes, as a means to track discriminatory activity for federal regulators and the public. The CRA and its implementing regulation require banks to loan, invest, and service all geographic areas in their defined markets.

The enforcement of the fair lending laws with respect to credit scoring models has been addressed in the regulatory examination guidelines of the Office of the Comptroller of the Currency (OCC).[2] Credit scores cannot take into account or segment the population by race, national origin, or any other prohibited basis, except for age in certain circumstances. In examining banks that use credit scoring models, the OCC states that its examiners "will focus particularly on overrides." The examination would involve determining whether or not denied and approved applicants with similar credit scores were similarly qualified in obtaining a loan. In addition, bank regulators require that the factors used in the scoring model have a business justification. According to the OCC, "if the variable is statistically related to loan performance and has an understandable relationship to an individual applicant's creditworthiness" it will conclude that a factor in the scoring model is "justified by business necessity and does not warrant further scrutiny."

---

2 OCC Bulletin No. OCC 97-24 Credit Scoring Models — Examination Guidance, *Appendix, Safety and Soundness and Compliance Issues on Credit Scoring Models.*

ent policies may be necessary for direct and indirect lending. It may be prudent to rely less on application factors and more on credit bureau factors in an indirect lending environment to avoid compromising the use of the scorecard by savvy dealers.

Second, it is critical to thoroughly understand the statistical properties of the scorecard. In particular, bank management needs to quantify the impact of individual input characteristics on score and understand the contribution of each factor to the final score in order to select the combination of application and credit bureau factors that are finally included in the scorecard. The selection of characteristics should be governed not only by statistical properties but also by considerations such as simplification, data availability and quality, operational risk, and legal compliance risk (disparate impact).

Next, bank management needs to develop a policy on scorecard overrides and enforce adherence to the policy. The following issues should be considered in developing override codes for underwriters and loan officers:

1. Limit override factors to a manageable number. It is good practice to keep the number of underwriting overrides (both low and high) to no more than ten, and of pricing overrides to no more than six. Of course, the exact number will depend on the product and the market.
2. Try not to use override factors that are included in the credit scoring model, to avoid double counting of the same characteristics.
3. Ensure that the explanation for each override code is clear and concise with no ambiguity about how it should be applied.
4. Avoid catch-alls like "Miscellaneous" and "Other" because they do not provide any information for retrospective analysis.
5. Develop policies on the level of authority for use of different override codes. The use of a code may be limited for example, to branch manager, senior executive, senior underwriter, or second review lender.
6. Develop guidelines on the coding of policy exceptions (i.e., override of an override).
7. A team representing business operations, legal, credit risk, information systems, and compliance functions should jointly develop the override policy.
8. Constantly analyze the use of override codes and continuously challenge current policy by eliminating codes that are used infrequently, while adding others that may expedite the lending process.
9. Develop a hierarchy of override codes that needs to be followed in situations where multiple override codes may apply.
10. Determine whether to allow documentation of only one underwriting and one pricing override code, or allow multiple entries depending on system capabilities and product type.

Though these general guidelines form a good starting point for developing an override policy, they need to be customized to specific differences by product, geographic market, and lending environment. At the very minimum, senior bank management needs to consider the trade-offs for deviating from these general guidelines.

Finally, bank management should introduce override discipline by setting tolerable override goals that are both realistic and practical given the product and market. A good practice requires setting these goals at both the global level and at the branch and region levels to accommodate differences in markets. The tolerable level of overrides will depend on a number of factors, but most banks attempt to keep the overall override rate within 10 percent.

## Designing Data Warehouse Systems

Table 14-4 above showed a pattern of disparity in the assignment of pricing concessions (overrides) due to depository relationship. If AnyBank does not retain information on depository relationship for all its applicants, it will find it difficult to defend itself against an allegation of discrimination without manually reviewing each loan file. Similarly, the ability to evaluate the impact of certain attributes (overrides or not) on loan performance is only possible if the underlying information about that attribute is consistently captured in the electronic data. For example, the impact of bankruptcy history on loan performance, and its interaction with credit scores, can be examined only if all applicants with previous bankruptcy can be identified.

These examples demonstrate that the performance of any system can be measured only if enough information is available to analyze issues in context. Adequate monitoring of overrides requires that for each authorized override code, the underlying code specific data be retained for subsequent analysis. This analysis is necessary to monitor consistent assignment of overrides, and understand risks associated with various attributes. As an example, if AnyBank retained information about the depository relationship for all applicants in conjunction with the below-par pricing override code, it would be able to:

1. Develop a better measure for analyzing whether the pricing policy of the bank is practiced consistently. The information can also be used to identify branches or loan officers who discriminate.
2. Evaluate the costs and benefits of offering the pricing concession to its depositors. For example, the bank can evaluate the differences in customer behavior of its depositors from those that were given the pricing concession and those that were charged the risk-based price.

A good practice followed by many institutions is to develop a list of override codes and the attributes necessary to fully explain the override code assignment. This list can also be used to identify and eliminate codes that require the same underlying data, and the final list of data attributes forms the basis for designing support databases. Other critical lending information varying by product is also stored electronically for easy monitoring of the system.

Therefore, for effective monitoring of the use of the scoring system and continuous evaluation of override assignment, it is imperative that databases be in place to support those objectives. Data captured on the front-end can help the bank reduce its legal and compliance costs in the long run, and also provide valuable information for increasing portfolio profitability.

## FRAMEWORK FOR MONITORING OVERRIDES

The credit scoring model is an efficient front line tool with which lenders and underwriters can make timely credit decisions. At a strategic level, senior management relies on the scoring systems to produce a consumer portfolio with risk and return attributes within the tolerance levels established by the risk management function. The bank's risk and return appetite is implemented through score cut-offs and pricing policies established by bank management.

Herein lies a significant risk for the bank, in that the actual implementation of the scoring models and overrides may produce a portfolio quite different from that anticipated by the management. Figure 14–3 shows that an effective operational risk management system (override monitoring and control) needs to interface as "middle-ware" between the front-end scorecard underwriting and back-end credit risk management functions.[3]

The operational risk monitoring framework can be developed to periodically access override information from the processing system. To maximize the benefits from this "middle-ware" investment, it is recommended that the system be integrated with the performance data to evaluate the impact of various attributes on loan performance and returns. This integrated approach can give the bank an effective management decision support tool to continuously refine its credit and pricing policies while monitoring on-going operational risk.

The impact of underwriting and pricing overrides on consumer loan portfolios should be analyzed systematically. The analytical framework should give the bank the flexibility to electronically monitor the override

---

3 Ernst & Young LLP has implemented the framework depicted in Figure 14–3 for monitoring compliance and operational risk that generates reports discussed in this section.

# FIGURE 14–3
## Management Decision Support System for Monitoring Operations Risk

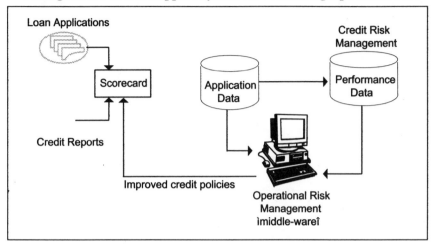

policy. The monitoring process should enable the user to identify overrides by geography and bank organization, identify systematic deviations from a benchmark such as average override rate, and use the underlying data attributes to understand the rationale behind the deviation. Statistical tests can be used to determine whether the assignment of overrides at various levels of authority, by override codes, and by geographical locations is significantly different from the benchmark. See Box 14–2 for a brief overview of statistical tests used to identify patterns in the assignment of overrides.

# BOX 14–2
## Statistical Test for Comparing Override Incidence

A statistical approach to the override analysis can be developed based on the Pearson Chi-Square and the Fisher's Exact statistical tests. The Pearson Chi-Square test analyzes differences between observed and expected frequencies to determine whether or not two groups differ with respect to some characteristic, and can be used to examine whether or not the proportion of overrides assigned is statistically significantly different from the benchmark proportions. The test can be thought of as a test of the difference between two proportions.

If the number of observations is small, the Fisher's Exact test may be used instead. This test also examines the difference between two proportions. For both tests, the statistical significance level indicates the level of confidence at which the test finds the proportions to be different across the two populations. An inference of a statistically significant difference across the borrower groups is reached if the Chi-Square or the Fisher's exact test has statistical significance greater than or equal to 95 percent.

## FIGURE 14-4

### Distribution of Loans by Credit Score for East and West Regions

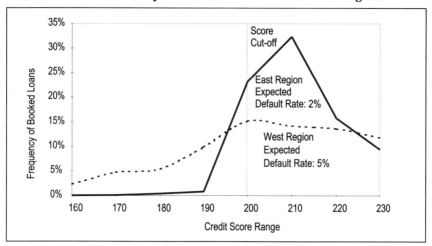

This process can identify lending officers with a pattern of override assignments that may violate the established credit and fair lending policies of the bank.

## Monitoring Credit Quality

One way to continually monitor the credit quality of the bank's loan portfolio is to identify the total incidence of underwriting and pricing overrides. Depending on how the institution is organized, the analysis needs to gradually focus on the details of override codes and their geographical or organizational distribution. For example, Figure 14-4 shows the differences in distribution of booked loans for AnyBank by credit score between the East and West regions using the same scorecard for the same product. The East region has a lower incidence of low-side overrides, and most of them are concentrated near the score cut-off; the West region appears to have a more dispersed distribution of scores below the cut-off score. As a result of differences in loan officer adherence to the scorecard decisions, the estimated default rate of loans using scorecard projections is 5 percent for the West and only 2 percent for the East.

The next layer of analysis is to determine the override reason that contributes to the disparity between East and West region. Table 14-5 provides a statistical analysis of the five low-side override codes used by AnyBank. The branch override code appears to be contributing the most towards the differences between the two regions, with statistical significance levels greater than 95 percent on both tests.

## TABLE 14-5

**Summary of AnyBank Low-Side Overrides By Race**
**Home-Improvement Loans, January, 1997**

| Low-Side Overrides Code | East Region Number | Percent | West Region Number | Percent | Significance Tests Chi-Square | Fisher's |
|---|---|---|---|---|---|---|
| Satisfactory loan hist. 1 | 1 | 0.1% | 7 | 0.5% | 91.3% | 85.1% |
| Strong co-signer 4 | 4 | 0.4% | 13 | 1.0% | 88.5% | 85.8% |
| Branch Override 2 | 2 | 0.2% | 258 | 19.4% | 99.9% | 99.9% |
| Banking relationship 4 | 4 | 0.4% | 12 | 0.9% | 84.1% | 79.3% |
| Low LTV 2 | 2 | 0.2% | 9 | 0.7% | 89.6% | 86.8% |

Additional analyses can also be conducted by the bank to determine branch and loan officer patterns in the West region that may explain its higher use of low-side overrides. Since the analyses use the bank's processing system data and can be automated to flexibly analyze various aspects of the system, senior management can quickly identify on a weekly or monthly basis practices that may compromise the scoring model.

The same framework can be used to evaluate the incidence and implications of deviations from the bank's risk-based pricing policy. Table 14-6 shows the distribution by branch of below-par pricing overrides for January 1997.

Compared to the average benchmark below-par pricing override rate of 12 percent, the non-metro branches are originating loans below the risk-based guidelines at significantly higher rates. The statistical tests combined with the magnitude of deviations from the benchmark provide information that management can use to take corrective action, if necessary. It is important to note that differing competitive conditions experienced by some branches may contribute to the higher incidence of pricing overrides.

## TABLE 14-6

**Summary of AnyBank Below-Par Pricing Overrides By Branch**
**Home-Improvement Loans, January, 1997**

| Branch | Number | Percent | Chi-Square Significance | Fisher's Significance |
|---|---|---|---|---|
| Metropolitan Branches | 324 | 12.0% | 10.7% | 10.5% |
| Non-Metro Branches | 460 | 25.0% | 99.9% | 99.9% |
| Regional Branches | 331 | 11.0% | 81.5% | 80.8% |
| Outer Branches | 326 | 13.0% | 88.5% | 88.0% |
| Inner Branches | 69 | 4.6% | 99.9% | 99.9% |
| AnyBank (Benchmark) | 1374 | 11.9% | — | — |

If the analytical monitoring framework is connected with a loan performance database, as in Figure 14-3, other risk management and profitability analyses can assist the bank to improve portfolio returns and maximize the benefits of a credit scoring system.

## Monitoring Fair Lending Compliance

The systematic approach to monitoring scorecard overrides can also be used effectively to oversee bank compliance with fair lending laws. The statistical framework should be flexible enough to identify patterns in the assignment of override codes by race, gender, age, or other protected class definitions. Figure 14–5 shows the steps in a systematic approach to analyzing fair lending compliance. Underwriting and pricing override codes are first analyzed at the aggregate level, then further examined at a more detailed level.

After identifying statistical differences, if any, in the assignment of override codes in the first step, the bank may choose to evaluate the data by override codes, score bands, underlying attributes, or product type, to isolate the reason for disparity at the aggregate level. The bank can also generate exception reports to identify the loans most likely to contribute to a discriminatory pattern for further review and corrective action. For example, it is unusual to expect a high-side override (pass score denial) for applicants scoring significantly higher than the cut-off. Therefore, such applicants can be classified as exceptions and reviewed one by one to confirm that underwriting criteria were applied consistently.

As an example, recall that Table 14–3 showed a pattern of excessive high-side override codes for home-improvement loans processed by AnyBank during January 1997. That analysis can be refined to examine if specific override codes were used in a disparate manner. Table 14-7 shows the differences in assignment of individual high-side override codes between minority and non-minority borrowers.

## TABLE 14–7
Summary of AnyBank High-Side Overrides By Race
Home-Improvement Loans, January 1997

| High-Side Overrides Code | Non Minorities | | Minorities | | Significance Tests | |
|---|---|---|---|---|---|---|
| | Number | Percent | Number | Percent | Chi-Square | Fisher's |
| Public Records | 10 | 0.5% | 37 | 2.5% | 99.9% | 99.9% |
| Insufficient collateral | 77 | 3.8% | 62 | 4.2% | 42.3% | 40.0% |
| Debt-to-Income ratio | 21 | 1.0% | 70 | 4.7% | 99.9% | 99.9% |
| Exceed loan terms | 54 | 2.7% | 29 | 2.0% | 83.1% | 82.1% |
| Total | 162 | | 198 | | | |

## FIGURE 14-5
**Systematic Overview of Fair Lending Analysis**

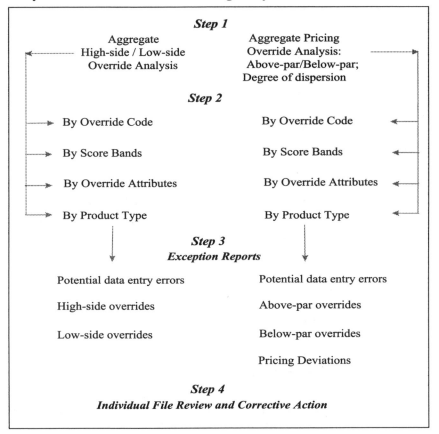

The results shown in Table 14-7 indicate a potential disparity resulting from two override codes: public records, and debt-to-income ratio.[4] Less than half of 1 percent of non-minority applicants who passed the credit score were denied loans due to presence of public record history, while more than 2.5 percent of minority applicants passing the credit score were denied using the same override code. Although informative, this analysis is insufficient in explaining whether there was discrimination in the assignment of this override code.

Instead of comparing the proportion of overridden loans to all loans that passed the credit score by race, a more appropriate test is to compare the proportion of passing applicants that were overridden for public

---

4 The significance of statistical tests exceeds 95 percent for both override codes.

## TABLE 14–8

**Anybank High-Side Overrides for Public Records by Race**
**Home-Improvement Loans, January, 1997**

| Applicants with Public Record History | Non-Minority | Minority | Chi-Square Significance | Fisher's Significance |
|---|---|---|---|---|
| Overrides | 10 | 37 | | |
| Total with passing score | 25 | 84 | | |
| Percent | 40% | 44% | 28.3% | 18.0% |

records, to those applicants that both passed the score and had a public record history. Table 14-8 shows the results of this analysis.

This table suggests that there is no statistical disparity between minority and non-minority borrowers for assignment of the public records override code when the analysis is conducted in the appropriate context. Roughly 40 percent of both minority and non-minority applicants that had a public records history and passed the score cut-off were denied loans. This example shows that while differences across populations in the distribution of under-lying attributes can contribute to a fair lending concern at the aggregate level, a conclusion of disparate treatment can only be reached if it is demonstrated that "similarly situated" borrowers are treated differently. Further refinements of this analysis can also be achieved by examining the treatment of applicants by credit score intervals.

It is important to note that the analysis presented in Table 14-8 was possi-ble because AnyBank had retained information about the presence of public record history not only for overridden loans but for all applicants. If the bank had not systematically captured this data electronically, a significant and labor-intensive manual review of all applications would be necessary. This example reinforces the need for banks to retain adequate electronic data for all applicants.

Similar fair lending monitoring can also be conducted on the assignment of pricing overrides to analyze potential disparities by protected classes. This comprehensive monitoring system can alert the bank to potential civil litiga-tion or regulatory exposure for non-compliance with the fair lending laws.

## CONCLUSION

Credit score model overrides give banks the opportunity to reduce their cred-it risk exposure, increase portfolio returns, and implement bank policies more effectively—using information not captured by the scoring systems. Banks need to continuously monitor their override policy and application to insure consistency in the judgmental discretion used by its officers. Inconsistent application of overrides can significantly erode credit quality and profitability, and potentially expose the bank to a legal compliance risk resulting from possible violations of the fair lending laws.

A systematic framework for monitoring underwriting and risk-based pricing process is an essential management decision support tool that can provide timely information for refining a bank's credit and pricing policies. Developing this additional data analysis framework is a prudent investment that complements the acquisition of credit scoring systems and maximizes their effectiveness.

## APPENDIX: SETTING RISK-BASED PRICES

Economic theory suggests that in a competitive market, prices will equal the incremental cost of delivering an additional unit of a product or service. If the market price is higher than the incremental production cost, the margin will induce competitors to enter the market and bid down the price until the market price equals the incremental production cost.

In the lending environment, the application of this principle implies that each loan is priced in accordance with cost of funds, origination/servicing costs, and the implicit costs associated with potential default and prepayment. While the fixed costs do not generally vary within the same product category, costs associated with default and prepayment risk can vary across credit scores and loan attributes.

The following example illustrates how a lender can use cost accounting data and credit risk measurement tools to price consumer loan segments. Although a portfolio may be segmented across different variables to arrive at risk-based prices, this example only considers differences in credit quality.

Table 14-9 illustrates the analysis necessary to develop a risk-based pricing mechanism for a 10-year consumer loan portfolio segmented into three risk ratings (low, moderate, and high). The amortized cost estimates over the loan term are generated by a simulation model that takes into account not only the differences in averages but also the differences in distribution of factors by credit ratings. A similar pricing framework can be developed using average values of the various cost attributes considered in this analysis. The average cost approach can provide accurate estimates if the loan attributes do not vary within each segment (i.e., the groups are homogeneous).

While servicing and other costs vary because of different loan amount distributions within each rating, the biggest cost difference is due to the default risk, which ranges from over 200 basis points for the highest risk borrowers to 10 basis points for the lowest risk borrowers. Credit scoring models provide the default probabilities by score as the basis for developing an objective risk-based pricing framework. In addition to allocating capital for expected defaults as loan loss reserves, prudent credit risk management requires that

## TABLE 14–9

Estimating Risk-Based Pricing for 10-year Consumer Product
by Credit Score Intervals

| Credit Scores —> | High-risk < 200 | Moderate-Risk 200-240 | Low-Risk 240 + | Combined All |
|---|---|---|---|---|
| Assumptions: | | | | |
| Average amount | $4,000 | $4,800 | $6,000 | $5,000 |
| Default rate (based on credit score) | 13.52% | 3.38% | 0.84% | 4.01% |
| Prepayment (in months) | 72 | 60 | 48 | 65 |
| Operating Costs1: | | | | |
| Origination costs | 0.08 | 0.07 | 0.06 | 0.07 |
| Servicing costs/overhead | 1.97 | 1.60 | 1.05 | 1.51 |
| Default risk | 2.08 | 0.28 | 0.10 | 0.49 |
| Prepayment risk | 0.03 | 0.03 | 0.04 | 0.03 |
| Other costs | 0.05 | 0.04 | 0.04 | 0.04 |
| Subtotal: Operating Costs | 4.21 | 2.02 | 1.29 | 2.14 |
| Cost of funds plus 2% | 7.00% | 7.00% | 7.00% | 7.00% |
| **Loan Price** | **11.21%** | **9.02%** | **8.29%** | **9.14%** |

economic capital be allocated to cover unexpected losses (related to the volatility of expected losses) depending on the risk tolerance of the lender. The total cost of capital allocation by segment reflects the lenders cost for assuming default risk. The amortized costs are then added to the cost of funds to generate an estimate of loan prices under each rating.

Table 14-9 shows that in order to obtain the same spread or net return, the bank could charge its lowest risk customers an interest rate of 8.3 percent and its highest risk customers 11.2 percent. If on the other hand, the bank decides to charge the same price to all borrowers, it could charge an interest rate of approximately 9.15 percent to earn the same spread. In a market with cost conscious borrowers, the bank may lose high-quality credit customers if it decides to charge them higher prices to cross-subsidize low-quality borrowers.

This illustration shows how a financial institution can use the information provided by credit scoring models to develop a risk-based pricing methodology and effectively compete in a competitive environment. In addition to credit score, banks can also use attributes such as debt capacity and loan-to-value to accurately estimate the risk adjusted loan prices.

---

1 Operating cost estimates are based on a pricing simulation model that takes into consideration the distributional differences in loan amount, default timing, and other factors.

# INDEX

401K plan, 99

## A

Above-par override, 228, 230
Above-par pricing override, 228
Acceptable risk, 83
Acceptance rate, 197
Acceptance region, 91
Accept-refer regions, 93
Account attrition, 220
Account balances, 174
Account lifecycle stages, 30
Account management, 32–34. *See also*
　Existing accounts.
　practicies, 204
　strategy, 34
　techniques, 209
Account number, 19
Account payment histories, 44
Account repayment, 27
Account retention strategy, 33
Account-related information, 24
Accounts, 17, 213. *See also* Bad accounts;
　Delinquent accounts; Good
　accounts; High-risk accounts;
　Inactive accounts.
　attrition-adjusted pool, 220
　identification. *See* Bad accounts iden-
　tification.
Account-selection process, 208
Acquisition. *See* Credit bureau scores.
Action reasons. *See* Adverse action rea-
　sons.
Action-driven objective, 143
Activation, 37
　rates, 30
Ad hoc database queries, 142
Adjustable parameters, 83, 88, 89, 101,
　108
Adverse action reasons, 47, 50
Adverse selection, 30
After-tax income, 159
Algorithms, 108
Aliases, 26
Alltell, 113
American Bankers Association, 155
Annual percentage rate (APR), 7

Applicant population, 60, 202
Applicant risk, 193, 202
　predictors, 200–201
Applicant score distribution, 196
Applicant-by-applicant characteristics, 50
Applicants, 60, 184, 188, 209, 214, 225,
　226, 242. *See also* Minority appli-
　cations; Rejected applicants;
　Underage applicants.
　evaluation. *See* New applicant evalua-
　tion.
　quality, 196
Application data, 204
Application fraud, 31
Application review, 30
Application review/booking, 31–32
Application score, 59–79
　application, 76–78
　conclusion, 78–79
　cross validation, 78–79
　data, 61–69
　development expertise, 69–74
　fair lending considerations, 74–76
　introduction, 59–60
　technology, 69–74
Application specific scores, 2
Approval rate, 20
Approval/decline decisions, 31
APR. *See* Annual percentage rate.
Asset classes, 2
Asset-backed debt, 160
Asset-backed securities, 160
Attrition, 33, 34, 37. *See also* Account
　attrition; Silent attrition.
　rates, 220
Automated data, 19
Automated learning, 82–85
　procedures, 83–85
Automated learning procedure, optimiza-
　tion, 100–105
Automobile lending, 158

## B

Back-end credit risk management func-
　tions, 236
Back-end data, 204
Back-end reports, 199–203